Out of Nowhere

*Published in cooperation with
the Center for American Places,
Santa Fe, New Mexico,
and Harrisonburg, Virginia*

Eric Purchase

Out of Nowhere

DISASTER AND TOURISM
IN THE WHITE MOUNTAINS

The Johns Hopkins University Press · *Baltimore & London*

© 1999 The Johns Hopkins University Press
All rights reserved. Published 1999
Printed in the United States of America on acid-free paper

2 4 6 8 9 7 5 3 1

The Johns Hopkins University Press
2715 North Charles Street
Baltimore, Maryland 21218-4363
The Johns Hopkins Press Ltd., London
www.press.jhu.edu

Library of Congress Cataloging-in-Publication Data

Purchase, Eric.
Out of nowhere : disaster and tourism in the White Mountains / Eric Purchase.
p.   cm.
Includes bibliographical references and index.
ISBN 0-8018-6013-X (alk. paper)
1. Tourist trade—United States.   2. Landslides—New Hampshire—Crawford
Notch.   3. Crawford Notch (N.H.)—History.   I. Title.
G155. U6P87   1999
338.4'7917304929—dc21   98-28897

A catalog record for this book is available from the British Library.

To Paula

If he sang of a mountain, the eyes of all mankind beheld a mightier grandeur reposing on its breast or soaring to its summit, than had before been seen there.

—Nathaniel Hawthorne, "The Great Stone Face"

Contents

ILLUSTRATIONS

Acknowledgments

Although writing is best done by oneself, no book ever gets written through the effort of a single person. This one needed the help of many to grow out of the smallest seed of curiosity. It started when I read footnote 167 in G. P. Marsh's *Man and Nature* (Cambridge: Harvard University Press, 1965)—although I should have been reading American travel literature for Ross Miller at the University of Connecticut. Ross didn't seem to mind. Since then, he has provided advice about great matters and small, and he always knows just the right books for me to read. Thomas P. Riggio early on gave my work a rigorous reading and encouraged me when I needed it most. I am also very grateful for the support and encouragement of Robert S. Dombroski. In the Inter-Library Loan Department at the University of Connecticut's Homer Babbidge Library, Robert Vrecenak and Lynn Sweet cheerfully tracked down many obscure books on White Mountain history. The Graduate School of the University of Connecticut gave me five hundred dollars for travel and research. This book also benefited greatly from the editor's pencil and critical eye of George F. Thompson, president of the Center for American Places. With her copyediting, Linda Forlifer made the writing much more readable and precise. Finally, I would like to thank my wife, Paula, for her indispensable support. We had a great time together reading land records in the brick vault at the Coos County Courthouse in Lancaster.

Out of Nowhere

Introduction

On Monday night, 28 August 1826, the entire Samuel Willey household—Mr. and Mrs. Willey, five young children, and two hired men—were killed by an avalanche in Crawford Notch in New Hampshire's White Mountains. Triggered by a fierce thunderstorm, the slide started near the top of Mount Willey (4,300 feet), carved a channel fifty feet deep, and obliterated the road at the bottom of the valley. Incredibly, the Willeys' house was spared: A boulder had divided the landslide directly behind the house so that it passed by on either side. But for some reason the family had gone outside and was buried under the stream of earth, stones, and uprooted trees. An open Bible, a burnt candle end, and unmade beds were later found as evidence of the family's sudden departure. No survivors witnessed the disaster.

The Willey slide quickly became known all over the nation. Throughout the nineteenth century, depictions of the event appeared in various forms: literature, paintings, drawings and engravings, travel writing, memoirs, local histories, newspapers, and scientific journals. People marveled at the sheer perversity of nature in destroying a whole family at a stroke while leaving its house untouched. The disaster resembled an inscrutable Euripidean tragedy. Like Hippolytus and Heracles, who were destroyed by the gods' pathological malice, the Willeys seemed to fall victim to a dysfunctional landscape. Yet, whereas Euripides penetrated to root causes by dramatizing the vicious symbiosis between men and gods, nineteenth-century observers seldom asked the right questions about the disaster. The story seemed easy enough to understand, but below the surface was the disturbing problem of humans' relationship to the earth.

Perhaps better than any other event, the Willey disaster marks the start of a new American awareness of landscape. When Americans hear the word *landscape* today, most commonly picture awe-inspiring formations of the Far West, such as Pike's Peak and the Grand Canyon. The vast dimensions of time and space revealed there typically induce in visitors a sense of their own insignificance. Europeans coined the term *sublime* to describe this feeling and the landscapes that provoke it. Europeans had begun visiting the Alps to find similar views a hundred years before the Willeys but, prior to 1826, few thought that America had its own sublime landscapes. The Willey slide provided stark evidence of nature's grandeur and force. Visitors started traveling to Crawford Notch and the White Mountains to experience the sublime. And the Willey House became one of New England's most popular attractions.

Then, as today, the sublime seemed to the viewer as natural as the land itself. Yet Europeans had lived in the shadow of the Alps for millennia and scarcely thought of them in these terms. The sublime, an aesthetic idea, was brand-new in the eighteenth century, and artists and intellectuals had to train tourists to appreciate nature in this way. In Europe, the rise of the sublime followed the commercial revolution and was a reaction against capitalism's view of nature as merely the source of raw materials. The sublime fulfilled the same function in nineteenth-century America, but in America it was not the artists and intellectuals who first applied the idea to landscapes such as the White Mountains. Rather, it was businessmen (speculators) who sought to lure educated, wealthy tourists to their inns. The sublime, the picturesque, and other aesthetic notions were convenient ways to sell travelers on landscapes in remote parts of the country. Capitalism manipulated Art for its own purposes.

The Willeys were among the first entrepreneurs of White Mountain tourism. Just ten months before the landslide, in October 1825, they had moved to Crawford Notch to run an inn and tavern for travelers. By choosing to live in isolated Crawford Notch, then, the Willeys had brought about their own destruction. Yet Americans never saw it that way. Instead, public attention focused almost exclusively on the family's behavior on the night of the slide. People wondered what the Willeys suffered and thought. People wondered why they fled from the safety of the house into the path of the slide. The real significance of the disaster, however, lay not with the choice the Willeys made *during* the slide, but with the one they had made ten months before. What needed explanation was not why the Willeys left the house on August 28, but why a middle-class family came to live there in the first place. If people had looked more carefully, they might have seen that, through everything, the only constant was the growth of the business of tourism. Even the landslide itself made White Mountain tourism more popular than ever. The Willey House served as both tourist attraction and hotel for three-quarters of a century after the disaster.

Capitalism had gotten to the American Alps first and used Art as both marketing ploy and camouflage. America's discovery of sublime landscapes early in the nineteenth century resulted directly from the speculative use of land, a purpose that nevertheless remained hidden. Entrepreneurs such as the Willeys used aesthetics to make their property attractive to customers and to give it economic value. At the same time, the artistic values projected onto the landscape by the tourist industry made Nature seem an antidote to crass business. For these reasons, the Willey disaster encapsulates America's complex attitudes toward land. There is a hidden motive beneath America's imagination of landscape, that of the speculator who finds new images in order to give value to otherwise worthless land. To see the speculator's influence, we need to go back in time to when the landscape itself arrived in American consciousness. Thus, the Willey disaster offers an excellent opportunity to examine the significant relationship between art, land, and capitalism in America.

CHAPTER ONE

The Significance
of the Willey Disaster

THE WILLEY DISASTER made a place in the middle of nowhere famous throughout the United States. Before 1826, Americans largely ignored the White Mountains as formless masses of rock that blocked travel and contained nothing of value or interest. The slide convinced the public that the White Mountains preserved Nature in its original, potent state. Hundreds, and then thousands, of people began traveling to the White Mountains every summer for vacations amid such a romantic landscape. Ironically, that is just what the Willeys had wanted to achieve when they first moved to the mountains to run an inn for tourists. This irony escaped the artists, writers, and scientists whose attention had been caught by the disaster because they forgot that the White Mountains were once nowhere rather than somewhere. As a consequence, intellectuals missed an opportunity to discover a bedrock truth about how Americans treat land.

The Willeys' Story

The story of the Willey family is really White Mountain history in brief, and one cannot understand the Willeys without knowing the place where they died. Crawford Notch forms a narrow, eight-mile passage through the White Mountains (fig. 1). For eighty years it was almost the only connection between farmers in the upper Connecticut River valley and markets on the Atlantic Ocean—especially Portland, Maine, and Portsmouth, New Hampshire. At its northern end, called the Gate of the Notch, two sheer rock walls (seventy feet high on one side, fifty on the other) stood a mere twenty-two feet apart during the first half of the nineteenth century. The Saco River begins from a pond located just north of the Gate and flows through the Notch on its 160-mile journey to the Atlantic. The Amonoosuc also begins in the same

Fig. 1. Thomas Cole, *A View of the Mountain Pass Called the Notch of the White Mountains (Crawford Notch)*, 1839, oil on canvas. Late in his career, Cole painted the Gate of the Notch from the north looking south; Mount Webster looms in back, and the inn run by Ethan Allen Crawford's brother Thomas is in the lower left. *Used with permission, Andrew W. Mellon Fund,* © *Board of Trustees, National Gallery of Art, Washington.*

area and flows west to the Connecticut. Two hunters, Timothy Nash and Benjamin Sawyer, discovered the Notch by accident in 1771 while chasing a moose. Pleased that a road through the mountains was feasible, New Hampshire's governor rewarded them with two thousand acres of land just beyond the Gate, called Nash and Sawyer's Location (fig. 2).[1]

Interest in the Notch grew slowly. The road through was probably not opened until 1785.[2] The Revolution delayed things, as did the difficulty of excavating stone blocking the Gate of the Notch. Thus, in 1792 when Eleazer Rosebrook moved to Nash and Sawyer's Location along the road to Jefferson, his nearest neighbor was Abel Crawford, twelve miles away at the southern end of the Notch.[3] But in 1803–4 the Tenth New Hampshire Turnpike was incorporated to upgrade twenty miles of road from Bartlett, below the Notch, to Jefferson, near the Connecticut River, at a cost of forty thousand dollars,

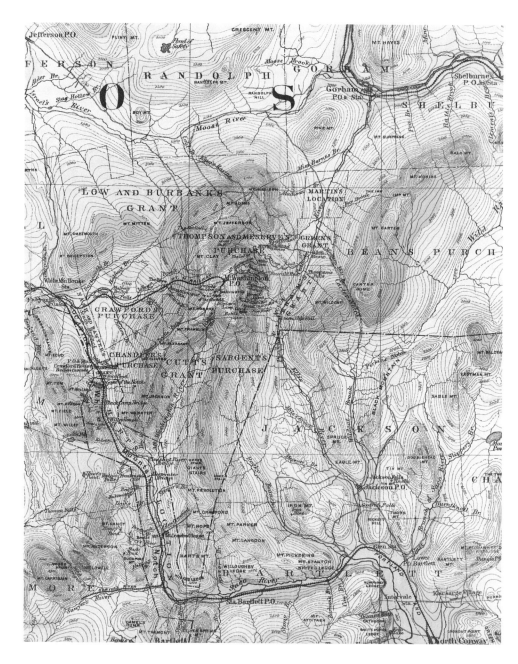

Fig. 2. Detail, *Map of the White Mountains of New Hampshire from Walling's Map of the State*, 1877, in *Appalachia* 1, no. 3 (June 1877): figure 7. This is by far the clearest, most detailed, and most accurate map of the White Mountains in the nineteenth century.

raised mostly from investors in Portland, Maine. Rosebrook saw an opportunity. He built a two-story inn to serve the travelers who would now be using the turnpike.[4] He and Crawford became the first innkeepers in the White Mountains.

The turnpike succeeded handsomely. During an era when tolls collected on most turnpikes did not return construction and maintenance costs, the Tenth New Hampshire Turnpike paid large dividends.[5] One measure of the turnpike's success is that it remained a toll road perhaps as late as 1876, several decades after most turnpikes in the United States had become free.[6] But it was even more valuable for Coos County, New Hampshire—incorporated three days before the turnpike itself—and the adjoining area of Vermont. According to Frederic J. Wood, "The Tenth New Hampshire Turnpike Corporation, chartered in 1803, was the means of bringing all the north country into communication with the seaports and of stimulating settlement and development to a greater extent than any other New England road."[7] In the forty years from its first settlement to its incorporation, Coos County had attained a population of only three thousand, but it grew steadily from then on, with the population doubling by the time of the Willey slide and reaching ten thousand by 1850. Though less dramatic than Oklahoma's land rush in 1889, this dynamic period of White Mountain settlement was possible only because of the turnpike.

The turnpike saw more and more traffic until, by the 1820s, farmers carrying goods would form long caravans, winter and summer. This heavy volume of traffic seems even more amazing in light of the absence of wheeled vehicles. The rugged road forced farmers to use two-horse pungs, a kind of sled made from two poles. The horses were harnessed to the front ends of the poles while the back ends were left dragging on the ground. The driver and his cargo were slung in between on a board. Edward H. Elwell, a nineteenth-century memoirist, remembered it this way: "From Coos, from Vermont, away to the Derby line, came down in winter long strings of red pungs, drawn by two horses, with a board projecting behind, on which stood the driver, clad in a long blue frock. In the pung were his round hogs, cheese, butter and lard, together with a round red box in which was stored his own provender for the journey, in the shape of huge chunks of cheese and big doughnuts . . . For a return load they took up flour, salt-fish, rum, and molasses." Elwell reports meeting someone in Portland who claimed to have "driven one of these pungs down through the Notch, in the night, in the midst of a driving snow-storm, when there were seventy-five of them in a string."[8] And, in *Incidents in White Mountain History*, Samuel Willey's brother Benjamin recalled "the long train of Coos teams which used to formerly pass through Conway. In winter, more particularly, we have seen lines of teams half a mile in length; the tough, scrubby, Canadian horses harnessed to 'pungs,' well loaded down with pork, cheese, butter and lard, the drivers rivalling almost the modern locomotive and its more elegant train of carriages in noise and bluster."[9]

The Willey family moved to the Notch in October 1825 and opened an inn in a house that had been occupied intermittently since being built in 1793. Two stories tall, with stables attached, the house sat on a small meadow on the west bank of the Saco River at the foot of the mountain later named for the family. The Willeys bought the house from Abel Crawford's son Ethan Allen Crawford. Ethan Crawford had married Lucy Howe, the granddaughter of Eleazer Rosebrook, who died in 1817, leaving them his inn north of the Notch. In 1846, Lucy Crawford published a memoir of her husband, entitled *History of the White Mountains*, which explains his decisive role in the region's growth. The Willey place, she wrote, "which is now nothing but sand and gravel [because of the landslide], was over a beautiful valley, covered with maple, and there used to be a great quantity of sugar made there."[10] Directly across the river loomed Mount Webster, a steep thirty-eight hundred feet high; much of its western face is sheer rock. Commanding a view of the valley from the south was Mount Crawford, and to the north Mount Willard stood behind the shoulder of Mount Willey. These large hills form a kind of canyon that narrows sharply toward the north and through which blow brisk winds, even on serene summer days. The house stood two miles south of the Gate of the Notch where the road reached its highest elevation, over eighteen hundred feet. Travelers welcomed the sight of the Willeys, especially in winter, because theirs was the only inn for six miles in either direction.

The parents of both Samuel Willey Jr. and his wife, Polly Lovejoy, lived in Conway, across the Saco River from each other.[11] They were among the original settlers of the town. Samuel and Polly grew up there, married in 1812, and moved up the valley to Lower Bartlett (now North Conway), where they owned a farm. They lived in Bartlett thirteen years and had five children before buying the Notch House.

By late summer in 1826, a drought had dried the mountain soil to a fine powder, loosening tree roots, so that the powerful storm of Monday, August 28, set off hundreds of landslides all over the mountains. A steady rain began about 4:00 A.M., continued all day, and climaxed near 11:00 P.M. in an intense cloudburst, which triggered the slides.[12] By midnight the clouds had gone, leaving a calm, star-filled sky, although the rumble of still-falling slides filled the valley.[13] The mountainsides displayed long gouges and bare rock where trees, soil, and stones had been stripped away. The valley bottoms were filled with massive snarls of earth, boulders, and full-grown trees whose branches and rootballs were hopelessly tangled. Yale geologist Benjamin Silliman reported that the largest slide, located just north of the Gate of the Notch, "was described to us by Mr. Abbot of Conway, as having slid, in the whole, three miles—with an average breadth of a quarter of a mile"; that is, it covered nearly five hundred acres.[14]

The normally small Saco River flooded, knocking out most bridges on the turnpike and inundating farms all the way to Conway, twenty-five miles from the Notch House.[15] The water in Conway had risen twenty-four feet in seven hours.[16] A group of men who had barely escaped on August 28, while attempting to climb Mount Washington, the region's tallest peak and primary attraction, returned there on the thirtieth. Their base camp "had been wholly swept away; and the bed of the rivulet by which it had stood, was now more than ten rods wide [165 feet], and with banks from ten to fifteen feet high."[17] From the hilltop near his inn, Ethan Crawford saw the valley below submerged under a two-hundred-acre lake; his farm sustained one thousand dollars of damage.[18] Abel Crawford's farm six miles below the Notch House suffered even more, according to Lucy: "The best part of his farm was entirely destroyed. A new saw mill, which he had just put up, and a great number of logs and boards were swept away together into the sand; fences on the interval were all gone; twenty-eight sheep were drowned, and considerable grain which was in the field was swept away. The water rose on the outside of the house twenty-two inches, and ran through the whole house on the lower floors and swept out the coals and ashes from the fireplace."[19]

In the Notch itself slides destroyed miles of the turnpike and altered the Saco's course. Such damage made traveling hard, so the Willeys' deaths did not become known for two days. The Reverend Carlos Wilcox of Hanover, New Hampshire, who stayed at Ethan Crawford's right after the slide, described the condition of the Notch: "In some places the road was excavated to the depth of fifteen and twenty feet; and in others it was covered with earth, and rocks, and trees, to as great a height. In the Notch, and along the deep defile below it, for a mile and a half, to the Notch House, and as far as could be seen beyond it, no appearance of the road, except in one place for two or three rods [30–50 feet], could be discovered." Coming down from Crawford's, a merchant named Barker was the first to go through the Notch. Having spent all of Tuesday scrambling over six miles of rubble, he got to the Willeys' at sunset, stayed the night in the empty house, and proceeded to Bartlett the next morning. With Barker's news that the Willeys were missing, neighbors and relatives set out on Wednesday but could not reach the Notch until Thursday morning, August 31. According to Reverend Wilcox, they found the house "entirely deserted; the beds were tumbled; their covering was turned down: and near them upon chairs and on the floor lay the wearing apparel of the several members of the family; while the money and the papers of Mr. Willey were lying in his open bar."[20] Clearly, the Willeys had left in a hurry and been buried.

The slide that killed the Willeys had started near the top of the mountain and traveled almost three miles to the valley floor.[21] Edward Melcher, a member of the search party who wrote an account in 1880, was impressed by the strange architecture of the slide: "The track of the slide reached to within three feet of the house, and had carried away one corner of the barn. Across the course of the slide, the rocks, gravel and trees were piled and mixed in awful confusion for a great distance. It seemed to have suddenly stopped, for the advanced part of the avalanche was more than perpendicular, the top projecting over that portion that rested on the ground—so much so as to form caves." The Willey House survived because an outcropping of rock had divided the avalanche into two streams, which rejoined a few feet below the front door. "As the Willey House stood directly in the line of the avalanche, it would have been swept away but for a rock near the corner of the house, well sunken in the ground, which proved to be a barrier that turned the current by first arresting a large spruce tree and then what was immediately behind, till the mass was piled up as high as the [two-story] house, and so near I could easily step from the rubbish to the top of the building."[22] The wreckage of the barn killed two horses and trapped a yoke of oxen. Several mud-soaked sheep and milk-laden cows were found on the small patch of clear ground in front of the house.

That first day, the searchers eventually found the bodies of David Allen and Samuel and Polly Willey, though they had looked all morning without success. Melcher gave the details of the discovery.

> It had got to be well toward noon, and in all this time we had seen nothing to indicate where the bodies of the unfortunate family could be found. Seeing large numbers of flies about the entrance, I was led to search one of the caves above mentioned. I crawled in quite a number of feet, and discovered a man's hand jammed in between two logs. I came out and indicated to Thomas Hart and Stephen Willey [Samuel's brother] where to dig. We soon came to the body of the man whose hand I had seen. It proved to be that of David Allen, a hired man of the Willeys. Directly behind the body of Allen was that of Mrs. Willey. Both were entirely denuded and terribly mangled, especially about their heads. The back part of Mrs. Willey's head was entirely jammed off . . .
>
> Mr. Allen's right hand was extended toward Mrs. Willey and about two feet from her left hand, and it appeared as though they had joined hands in his attempt to save her, but when found were not joined. Both were lying on their

faces. Mr. Allen's left hand was fast between two logs. It being dark in the place, nothing could be seen, but by reaching in, to discover if I could, what attracted the flies, I took hold of a hand and examined each finger and thumb to satisfy myself that it was a man's hand, and it proved to be Mr. Allen's.

Others soon found Samuel Willey's body in good condition, fully clothed "with the exception of one coat sleeve, which was torn entirely off."[23] He was pinned under a beam from the barn and submerged under the river. He was thirty-eight years old. Polly Willey was thirty-five. David Allen, thirty-seven, left a wife and four children in Bartlett.

Other bodies were not discovered until Sunday, September 3, when searchers found the oldest and youngest children: Eliza, aged thirteen, and Sally, three years old. Sally was found under three feet of rubble after searchers accidentally disturbed more flies. Eliza was found in the river. "When she was removed from the water," wrote Floyd W. Ramsey, "she was wearing only a large handkerchief tied around her waist, presumably to permit someone to lead her. She was unbruised and had evidently drowned."[24] The other hired hand, David Nickerson, twenty-one years old (also from Bartlett), was not found until the following Tuesday. The bodies of the rest of the Willey children—Jeremiah, eleven; Martha, ten; and Elbridge, seven— were never recovered.

Pending burial in the family cemetery in Conway, searchers temporarily interred the four Willeys where the first bodies had been found. With a piece of red chalk, Ethan Crawford wrote on a board "THE FAMILY FOUND HERE" and nailed it to a tree nearby.[25] Visitors would customarily toss a stone under the sign so that a large tumulus soon grew up. But the Willeys' greatest memorial was their undamaged house, which remained one of the most popular tourist attractions in the White Mountains until it burned down in 1899.

A Tragedy without a Plot

The Willey disaster baffled and fascinated nineteenth-century Americans. Local residents and the Willeys' relatives struggled to understand what led the family to rush outside to its death, but explanations varied. In *Incidents in White Mountain History*, published thirty years after the slide, Benjamin Willey propounded three different versions of the Willeys' final moments. Like a theatergoer who arrives after the final curtain and asks someone in the audience about the play, Benjamin was forced to imagine the Willeys' tragedy at second hand. The mere fact of the destruction of his brother's family did not represent a proper conclusion; catharsis can come only from seeing firsthand the action that leads to a calamitous ending.

Thus, Benjamin's narrative places the reader as if in the house itself, watching the family's last hours.

> The family, at first, designed to keep the house, and did actually remain in it till after the descent of most of the slides. From the commencement of the storm in its greatest fury they were, probably, on the alert, though previously to this some of them might have retired to rest. That the children had, was pretty evident from appearances in the house when first entered after the disaster. My brother, it is pretty certain, had not undressed; he stood watching the movements and vicissitudes of the awfully anxious season. When the storm had increased to such violence as to threaten their safety, and descending avalanches seemed to be sounding "the world's last knell," he roused his family and prepared them, as he could, for a speedy flight, trembling every moment lest they should be buried under the ruins of their falling habitation.
>
> At this hurried, agitating moment of awful suspense, the slide, which parted back of the house, is supposed to have come down, a part of which struck and carried away the stable [attached to the house]. Hearing the crash, they instantly and precipitately rushed from their dwelling, and attempted to flee in the opposite direction. But the thick darkness covering all objects from their sight, they were almost instantly engulfed in the desolating torrent which passed below the house, and which precipitated them, together with rocks and trees, into the swollen and frantic tide below, and cut off at once all hope of escape.[26]

Benjamin's story accounts for the known facts and makes reasonable conjectures about what happened. The narrative is also emotionally convincing: Just a few words—*anxious, trembling, frantic*—persuade us that Benjamin grasps how the family's emotions must have escalated. There can be no clearer description of the Willeys' movements and state of mind.

Yet experience is so idiosyncratic, one can never be sure what another has felt. Even after so many years, Benjamin's curiosity was too intense for one dramatization to satisfy; therefore, he rehearsed other explanations of their flight:

> Others have supposed that, as the storm increased during the night, thinking the stable a safer place than the house, being constructed of stronger materials, they went into the stable before the destructive slide came down which carried them away; and there they met death by the part of it which fell, and the mingled current of sand and timber which produced the fall, and were borne along on its course to where they were afterwards found. This conjecture arose, probably, from the fact that the remains of such of the family as were discovered were found very near the timbers of that portion of the stable which was carried away.

Close attention to the disaster's details produced a different, though still reasonable, explanation of the family's movements. Benjamin had become a kind of playwright, searching for the best way to work out the plot of his drama. Still not satisfied, he took a larger leap of imagination:

> There is still another conjecture respecting the manner of the great disaster, suggested by a dream of my eldest brother, James Willey. In his dream he thought he saw the brother that was destroyed, and asked him why he and his family left the house as they did, and thus exposed themselves to dangers abroad, when they might have been more safe at home . . . In reply to this, my brother remarked that they did not leave the house until the waters rose so high in front, and came up so near, that they found they would carry away the house; so, to avoid being drowned, they took some coverings for shelter against the storm, and went out to the foot of the mountain back of the house, and from thence, soon after, were carried away by the great slide that came down in that direction.

The Willeys fled from the house in panic when the avalanche struck the stable; or, perhaps, they had taken refuge in the stable, where the slide overwhelmed them; or, alarmed by the river's sudden rise, they sought higher ground, only to be buried by the slide. The many possibilities preempt any feeling of certainty. After all, as Benjamin concluded, the *dream* "adjusts itself better to the great facts in the case than either of the theories we have hitherto considered."[27]

The Willey disaster also baffled American intellectuals, who created their own dramas about it. A few invoked Providence, yet without much conviction. After all, God must have a capricious, malignant sense of humor to target a house with a landslide only to spare the house at the last second and destroy its fleeing occupants. For most, the slide challenged fundamental beliefs about the relationship between humans and the natural landscape, and it refuted common-sense notions of how nature and the economy work. Before the Willey disaster, popular opinion rarely questioned the fundamental compatibility of Man and Nature, but the slide pointed up the disparity between America's agrarian philosophy and the lived experience of ordinary people such as the Willeys.

Nineteenth-century Americans inherited their agrarianism from Thomas Jefferson and other Founding Fathers. Since the earth is the original source of all wealth, Jefferson thought, the farmer—who draws riches directly out of the soil—must be the most productive citizen. His efforts increase the whole nation's wealth.[28] Moreover, growing wealth makes possible higher forms of civilization so that the development of a landscape mirrors and complements this upward progress.[29] Human improvement depended on a corresponding improvement in land. In contrast, the Willey disaster highlighted the disparity between the landscape and its inhabitants. From the enormous forces unleashed in the slide, intellectuals saw that Nature operated on a much vaster scale than previously imagined. Instead of enjoying a snug relationship, people were dwarfed and threatened by an earth that seemed utterly indifferent to human concerns. Furthermore, if the earth is not innately congenial to humankind, perhaps Jefferson was wrong to think that wealth—and civilization—originates in the soil. Perhaps the farmer is not the prototype of the good citizen. Indeed, the Willeys were not farming in Crawford Notch but running an inn. They had left their farm to do so, and the choice contradicted agrarian common sense. Yet nineteenth-century Americans scarcely wondered what the Willeys' choice meant, even though it had serious implications for the prevailing wisdom about political economy.

As a result, the Willey disaster prompted nineteenth-century intellectuals to develop stunning new images of Nature while overlooking the correlative question of how Americans use the earth. Or, rather, the economic issue appears in these new images but in suppressed form. Newly attuned to landscape, painters, writers, and scientists remained unconscious of the influence of entrepreneurs such as the Willeys, whose use of land differed fundamentally from that of Jefferson's farmer. Thus, speculative practices appear in nineteenth-century landscapes as irrational departures from the upward course of development predicted by agrarianism. The operatic canvases of the Hudson River School, for example, cannot be understood fully without understanding how land speculators suddenly change the prevailing narrative of a landscape to make it seem more desirable to customers (tourists, in the Willeys' case). Art, literature, and science, in turn, also helped the entrepreneurs of tourism because the new landscape images aroused the interest of the traveling public and raised the land's pecuniary value. Convinced by intellectuals that Nature, raw and pure, could be found in the White Mountains, the new elite from Boston, New York, and other cities paid good money to vacation away from urban filth and noise. The new landscape images were much more effective because of their apparent detachment from the sordid concerns of business.

In reality, no clear lines separated intellectuals, tourists, and businessmen. They fertilized each other's imaginations. Many Hudson River School painters acted as entrepreneurs and made good livings selling White Mountain views to patrons who vacationed there—or dreamed of doing so. These painters also taught geologists and botanists how to look at landscape analytically. Earth scientists tried to pry money from state legislatures by arguing that scientific appreciation of scenery boosted tourism and contributed to the economy. In professional journals some scientists published popular notices of White Mountain scenery that had been inspired by their research there.

Many tourists were also amateur scientists, and science influenced the way tourists thought about the landscape. Such serious writers as Nathaniel Hawthorne often went to the White Mountains as tourists, and many tourists read literature about the region. This exuberant swapping of ideas among normally separate fields shows the energy with which nineteenth-century Americans pursued their "discovery" of landscape.

The Willey slide, then, became a kind of red herring. Although the disaster drew attention to an area where America's entrepreneurial spirit was at work, it led intellectuals to look for natural, rather than human, explanations of the White Mountains, the Willeys, and their death. To learn the truth, tourists and intellectuals should have visited the Willeys *before* the slide. Joseph T. Buckingham did. The editor of two Boston newspapers, Buckingham stayed with the Willeys in June 1826 and, twenty-four days before the slide, published a report that framed the core issue: "Can philosophy or conjecture account for or explain the motives that can induce a man thus to plant himself at a distance of six miles from the habitation of any of his race, and in a spot where it is next to impossible he can ever have a nearer neighbor?"[30] The Willeys' situation puzzled an age that believed in Jefferson's prosperous, public-spirited farmer; indeed, it seemed to contravene economic law. As Buckingham guessed, to see the Willeys' choice of life and location as rational requires a new philosophy of landscape.

The Defeat of History

After the disaster, few would have questioned the desirability of living in the White Mountains (risky though it might be) because the slide had demonstrated their sublime and romantic attraction. Americans quickly forgot the earlier consensus, which Buckingham shared, that Crawford Notch was the middle of nowhere. Yet the Willeys' story makes sense only if it is remembered that the White Mountains were originally a nowhere rather than a sublime somewhere.

The agrarians, at least, understood what *nowhere* meant. They took key ideas about the status and value of land from John Locke, who considered the issue strictly from the farmer's perspective. In his *Second Treatise of Government*, Locke famously remarked that "in the beginning all the world was America." "His often misconstrued point here," explained Leo Marx, "is not so much the general resemblance between the American wilderness and the prehistoric state of the world, it is the function of commodity exchange as a necessary precondition of all social value." According to Locke, "a hundred thousand acres of excellent land, ready cultivated, and well stocked too with cattle, in the middle of the inland parts of America" would have no value because the farmer could not bring his products to market.[31] In Locke's vocabulary, America meant "worthless," an early version of the fabled swampland of real estate swindles. Crawford Notch fell into this category in Locke's and Buckingham's reckoning.

Following Locke, the agrarians believed that land had value only through what it produced; they did not see that land—when freed from feudal restrictions, as in America—would become a commodity in its own right.[32] Moreover, the very worthlessness of land in America makes it immune from the supply-and-demand equilibrium and therefore all the more attractive to speculators.[33] A piece of property worth next to nothing has the highest potential profit margin. The key lies in finding a way to *make* that property valuable, to convince others of its value. This is what motivated the Willeys: They left the farm they owned in Bartlett and moved to Crawford Notch to exploit a piece of land that was worthless because it was situated in the middle of nowhere. They saw that tourism could add value to this unproductive land. The future belonged to those such as Buckingham who traveled to the mountains for curiosity or pleasure. For visitors wanting to climb Mount Washington and to enjoy other White Mountain sights, the Notch road provided the easiest access before the railroad was built. Ethan Crawford had already made the first trails to the top of Mount Washington and always tried to make stays at his inn more comfortable and entertaining for guests. He asked the Willeys to buy the Notch House to help serve the tourists, who came in increased numbers every year.[34] The Willeys bought the house because they figured they could make more money there than on the farm.

The choice made by this typical, middle-class family illustrates the uniquely American approach to land. Like the Willeys, speculators find land that is worth little from one point of view and invent a new image or narrative to make it desirable. In the nineteenth century, the settling of the West produced America's most powerful landscape narrative. With his famous "frontier thesis," historian Frederick Jackson Turner exalted this process by sketching the westward movement with epic scope and regularity. But if his tale of crossing from savagery to civilization, from nature into culture, is America's greatest myth about land, it is still just *one* myth—and not the only profitable one. As entrepreneurs of White Mountain tourism, the Willeys tried to make money the other way around, helping consumers to cross back into nature from culture. People—mostly urban and wealthy—went to the White Mountains to buy relief from the daily grind, and they took home purchases wrapped in Arcadian images of the wilderness and of hardy pioneers. Though promoting

Nature in its unimproved state, the Willeys made their initially worthless land valuable.

The White Mountains demonstrate speculation's powerful, continuing hold over the American economy and imagination. The business that Crawford and the Willeys created has lasted nearly two centuries. Thousands of vacationers still go to the White Mountains each year, and tourism dominates the local economy today as it has since the 1820s. As White Mountain history shows, speculation is so commonplace in America—indeed, so much the norm—that most overlook it, despite its pervasive effects. Speculation lulls both intellectuals and ordinary Americans because it offers them more attractive landscape images and narratives in place of an area's real history, and no one is immune from this appeal. When nineteenth-century America's most critical minds—including Ralph Waldo Emerson, Henry David Thoreau, Nathaniel Hawthorne, and Henry James—vacationed in the White Mountains, they accepted the basic myth the tourist industry was selling: that the White Mountains preserve Nature in its aboriginal state. These writers enjoyed the scenery unreservedly even as they deplored tourism's vulgarity. None reflected that *both* the pleasure and disgust of tourism originated from entrepreneurs such as the Willeys having invented the business of selling the enjoyment of Nature in the White Mountains.

Perhaps James's experience best illustrates how thoroughly speculation controlled the way Americans imagined the White Mountains; he was in the perfect position to recognize it, yet failed to do so. James visited the White Mountains in September 1904—long after the Willey slide, when tourists paid dozens of times more to stay in grand hotels, rather than in the small, ramshackle inns of the 1820s. The grand hotels, each of which contained hundreds of standardized guest rooms, were horizontal cousins to the skyscrapers of New York and other American cities, which contained standardized office space. Both grand hotels and office skyscrapers came into their own after the Civil War as a way to maximize the income from a given piece of real estate.[35] However, despite their outward sophistication, the grand hotels simply perfected the business that Crawford and the Willeys had invented.

James's visit to the White Mountains occurred during a long tour through the United States, his first U.S. trip in more than twenty years. He stayed in Chocorua, New Hampshire—on the White Mountains' south side—in the summerhouse owned by his brother, William James (fig. 3). During his stay Henry James made a circuit of the mountains by carriage and train. In *The American Scene* (1907), James compared the White Mountains favorably to New York City and suggested that conditions in the White Mountains came closer to the (European) ideal than those in any other part of America. His long absence from America and his admiration for Europe's more settled landscape allowed James to spot speculation's baneful effects as soon as he landed in New York City. James disliked New York's uncontrolled growth and the gaudy mansions of the "new rich." European institutions had evolved over centuries and had roots in pastoral and agricultural traditions. In Europe, history and landscape coincided and, therefore, permanently exhibited the highest values attained by civilization. But Americans seemed to destroy their landscape before it could become part of history and culture. James especially hated to see distinguished buildings torn down to make room for bigger, newer, more vulgar structures. Proper social "forms" could not develop in an America that reinvented itself every few years. James named this uniquely American phenomenon "The Defeat of History."

In American cities, James saw, the speculator treats landscape as a void to be filled by his own invented narrative. The speculator erases (actually or con-

Fig. 3. Asher B. Durand, *Chocorua Peak*, 1855, oil on canvas. A notable sight in the White Mountains, Mount Chocorua dominates the area where William James owned a summerhouse. *Used with permission, Museum of Art, Rhode Island School of Design. Gift of the Rhode Island Art Association.*

ceptually) what the landscape contains to make room for something new.[36] Manhattan's skyscrapers were "consecrated by no uses save the commercial at any cost," and through sheer size they overwhelmed such older buildings as Trinity Cathedral which embodied tradition and humane values.[37] In return, skyscrapers offered mere blankness. New York City's "whiteness," said James, "is precisely its charming note, the frankest of the signs you recognize and remember it by" (75). New York resembled a city of marble towers, whose brightness was designed to impress, but which did not possess the substantial, enduring beauty of Old World architecture, such as Giotto's bell tower in Florence.

Skyscrapers also lacked individuality. They were all basically steel-framed boxes overlaid with a thin curtain wall of concrete ornamentation and glass, molded in the prevailing architectural fashion. In effect, this skin was a building's advertising and served to make it stand out from all the other office towers, which had the same use and structure. James was shrewd to notice the prodigious use of windows in skyscraper design. He wrote that the skyscrapers' "essentially *invented* state, twinkles ever, to my perception, in the thousand glassy eyes of these giants of the mere market." Thus, the successful skyscraper flaunted its superior size, newness, and style, but these superficial qualities also invited a still-newer structure to make it quickly obsolete. Accordingly, New York City's buildings stayed in fashion no longer than bestselling novels. In fact, skyscrapers *were* novels. "One story is good only till another is told," James observed, "and sky-scrapers are the last word of economic ingenuity only till another word be written" (77). Such disposable buildings gave New York a contrived feeling—and, of course, contrivance, or invention, is the speculator's hallmark.

In contrast, the White Mountains suggested European references. "Why was the whole connotation so *delicately* Arcadian," James marveled, "like that of the Arcadia of an old tapestry, an old legend, an old love-story in fifteen volumes, one of those of Mademoiselle de Scuderi?" (14). Henry James—man of letters, art lover, and devotee of polite society—felt right at home in the American woods. Although the new rich summered there, they did not overwhelm the landscape the way New York skyscrapers do. The landscape retained its integrity and cultural associations. Perhaps these would eventually instruct the summer people in values more admirable than conspicuous consumption. Indeed, for James himself, the White Mountain tour had a sacred cast. The natural scenery recalled for him the spirit of American romanticism. Like Henry David Thoreau, James especially liked solitary ponds. James could not "resist the appeal of their extraordinarily mild faces and wooded brims, with the various choice spots where the great straight pines . . . yielding to small [beaches] as finely curved as the eyebrows of beauty, make the sacred grove and the American classic temple, the temple for the worship of the Indian canoe, of Fenimore Cooper, of W. C. Bryant, of the immortalizable water-fowl" (17–8). This experience of the ponds represented the simple, naive relationship to land James believed necessary for higher forms of culture to develop.

Of course, the Arcadian ideal that delighted James had been imported to the White Mountains by the tourist industry and used to reinvent the region in just the way that New York City reinvented itself with every new skyscraper. Fastidious, acute Henry James never suspected that his White Mountain idyll had been written eighty years before by locals such as the Willeys. But James's bias toward high culture made him the perfect White Mountain consumer: someone with money to spend who understood the area's highbrow appeal.

The seductive power of the speculator's fiction even caused James to blink the evidence that remained in the landscape of the region's true history. "The history was there in its degree," he wrote, "and one came upon it, on sunny afternoons, in the form of the classic abandoned farm of the rude forefather who had lost patience with his fate."[38] James noticed the poverty of the countryside away from the grand hotels. He saw that farms had been abandoned because of competition from the Midwest and that the region would have been a backwater except for tourism. "Everywhere legible," James wrote in *The American Scene*, "was the hard little historical record of agricultural failure and defeat . . . One was in presence, everywhere, of the refusal to consent to history, and of the consciousness, on the part of every site, that this precious compound is in no small degree being insolently made on the other side of the continent, at the expense of such sites" (21). Instead, James saw "the disinherited, the impracticable land throwing itself . . . on the non-rural, the intensely urban class, and the class in question throwing itself upon the land for reasons of its own" (22). In short, wealthy tourists from the city were rescuing the White Mountains from inevitable poverty.

Yet there was something odd about the way the tourist's Arcadia and the abandoned farmhouses existed side by side in the landscape: "These scenes of old, hard New England effort, defeated by the soil and the climate and reclaimed by nature and time—the crumbled, lonely chimney-stack, the overgrown threshold, the dried-up well, the cart-track vague and lost—these seemed the only notes to interfere, in their meagerness, with the queer *other*, the larger, eloquence that one kept reading into the picture" (14–5). Despite their reclamation by nature, the abandoned farmsteads did not have a genuine relationship with the Arcadia that James imagined the White Mountains were. This pastoral landscape seemed to exist by itself, fully formed and perfect: "Why . . . did all the woodwalks and nestled nooks and shallow, carpeted dells, why did most of the larger views themselves, the outlooks to purple crag and blue horizon, insist on referring themselves to the idyllic *type* in its purity?" (14).

If he had looked harder, James might have seen that the terms he used to describe New York City also fit the White Mountains.[39] But he underestimated "the rude forefather," pitiful inhabitant of the derelict farmhouse. Ethan Crawford and the Willeys had brought about a conceptual renewal of the landscape. The White Mountains became Arcadian because speculators had started advertising them that way. They invented a new use for the land which went contrary to its expected, agrarian development, and this reinvention of land differed little from the examples of speculation James detested in New York City. He did not recognize speculation in the White Mountains— even when faced with one of its typically abrupt changes—because he was suckered by his own educated tastes. "When you wander about in Arcadia," he confessed, "you ask as few questions as possible" (13). James could have found the truth plainly revealed in the fateful choice of the Willey family to move to Crawford Notch.

CHAPTER TWO

The Tourism
Frontier

LOCAL HISTORIANS could never quite explain how the White Mountains got their name. Some suggested an Indian origin; some thought that early sailors to New Hampshire's Atlantic coast had seen snow on the distant hilltops; others believed that sunlight reflecting off the granite slopes had inspired the name. Perhaps Henry James would have said that *white* simply referred to the region's blankness or barrenness. In any case, New Englanders perceived the mountains as a void for two centuries. Although people expected hills of such prodigious size to yield much, the White Mountains produced little. They aroused little interest and went virtually unexplored until the end of the eighteenth century.

Disappointment and failure had been the White Mountains' legacy from the beginning. John Winthrop recorded in his journal that Darby Field, with Indian guides, became the first white man to visit Mount Washington, making two trips in June 1642. "They brought [back] some stones which they supposed to be diamonds," wrote Winthrop, "but they were most crystal." Nevertheless, Darby Field's return started a rush to the mountains. Like Coronado intoxicated by stories of Eldorado, many could not resist the urge to follow up on Field's claims. "The report he brought of shining stones, etc., caused divers others to travel thither, but they found nothing worth their pains."[1] The fortune hunters included two of Maine's top magistrates: Thomas Gorges, the deputy governor acting on behalf of the colony's proprietor, his uncle Sir Ferdinando Gorges, and Richard Vines, a member of the governing commission and acting governor himself from 1643.[2] Their failure dampened any interest in further exploration and convinced everyone that the mountains contained no extractable wealth. Since then, the White Mountains' romantic nickname "Old Crystal Hills" has reminded people of that delusion.

Other uses developed slowly. Hunting and trapping flourished in the White

Mountains before local historians could record it. References are scarce, but the best source is James W. Weeks's *History of Coos County, New Hampshire* (1888), which draws on the memoirs and reminiscences of early settlers. According to Weeks, two brothers, John and Israel Glines, who gave their names to John's River and Israel's River in Lancaster, New Hampshire, trapped beaver there before 1750. "The beaver inhabited this region in immense numbers," wrote Weeks. He reported that, even at the time of his writing, the dams, meadows, and canals built by beaver were still visible all over the region. Beavers must have been hunted intensively because they were "substantially exterminated prior to the settlement of Lancaster" in 1763.[3] Sables were trapped in Coos County well into the nineteenth century. Ethan Allen Crawford reported catching twenty-five in one year and seventy-five in another.[4] Other animals hunted include the black bear, wolverine, moose, geese, pigeons, and partridges.[5] Before dams were built across it to the south, the Connecticut River as far as Coos contained salmon, which ranged up tributaries such as the Amonoosuc River almost to the Notch. "Trout," wrote Weeks, "the natural and delicious fish of New England, once peopled in crowded abundance every stream of our hills and every pond of our valleys" (118–9).

Despite these resources, interest in permanent settlement developed slowly. In the eighteenth century there were only a handful of expeditions to scout out locations for new settlements and roads or to eliminate the Indians.[6] In 1763 David Page, Edward Bucknam, and Emmons Stockwell settled Lancaster, the first town in Coos County and later the county seat.[7] Soon after, settlers moved into other towns farther up the Connecticut River, such as Northumberland, Stratford, and Columbia, although the area around Mount Washington remained virtually uninhabited. According to the 1775 New Hampshire census, towns later included in Coos County reported a total population of 171.[8] Coos was a frontier in the classic sense from the end of the Revolution until incorporation, and during this time settlers first entered the inland towns in significant numbers. The 1790 federal census lists about 700 inhabitants in Coos, with another 248 in Bartlett immediately south of the Notch (and included in Coos County for a time later on), and 574 in Conway, the next township below Bartlett on the Saco River. The figure for Coos alone represents nearly a fourfold increase in fifteen years. The population doubled by 1800 to about 1,450, with an extra 548 in Bartlett, 705 in Conway, and 180 in Adams (now called Jackson) on the southeastern corner of Mount Washington. The 1810 census, the first in which Coos County properly appears, lists its population (now including Bartlett and Adams) at 3,991. All told, one generation saw the population in Coos and in the vicinity of Mount Washington increase more than twenty times.

In general, the economic fortunes of Coos County in the nineteenth century changed along with those of the rest of northern New England. At the beginning of the period, northern New England's unused, cheap land drew many pioneers because it seemed excellent compared to what was still available in the long-settled south. Benjamin Willey even boasted of Coos's fertility. "Along its rivers are beautiful intervals, and on its uplands are the finest wheat farms in New England."[9] Land clearing continued into the 1820s, and the timber supported a large potash industry.[10] An English immigrant to New Hampshire, writing home about his experiences in 1821, noted the prosperity of hill country farms: "There is a great deal of traffic upon the Merrimac; in the winter from 50 to 100 sleighs pass from Vermont in the upper part of this state [sic] to Boston, with dead hogs, pork, butter, cheese, &c. and load back with store goods."[11] His evidence confirms the accounts of Benjamin Willey and Edward Elwell about the large volume of traffic moving through the Notch in the 1820s (see chap. 1, nn. 8–9).

After this peak came a long decline as Midwestern farmers, sending their staples east by train, began to undersell hill country farmers. "Although the price of corn, rye, and flour declined little between 1820 and 1845," wrote Harold Fisher Wilson in *The Hill Country of Northern New England* (1936), "in the latter year pork and beef commanded scarcely more than half as much as in 1820."[12] Eventually, northern New England gave up growing grains as well. Wilson described the resulting transformation of the landscape: "The difficulty of working the soil in competition with the richer land of Western farms was one of the principal reasons . . . for the abandonment of agriculture on much of this broken land and for its subsequent reversion to forest. Most of it is better adapted to timber growing than to farming, but portions of it are utilized today [1930s] for farm pasturage as a support to the dairy industry" (6). Thousands of farms were abandoned, especially in the late nineteenth century, and this last-settled area of New England soon returned to a state of nature.

But the greater ruggedness of the White Mountain region placed it even farther out on the economic margins than most other parts of northern New England. The land around the mountains was not settled until quite late. For example, Mount Washington's eastern valley was not settled until 1827, when Hayes D. Copp moved in—despite the fact that a road had existed there since before the Revolution.[13] Not surprisingly, in the 1830s, when the state of New Hampshire finally got around to selling the large tracts of land immediately surrounding Mount Washington, they went for pennies an acre. Moreover, the upland farms that Benjamin Willey praised looked less and less attractive over time until, at the end of the century, as Wilson noted, "people were amazed that these locations were ever chosen."[14]

Coos County also missed out on the boom in sheep raising. Northern New England, especially Vermont, became a world leader in wool production soon after Merinos were imported from Europe following the War of 1812.[15] Nevertheless, Coos scarcely participated. "The wools in this County," reads an 1837 survey of the U.S. sheep industry, "are generally coarse, and mostly in bad order."[16] Coos possessed just a tenth as many sheep as neighboring Grafton County and had no woolen factories at all (109–10). People in Coos were most likely too poor to buy the new stock.

The Entrepreneur

It took the illiterate, heavy-drinking Ethan Allen Crawford to figure out that land which produced little could still generate wealth. Crawford was a "mountain man" who epitomized Jacksonian America's rage for enterprise and speculation perhaps even better than did the trappers William Goetzmann wrote about in his famous article.[17] Almost single-handedly, Crawford transformed the White Mountains from a barrier to commerce into a great attraction for wealthy travelers. Unlike the trappers, who started with a ready-made market for furs, Crawford had to make his market from scratch. He saw that wealth did not lie in the mountains but would have to be brought in from the outside. Accordingly, he spent twenty years building better roads and improving accommodations for travelers, and his legacy to the tourist industry seems almost heroic. In the end, however, his enterprise failed because he had succeeded too well. By the time of Crawford's bankruptcy in 1837, so many tourists were coming to the White Mountains that the business had to be run on a much larger scale than he could afford. The rustic inn and the turnpike had to give way to the grand hotel and the railroad.

Ethan Allen Crawford's life encapsulates the problems faced by the whole second generation of hill country pioneers. Abel Crawford, who had been almost the first settler in the White Mountains, fathered eight children besides Ethan, who was born in 1792. Because of Coos's shortage of good land, many of the large family would have to head west to find better prospects, a typical choice for young northern New Englanders. A veteran of the War of 1812, Ethan went west to join his eldest brother, who was already living in upstate New York in 1815. The following year Ethan bought land to farm and settle on in Louisville, New York, near the Canadian border. Thus far, his choices were the same as those of thousands of others. But unexpected circumstances brought Crawford back to face the difficulty of making a living in the White Mountains. He was called back to care for his grandfather, Eleazer Rosebrook, who was dying of mouth cancer. Ethan took the title and a mortgage on Rosebrook's small farm and inn located four miles north of the Gate of the Notch on a knoll called Giant's Grave. In the fall of 1817, Rosebrook died and Crawford married his cousin Lucy Howe.[18]

At the time, the inn mainly served farmers and merchants who had to travel through the Notch to sell their goods. But two small groups in 1818 and a third in 1819 came all the way from Boston to climb Mount Washington. They found it exhausting to push through the thick brush on the mountain slopes. "As this was the third party which had visited the mountains since I came here to live," wrote Crawford, "we thought it best to cut a path through the woods; accordingly my father and I made a foot path from the Notch out through the woods, and it was advertised in the newspapers, and we soon began to have a few visitors."[19] Cutting this first path to the top of Mount Washington—and advertising it—marks the beginning of the White Mountain tourist industry.[20] Crawford saw that the aesthetic appreciation of mountain scenery by wealthy travelers would make the White Mountain landscape valuable. Land, which had merely obstructed the flow of commerce up to then, now became an object of business, a commodity in its own right.

The number of visitors increased so rapidly that the house could barely hold them: "Company coming from all quarters, we now suffered for the want of house room, and many times our visitors were so numerous that, for the want of beds and lodging rooms, Lucy would have to take the feather beds from the bedsteads and make them up on the floor, and then the straw beds would answer for the bedsteads. In this way we would accommodate two, and sometimes four, and frequently she would give up her own bed and lie down herself upon the floor."[21] The head of a military school in Norwich, Vermont, brought fifty-two cadets to climb Mount Washington in 1824, and Crawford reported sleeping seventy-five guests in one night in 1833.[22]

More importantly, the guests served at Crawford's included many celebrities. James Kent, the chief justice of New York's Supreme Court, came in 1823. America's leading scientist, Benjamin Silliman, came in 1826 to learn how massive deluges like the Willey slide affected the earth's topography. Thomas Cole, founder of the Hudson River School, visited in 1827 and 1828. In 1831 Crawford personally escorted Daniel Webster to the top of Mount Washington and got a twenty dollar tip for his effort.[23] During his stay with the Crawfords in July 1832, Ralph Waldo Emerson decided finally to quit the ministry.[24] Washington Irving visited about the same time.[25] Hawthorne found material for several sketches and stories when he came two months later. The long list of celebrities whom Crawford entertained demonstrates that he had tapped into the right class of people—the wealthy and educated of the eastern cities.

Nevertheless, the accommodations at Crawford's inn remained quite plain despite Ethan's efforts to improve them. Crawford's place differed little from farmhouse-taverns found throughout the United States—at a lonely southern crossroads, perhaps, or along the National Road. Such inns were usually private houses that had been converted into taverns superficially. Serving travelers was a sideline. Landlords farmed for a living and sold refreshments or put travelers up for the night only because their houses happened to lie along a through road. A typical inn had a front room with a counter across the middle where the public could buy drinks or food. Those who wanted to spend the night might have to share a bedroom with several strangers, depending on how many others were staying at the inn. Guests were served the same food their hosts ate, the kind that any farm family would eat—salt pork or ham, baked beans, brown bread, eggs. Dinner and a bed did not cost much. In Mount Washington's eastern valley, Dolly Copp (Hayes's wife) served travelers for years from her farmhouse: "The price of entertainment was not exorbitant— 'a shilling all round,' that is, twenty-five cents for a meal, the same for a bed for each person and a quarter for the feed and care of a horse."[26] In the early period of White Mountain tourism, genteel visitors found about the same level of material comfort as did the backwoods farmer hauling a load to market.

Mary Jane Thomas (Ralph Waldo Emerson's sister-in-law) left a detailed reminiscence of the conditions encountered by a visitor during the early period of tourism. Their curiosity aroused by "the sad catastrophe at the Willey House," she and her new husband, Moses, toured the mountains in 1831 and stayed at both Ethan Crawford's and Abel Crawford's inns. They traveled the slow, backcountry roads in a "one horse shay" borrowed from her father. It took a day to drive the fifteen miles or so from North Conway to Abel's. Writing from the perspective of the 1880s, when the White Mountains ranked among America's most luxurious resorts, Thomas recalled the inn with a mixture of disdain and nostalgia.

> I can distinctly remember the appearance of the house of Abel Crawford as we entered it—The inevitable bar room on the right—its white floor carpeted with sand, where those of the "male persuasion" mostly congregated—the goodly array of bottles behind the bar, and the tempting display of pipes and tobacco on the mantel shelf . . . [In the room on the left] the nicely scrubbed white floor guiltless of carpet or even mats—6 hardbottomed wooden chairs, one common rocking chair with its plethoric cushion of feathers, the fireplace filled with green branches, the mantel with two oil lamps at one end, and two [homemade] candles . . . at the other—some ordinary prints on the wall, a small looking glass, under which was a table containing the mental pablum for the family, viz. a Bible, a hymn book, an almanac and some New Hampshire Patriots.[27]

Fig. 4. William Henry Bartlett, *The Willey House*, in Nathaniel P. Willis, *American Scenery* (1840), 111. Bartlett accurately depicted the Willey site during the twenty years after the slide: Rubble surrounds the shabby house, and tourists wander about freely. John Pendexter, who briefly occupied the house, built the barn about 1829. *Courtesy, Homer Babbidge Library, University of Connecticut.*

Thomas wistfully named the simple foods that were all grown and made right on the premises: brick-oven-baked beans, wheat bread, "berries in abundance," honey, "cream and butter" (48).

The next day the Thomases went to the Willey House, which must have appeared to them much as it did six years later to William H. Bartlett (fig. 4). The Thomases found it locked shut against vandals, "relic hunters, with yankee blades" who liked to hack off pieces of the furniture to keep as souvenirs. Thomas described what they saw from the outside: "we could see through the windows, the table, with the crockery left as by an unfinished meal, a tea kettle, iron pot, and some other cooking utensils on the hearth and the brands that had fallen apart and died out."[28] They went on to Ethan Crawford's for the night.

Driving up to the inn, they met the six and a half foot "stalwart Mountaineer, framed in the doorway . . . He did not welcome us with much suavity of manner," Thomas remembered, "it was not his way—He had a brusque, *un*courteous, but not *dis*courteous manner, but as we afterward had abundant opportunity to verify, a great deal of native Kindness of heart—He was strong in his prejudices and resented any assumption of superiority—but always ready to meet and reciprocate any friendly advances." The Thomases could not have minded Crawford's inelegance too much because they stayed with him three summers. Nevertheless, Ethan Crawford's place was cruder than his father's. "Crawford did as well as was then in his power," Thomas remarked, "but our fare and accommodations were of the most primitive character." Besides the fresh trout he caught in the Amonoosuc River, Crawford could give his guests only "cold corned beef and salt fish."[29]

Ethan Crawford had a great location, and that brought in tourists such as the Thomases despite the poor food and service. The Thomases stayed there almost a week waiting for the weather to clear so that Moses could climb to the top of Mount Washington. (The ascent was too rugged for Mrs. Thomas.) And the wait was worth it. When the rain finally cleared, Ethan took Moses up. "He returned at night wonderstricken, awe stricken, and inexpressibly impressed by his first view from the summit of the mountains," wrote Mrs. Thomas. When Moses went back to Crawford's by himself in 1834, he found the bridle path almost finished. He and Mary Jane came the next summer and rode up the long path, which wound over several lower peaks. "I shall never forget my emotions," she wrote, "when I came out of the woods on the top of Mt. Clinton and saw what seemed to me like Mountain *billows* all around me."[30] That kind of entertainment was the essence of Crawford's success.

Crawford realized from the beginning that people came to the mountains primarily for diversion, so he tried out many ideas for making their stay more enjoyable. Some of these schemes seem quite cheesy; others anticipate the greatest attractions of White Mountain tourism. To entertain his guests at the end of a day's sightseeing, Crawford set up an alley for nine-pin bowling and arranged dancing when there were enough guests.[31] He would often sound a large tin horn or shoot off a small cannon from the top of Giant's Grave, creating booming echoes in the valley.[32] He tried to assemble a "menagerie," or petting zoo, from animals captured in the surrounding woods, including a deer that allowed guests to feed and pet him, a wolf, peacocks, and a bear cub. Occasionally, he would tie the wolf on a long chain and let it attack sheep, hogs, or calves (123–5). Crawford also ran the area's post office—ideal for tourists who wanted to write home about their trip (137). If these amusements failed, Crawford told a good story.

Crawford's capital improvements show how clearly he saw that in the future the tourist industry would operate on a larger scale and in a grander style. Almost every year Crawford added to travelers' convenience by building better roads or improving accommodations. He bought the Notch House in 1823 as a way station for those going the twelve miles between his own house and his father's (64). The next year he tried to erect an eighteen-man tent on the top of Mount Washington for guests who wanted to stay the night and see the sunrise, but the summit's powerful winds blew the tent down (67). In the following two years he built an addition onto his house and added stables (70, 82). He persuaded the Willeys to buy and operate the Notch House in 1825 in order to help serve tourists. In 1827 he began the ambitious project of building a road for guests to ride in carriages all the way to the top of Mount Washington. He planned to do a little himself every year, but the job was far too big for one man. He settled for making just a bridle path.[33] In 1828 Crawford and his father built an inn near the Gate of the Notch and installed his brother Thomas J. Crawford as the proprietor.[34] In 1831 and 1832 Ethan Crawford put up a new barn and made further additions to his own house (131, 138). And on top of all this, he was always active in repairing and maintaining the turnpike through the Notch (107–8).

Although Crawford displayed great energy and ambition in these improvements, he had little money of his own and quickly fell into debt. The large scale he had envisioned for White Mountain tourism required enormous investments of capital up front, which he could never hope to make. Accordingly, Crawford's projects were modest compared to what the industry achieved in the 1850s, when it first became really profitable, and in the end Crawford lost control of his enterprise. Crawford had put $280 of his own into the Rosebrook farm and had assumed a mortgage of over two thousand dollars.[35] He borrowed several hundred dollars from a bank in 1828 to make repairs to the turnpike, which a storm almost as fierce as the one in 1826 had washed out (108–9). These expenses, in addition to what he paid out of pocket for his other projects, burdened Crawford for years. Nevertheless, he continued to sink money into his business, believing it would eventually pay off. In 1832, to enlarge his inn, he borrowed fifteen hundred dollars from a Concord bank—with his farm as collateral. This debt finally forced Crawford into bankruptcy, imprisonment for debt, and exile to Vermont.

Crawford's story illustrates the nature of American capitalism in the 1830s. By the middle of the decade, Crawford could no longer afford the payments on his debts and wanted to sell. In 1835 he signed a "bond" allowing someone to try to sell his inn for ten thousand dollars to a Boston stagecoach line. He was offered twelve thousand dollars for the property in the meantime, which he refused, having given his word to the first man.[36] These years marked the height of the real estate speculation preceding the Panic of 1837, and the original deal was never completed. Crawford was left with big debts but could convince no one to buy the inn at its true value. After creditors had him imprisoned in Lancaster for twenty-five days, he was forced to sell off the business it had taken him twenty years to build for a mere three hundred dollars.[37]

The Inn Goes Out

Similar failures awaited most of the early hotel operators because the coming of the railroad in 1851 hastened the transformation of tourism into big business. Thomas J. Crawford, who owned the inn at the Gate of the Notch, overloaded himself with debt to expand his hotel and went bankrupt in 1852. After Abel Crawford's death in 1851, a son-in-law ran the inn at the southern end of the Notch. He, too, went bankrupt by the early 1870s.[38] Horace Fabyan, a provisions dealer from Portland, Maine, took over Ethan Crawford's inn in 1837. He bought the Willey House in 1844 and built onto it a larger hotel (fig. 5). In 1848, he expanded Crawford's inn into the Mount Washington House by adding fifty rooms to accommodate 100 guests. But, though Fabyan built on a larger scale than Crawford, he, too, lacked the funds to maintain his business. After a fire and some legal trouble, Fabyan went out of business in 1853.[39]

The string of bankruptcies was part of the shaking out of the White Mountain tourist trade between 1837 and 1851. These years of deep recession and slow recovery saw a transition to a sharply more up-scale business. In attempting to attract a wealthier clientele, the tourist industry had to replace the wayside inn, such as the Willey House and the Crawfords' inns, with the hotel—designed specifically to cater to the tourist. "Although no rigorous distinctions were made among inns, taverns, and hotels in the early nineteenth century," explained Dona Brown, "the word *hotel* clearly indicated that the landlord was offering (or attempting to offer) a new style of privacy and luxury that had recently become popular in the larger cities."[40] The introduction of the hotel into the White Mountains represented a large increase in sophistication. Tourism became more self-conscious. It had to project just the right image to the public and carefully foster a more refined tourist culture. At the same time, tourism became a more calculating and systematic business.

Tourists in the stagecoach era had to have stamina. For them, eating coarse food and meeting rustic characters such as Ethan Allen Crawford were part of the fun. Touring through the White Mountains appealed, for example, to young men looking for a little adventure, such as Nathaniel Hawthorne and Francis Parkman, the future historian. After all, going into the mountains at

Fig. 5. The Willey House, Benjamin W. Kilburn, stereograph (detail). In 1845,
Horace Fabyan built a hotel onto the Willey House that was half the size of his
Mount Washington House, the first grand hotel.
Used with permission, New Hampshire Historical Society #F1371.

that time was not a casual outing; it could easily turn dangerous. One July day
in 1841, Parkman climbed far up into the ravine carved by the Willey slide in
an attempt to outdo Benjamin Silliman's climb fifteen years before. "But I was
enclosed," Parkman explained in his journal, "between two walls, fifty feet
high and so steep and composed of such material that an attempt to climb
would only bring down the rotting granite upon my head." Below, however, a
forty-foot sheer cliff barred the way and forced him to climb out of the ravine
anyway by scaling its walls. "I got halfway up and was clinging to the face of
the precipice, when two stones which supported my feet loosened and leaped
down the ravine." Only a jackknife helped Parkman dig and claw his way to
the top. "I confess I shuddered as I looked down at the gulf I had escaped," he
concluded.[41] Although none died, climbing in the mountains was exhausting
at best and always treacherous because of the area's highly changeable
weather. Few women attempted Mount Washington before the bridle path
was finished in 1840, and that limited the area's appeal as a vacation spot.

The innkeepers who followed Ethan Crawford tried hard to make mountain travel seem easier, safer, and more genteel. Horace Fabyan marketed his

hotel with a sophistication and polish that Crawford could never have matched. In 1852 Fabyan had a New York City printer prepare a small pamphlet—really, an early version of today's glossy travel brochures—to make a careful sales pitch. Fabyan went out of his way to reassure women (or their husbands) about Mount Washington's bridle path: "Over fifteen thousand people—and one-third of the number ladies, many of whom were entirely unaccustomed to the saddle—have ascended by this path, and no accident causing the slightest personal injury has occurred in the mountain ride."[42] Such slow, correct prose suited the new highbrow appeal of White Mountain tourism. On the very spot where Ethan Crawford a short time before had offered only simple comforts, Fabyan provided luxury and relaxation:

> The Mount Washington House, kept by Mr. H. Fabyan, has been recently rebuilt and refurnished entirely, introducing all the modern improvements, affording the visitor all the luxuries of the first hotels in the country, within the quiet of a Home.
>
> The House is over two hundred feet long, fronting the mountains, has two piazzas running the entire length of the building, and contains some hundred and fifty rooms, large and airy (14–5).

Although Fabyan's diction sounds a bit old-fashioned, it makes the same basic appeal that many resort hotels do today. Like them, Fabyan hoped to attract well-to-do couples and families willing to pay a premium for good living. The young bachelor out for adventure no longer mattered much to the tourist industry.

Although, like Ethan Crawford, he was finally defeated by limited funds and overreaching, Horace Fabyan developed Crawford's business a step or two farther. Whereas Crawford had had to build the business haphazardly as his few resources allowed, Fabyan thought out how best to maximize the return on his investment. Under Fabyan, the hotel itself became a deliberate financial instrument, generating a calculable profit.

Born in Scarborough, Maine, in 1807, Fabyan worked buying provisions for hotels in Portland. On the side he engaged in land speculation without much success. After marrying a woman from Conway, New Hampshire, he moved there to work as an innkeeper for a couple of years. When Crawford bankrupted in 1837, Fabyan rented the hotel from Crawford's creditors for five hundred dollars a year and later bought it outright. As the long recession of 1837 eased off, Fabyan expanded aggressively. He bought the Willey House in 1844 and added on a twenty-five-room hotel. Onto the old Crawford inn he built a fifty-room hotel, which he named the Mount Washington House. "Finally," Bulkley writes, "Fabyan remodeled the old Crawford Hotel's interior, creating a sixty foot dining room which was fully carpeted, furnished with curtains, and set with full length tables."[43]

Horace Fabyan's Mount Washington House accommodated the most guests in the greatest luxury. Even more impressive, the large number of rooms of uniform size minimized construction costs while making it possible to calculate per-unit profits and expenses. For these reasons, Bulkley credits Fabyan with inventing the grand hotel—symbol of the Golden Age of White Mountain tourism. "Most of the important hotels constructed in this period followed the dimensions established by the Mount Washington House formulation, attaining a length of 140 to 200 feet, a height of three stories, and usually comprising 100 rooms which could accommodate 200 guests. Thus, by 1851 something like a standardized hotel had appeared in the White Mountains which was built as the first working approach to mass tourism."[44] An inopportune fire that gutted his hotel in 1853 and a lawsuit over a competing claim on the Crawford property kept Horace Fabyan from making much money out of his cleverness. Nevertheless, Fabyan's grand hotel was the instrument with which big business later pumped cash out of the White Mountains.

The Abolitionists' Vacation

Tourism's structural changes scarcely affected the tourist's own experience. Visiting the White Mountains in the 1840s was not too different from visiting them in the 1820s. Although stagecoaches offered better access to the area, travelers in Fabyan's time still walked or rode the circuit past Mount Washington. A few more hotels offered slightly better accommodations, but travelers had to endure the wayside inn's plain food and traditional discomforts for most of their route. And, of course, entertainment remained the same. Visitors hiked or rode to the top of Mount Washington as the Thomases had in Ethan Crawford's time. Horace Fabyan even maintained Crawford's petting zoo and still blew a trumpet from Giant's Grave so that his guests could hear the notes echoing in the valley. What tourists found in the mountains changed little in the quarter century after the Willey slide.

This situation is made clear by Nathaniel Peabody Rogers, who wrote the most fact-filled description of the White Mountains from the tourist's viewpoint. A zealous abolitionist, Rogers rode through the mountains with his close friend William Lloyd Garrison in 1841. On his return, Rogers published an account in four installments in the *Herald of Freedom*, the antislavery newspaper he edited. Garrison and Rogers set out from Concord, New Hampshire, on August 23. They reversed the usual route taken by visitors by going through the mountains from west to east. They first visited Plymouth, New Hampshire, then rode north through Franconia Notch to Littleton (twenty miles down the Connecticut River from Lancaster), and finally headed east toward Crawford Notch. Rogers reacted to the scenery as did most Americans of the time—with awe and pride. He pronounced the White Mountains superior to the Scottish Highlands made famous by Walter Scott's novels. "They are but *island* mountains," he declares. "Ours are *continental.*"[45] Rogers even made a gentlemen's bet on the superiority of the White Mountains with a skeptical Garrison.

Franconia Notch was a kind of appetizer for Mount Washington, the main course. Franconia contained two of the region's most popular attractions, the Flume and the Old Man of the Mountain. Located fifteen miles west of the Notch, the Flume is "a tremendous chasm," explained Rogers, "cut directly up into the bosom of the mountain—the walls rising on each side, in the highest parts sixty or a hundred feet . . . We took no dimensions, but should say the great sluice-way was fifteen or twenty feet wide, and as many rods long [250–330 feet]. It may be longer. The stream was along the bottom of it, among enormous rocks that have got there, we could not conjecture how."[46] The Old Man of the Mountain lies about five miles from the Flume at the north end of Franconia Notch. The Old Man is a granite formation projecting from the top of a tall cliff. "It is on your left," Rogers wrote, "up, say fifteen hundred feet, a perfect profile of an aged man, jutting out boldly from the sheer precipice, with a sort of turban on the head and brow; nose, mouth, lip, chin and fragment of neck, all perfect and to the life . . . It needs no imagination to complete it. It is perfect, as if done by art. But it is up where art has never climbed" (172–3). The following day Rogers experienced sublimity of a different sort; Garrison spoke to an antislavery convention in Littleton. "It was exalting and soul-refreshing to hear him," Rogers proclaimed. The next day the two friends rode toward Crawford Notch.

It was overcast and threatening rain. Approaching Mount Washington and the lesser peaks, Rogers and Garrison "descried through the thick atmosphere a gloomy range of mountain—its summit, or summits, hid in thick clouds, and its awful breast gashed and lacerated with the mighty slides." The climate had suddenly changed to something Alpine and romantic; the terrain had enlarged to the dimensions of a folk tale. "Everything around us," Rogers continued, "had for some time betokened that we were in the suburbs of one of the capitals of nature. The majestic woods, the tremendous elevation of the mountain ranges, and the vastness of the forest—the stillness in the air, and its altered temperature; and the majestic roar of the Ammonoosuck along its bed of precipices spoke of its mountain *descent*, and that its fountains could not be far distant. It was a glorious hour" (182). Garrison conceded the gentlemen's bet: The White Mountains beat the Scottish Highlands.

They spent the night at Fabyan's inn, which remained much as it had been under Ethan Crawford, and Rogers found several melancholy reminders of him there. "We sallied out to view the objects of interest about the house. A pair of immense moose horns hung suspended on the front of the inn." Crawford had shot the moose himself. "Near them hung the sign of the 'White Mountain Post Office.' A pleasant idea—as it was for the accommodation of the visiters [*sic*] while here away from their homes." Crawford was the first postmaster. In the yard they saw the remnants of Crawford's petting zoo—a raccoon on a short chain and a bear tied to a post. The abolitionists wanted the animals freed. "We crossed the road," Rogers continued, "and went up on to the Giant's Grave—the appropriate name of a mound rising out of the level plain, one hundred and fifty or two hundred feet long, some sixty broad, and thirty or forty feet high . . . Ethan Crawford used to fire his swivel [gun] on the top of it at nightfall, to thunder up the mountain echoes. We found the breech of the old gun, blown off about mid way from the mouth" (183).

Rogers and Garrison enjoyed Fabyan's in spite of themselves. Their sharp Christian disapproval of the pleasures of the flesh led them to condemn many of the pastimes that tourists enjoyed. They objected to hunting and fishing along with the cruelty of the petting zoo. "Let no man cast a *knavish* hook into these peopled waters," Rogers preached, "or discharge a *felon* gun at the gentle deer that stoops to drink on their wild margin" (176). When they caught a fellow abolitionist smoking, they shamed him into repenting and quitting the habit entirely. But most of all they detested liquor. "We found a very neat and elegant table at Fabyan's, and every accommodation about the house of corresponding character, except that *drink* was to be had at his bar. It was drink that brought down the great strength of Ethan Crawford to the ground. Let friend Fabyan take timely warning, and banish that DEVIL from his premises" (183). That was not going to happen, of course, because most visitors were not ascetics like Rogers and Garrison.

Nevertheless, the two managed to enjoy themselves by spiritualizing activities as much as possible. Nineteenth-century tourists often sanitized their experiences in this way. They simply considered the quite physical, sensual White Mountain tour to be part of their moral and aesthetic education. Thus, Rogers described the blasts from Fabyan's tin horn as a kind of sacred music. Like Crawford, Fabyan entertained guests by sounding the horn from Giant's Grave. Bracing the horn, Fabyan would blow with an energy and spirit that made us start from our feet, after a few moments the answer would come from the mountain—first in distinct but softened echo, tone for tone, and as if from the extreme right of the woods, shortly after it echoed again, less distinctly and from a little toward the left—shortly after again still farther on, and still less distinctly, and so moving along the face of the woods as if a band of the Spirits of the mountain were marching there, to their unearthly alchemy, till it terminated in a blast of all the echoes at once, mingled together and shed forth from the whole woods in one harmonious, trembling, ravishing strain, dying away over the ridge among the hollows of the mountain.[47]

The echoes "surpassed all music we ever heard from man," asserted Rogers. They were better than "Handel and Hayden," better even than the choir at Westminster Abbey. The claim recalls Shelley's image for the innate harmony of things—the Aeolian harp, whose music comes from the wind's blowing randomly across it. Rogers likewise thought the echoes uplifting and spiritual because made with Nature's assistance.

The next day Horace Fabyan's brother Oliver led Rogers, Garrison, and six others up Mount Washington's bridle path. The party included three women. They set out early in the morning and would not return until sunset. First, they rode along the Amonoosuc about four miles to where the path began its ascent. Then, as Rogers described, "The guide ordered us to mind our distance, to bear forward as hard on the mane as possible, give the horses the entire reins, and take courage. We commenced our clamber, and found it an awkward business to keep the saddle" (186). They stopped several times for rest and water.

> We persevered—not talking much—for it was terrible steep, and we had to mind our ways, crawling up precipices, and between trees, and round sharp rocks and among roots . . . The lessening trees at length announced that we were nearing the bare mountainside . . . The trees diminished till our heads were among their boughs, and kept lessening—preserving their entire form, till they were mere dwarfs—very ugly looking, with their stout trunks not more than a foot high, and their sturdy, scraggy boughs. At last they became mere roots, crooking about on the surface of the soil (186–7).

Mount Washington's unique dwarf vegetation added to the sense of extreme bleakness. "After we got onto the naked ridges, the climbing was appalling. We did not dare look at it. Occasionally, as we cast an eye right and left, *across our hip*, we saw clear down the mountain a thousand feet or two, and so horribly precipitous that a false step would seem to have sent us to the very bottom" (187). All they could do was entrust their lives to the practiced horses until they reached the top.

They ate lunch a quarter mile from the summit in a little shelter "built of stones laid in moss, and roofed with rafters and long shingle." The isolation was overwhelming. "We left the horses here," Rogers wrote, "and proceeded to the summit on foot. We can hardly conceive a more desolate spot than that stone tavern, or idea than that of being alone there in the night, in a storm, or in winter." Fog heightened this impression. "We could see nothing but a few rods of bare rocks around us, so thick was the white mist. A pile of stones, sur-mounted by a limb of a tree stuck up for a flag staff perhaps,—a few feet high, marked the highest spot on the summit . . . We found some disabled honey bees crawling about on the stone heap. The surface of the rocks was exceed-ingly ragged. Some cold water lay in the hollows worn into them" (188).

After an hour on the summit, they had to start down without the fog lifting to let them view the landscape below. "Somewhere near the stone tavern, however, the clouds went off and disclosed us a glorious prospect off to the westward. We could see the Franconia mountains, the entire White Mountain range as far as to the Notch, the successive peaks Jefferson, Monroe and oth-ers, and the vast sweep from top to bottom of their sides, immense ridges, covered with woods and torn with slides, extending from each summit down to the world below" (188). The descent on horseback proved much easier than expected, and they made it back to Fabyan's in good spirits.

Rogers and Garrison set off the next morning (August 29) for Crawford Notch and the Willey House, fifteen years and one day after the slide. At the Gate of the Notch, Rogers wrote, "we entered a chasm in the rocks—a preci-pice, almost perpendicular on the left hand and sloping but little on the right. The pass is just wide enough to admit the narrow road and the narrower stream which flows beside it, and which is the river Saco. Passing a little on, the road turns suddenly to the left, and leaves you abruptly upon a frightful abyss. It opens directly before you, and you seem about to plunge into it. It is a gulf some hundred feet in depth." On the other side of the pass, the scars from the slides of 1826 had been slow to heal: "Every thing looks as if thun-der and lightning had struck it, or volcano hove it up—or earthquake rent it, or deluge flooded and washed it away. Rocks gravel and sand, that have come down in slides from the mountains all along the Notch for half a dozen miles, present you with a hideous picture, relieved by nothing but its *vastness*" (191).

The Willey House "was in full keeping with the scenery around" (193). Coming toward it, the travelers "descried a solitary house—standing a little elevated from the road on the right—uninhabited, and grown about with raspberry bushes." Rogers gave almost the only account by a tourist of the interior:

We went into the bed rooms where the slumbers of the ill-fated inmates had been broken on that terrible night by the voice of the slide, and into the kitchen where they had lived, with the desolate hearth around which they had often gathered and heard the evening storms howling along the Notch. The old cupboards and the chambers—we explored all, where these our fellow creatures had once occupied. The walls and plastering were scrawled over with names. We wrote brother Garrison's and our own *linked together* on the wall with a fragment of coal (192).

After spending the night at Abel Crawford's, where they stared down a group of hostile southern slaveholders, Garrison and Rogers rode home. But their uncompromising antislavery and Christian views had not much interfered with their vacation. They experienced the White Mountains as did most other tourists of the time. That experience included a curious mixture of familiarity and solitude. On the one hand, the sights were all well known—the Willey House, Mount Washington, the Old Man of the Mountain. Most tourists would have read about them in newspapers and guidebooks or heard stories from those who had already visited. Innkeepers such as Horace Fabyan and Abel Crawford maintained a homey relationship with their guests that was anticipated by first-time visitors. On the other hand, there was little traffic to the various attractions. Since the railroads were not yet hauling trainloads of people to the mountains, most went through in small groups, in pairs, or alone, so a group often had the sight it was visiting all to itself. Like Rogers, people during the first half of the nineteenth century saw the White Mountains as a place of beautiful desolation.

The Willeys' Choice

Rogers would have been amazed if he had seen the White Mountains a generation later. The landscape he described in 1841 resembles that of Shelley's poem "Alastor, or the Spirit of Solitude"; in this poem the hero-poet wanders alone through a prodigious natural landscape—a world devoid of human traces. Only a couple of decades later, Rogers would have found that Culture had triumphed over Nature. On Mount Washington alone, two 100-room hotels, a carriage road, a railroad, an observatory, a telegraph, and even a daily newspaper had claimed the desolate peak, at least during the summer months. Moreover, these engineering marvels had become just as popular with tourists as the view from the summit itself. Yet building a train that could go up the side of a mountain or a hotel that could withstand long winters of hurricane-force winds represented just the second and lesser revolution that took place in the White Mountains.

The first and more important revolution had almost been completed by the time Rogers took a vacation there, but he did not notice it because it had not changed the landscape outwardly. Instead, it had occurred in people's perceptions of the mountains and in the way they went about getting a living from them. Ethan Allen Crawford, Horace Fabyan, and others had engineered this revolution in the popular perception of the White Mountains as deliberately as those who built the cog railway and the Tip-Top House. These smalltime entrepreneurs had transformed the White Mountains from a marginal agricultural area into a profitable commodity. Although they made little money themselves, they prepared the ground for the establishment of tourism on a large scale in the second half of the nineteenth century.

The means by which they accomplished this illustrates a speculative attitude toward land. After all, this transformation depended on there being no very visible changes in the landscape, since tourism fed off of the region's backwardness. Tourists did not visit the mountains to see the well-cultivated fields of a southern plantation or an industrial landscape such as Mauch Chunk.[48] They went to see earlier epochs of civilization firsthand. The frontiers of hunters and trappers, subsistence farmers, and teamsters survived as images that made the later nineteenth-century landscape attractive to such visitors as Henry James—and profitable to railroads and hotels. Crawford and Fabyan realized that the White Mountains could bring in a lot more money by remaining undeveloped and unproductive. So, for the tourist's benefit, they reinterpreted the landscape: The area is not a desert or an obstruction, they said in effect, but a place of unspoiled natural wonders.

The entrepreneurs of White Mountain tourism had cultivated the right image. They induced tourists and travel writers to think of the undeveloped landscape as an antidote to the hustle and grind of new industrial cities. There one could escape from the mundane world of "getting and spending." There one could worship nature according to the age's romantic sensibility. "What a place for the invalid from the pent-up city to come and sail on, in the hot summer months, in a beautiful highland barge!" enthused Rogers of the pond where the Amonoosuc rises.[49] The tourist industry used visitors' own tastes as its main tool for making the White Mountains into a commodity. Inns and stagecoaches, hotels and railroads simply offered different degrees of convenience to those who wanted to refresh their souls through the aesthetic appreciation of nature. Of course, most visitors overlooked the fact that commercial tourism made a profit from the pure "beauty" they thought had existed there immemorially.

Culture performed the work of speculation by creating a demand for previously unproductive and undesirable land. In fact, culture has long played a dual role in speculation, inasmuch as the speculator invokes cultural values both to promote his own real estate and to hide the fact that his venture is just a business deal. Culture's usefulness remains a constant—whether in this century or the last, whether in the country or the city.[50]

A speculator's covert attitude differs radically from the popular understanding of land. The speculator seeks to maximize profit by drastically *changing* the land's use, whereas the public believes that land is valuable because of what it *produces*, namely, crops or ground rents. The speculator works for sudden, often catastrophic change in the landscape; the public thinks land needs steady development. The latter idea influenced the first land grants awarded by the English government in Coos County. The terms of these grants state that they were "for encouragement of settling and cultivating." The crown ordered grantees to build a carriage road through the land within a year, to settle at least nine families in five years, to save trees fit to be masts on navy ships, and to pay one ear of corn per year "if lawfully demanded." The last provision is purely symbolic, but it drives home the point: Land should be made to *produce*.

The American grantees saw things differently. In nearly every case, they sold off their holdings within a short time. Information contained in the deeds suggests that they had been speculators all along. In 1774, for example, King George III granted 8,740 acres in Mount Washington's eastern valley to Mark Wentworth, Daniel Rogers, and Jacob Treadwell, who were relatives and associates of New Hampshire's governor, John Wentworth. Ostensibly a reward for their service in the French and Indian Wars, the grant smacks of cronyism. In any case, within five years Wentworth, Rogers, and Treadwell had sold their rights to John Brown, a merchant from Providence, Rhode Island, for £5,244. The Revolution had intervened, of course, but even so they had made not the slightest attempt to fulfill the terms of the grant. The same thing happened again and again. On 20 May 1773, Governor Wentworth rewarded Timothy Nash and Benjamin Sawyer for their discovery of Crawford Notch with a two-thousand-acre grant just north of the Gate of the Notch. They quickly sold the land to James Richardson of Dover, New Hampshire, who in turn sold it for £900 to two Boston men on 3 June 1774. Although the land had had three different owners in a single year, no one actually occupied it until Abel Crawford moved there eighteen years later.[51]

Land sales by the state of New Hampshire in the 1830s repeat the pattern. The buyers, who paid pennies an acre, scarcely tried to make the land productive. That was not practical because the land was too hilly and remote. Still, buyers paid so little that they could not go wrong. They resold the land in hundred-acre parcels for about a dollar an acre, a considerable markup despite the modest price. When no one wanted to buy from them, which was common, owners did not even bother to pay the taxes. The sheriff of Coos County would seize the land and auction it off for a few dollars to a new owner (often a friend or relative), who would start the cycle over. That was speculation in its barest form. The speculator's math was the inescapable reality of land in the White Mountains. It went unacknowledged by a public that believed in farming and hard work.

What makes the Willeys such key figures is that they faced a clear choice between a speculative and an agrarian use of land. They had to decide which would bring in more money, and tourism looked better to them than farming. The choice was unmistakable, and the Willeys made it freely. They did not move to the White Mountains because of an obligation to a dying relative, as Ethan Crawford had done. Nor did they take up tourism because, like Horace Fabyan, they had failed elsewhere. Instead, they quit a good enterprise for a better one.

Before the move, the Willeys owned what was for that area a decent farm. An 1848 deed records the sale of three parcels that had once belonged to Samuel Willey. He had owned a 60-acre farm on the west side of the Saco River, 18 acres of adjoining intervale (a low-lying tract of land along a river), and an upland woodlot of 32 acres—110 acres in all. The size was typical for a family farm in New England, and the three parcels suggest the standard combination of three kinds of land: cropland, pasture, and woodlot. The 1848 sale price of seven dollars an acre indicates that the land's quality was poor compared to farms in other parts of the country. (Improved farmland generally sold for ten dollars an acre.) Even so, the Willeys' farm was located in the region's widest, most fertile valley, and owning it made the family solidly middle class. It meant that they had escaped the fate of so many second-generation settlers forced to travel west into New York State and beyond to find enough good land. And so nothing compelled the Willeys to move to the Notch and serve the tourists, nothing except the calculation of their own best interests.

Modern readers used to the many choices offered by an urban, industrial economy may find the Willeys' decision unremarkable, yet one can hardly overstate the nineteenth century's incomprehension. To the average American in the 1820s, the Willeys would seem to have given up the tangible, reliable productions of a farm and the benefits of community to endure isolation while engaged in a business that produced nothing. Joseph Buckingham's incredulity reflects the outlook of the times: "Can philosophy or conjecture account for or explain the motives that can induce a man thus to plant himself at a distance of six miles from the habitation of any of his race, and in a spot where it is next to impossible he can ever have a nearer neighbor?"[52] Nineteenth-century Americans could think of only two sensible explanations—poverty or a romantic withdrawal from the world—and most writers portrayed the Willeys that way. They did not realize that the Willeys' sophisticated understanding of land far outstripped their own.

The Willeys' choice to reinvent land rather than to improve it represents in miniature the approach to land that dominates in America. Yet the very nature of speculation includes disguise or dissimulation. More than a century ago, Frederick Jackson Turner mistakenly reversed the relationship between culture and economics. His image of the frontier sweeping grandly westward expressed a deep faith in the primacy of culture; business simply represented the means by which America realized its cultural imperatives. To Turner, the speculator operated in the interstices of the larger movement. A mere opportunist, he interfered with the honest business of settlement. However, the example of the White Mountains shows that anomaly is more than just a symptom of speculation. It lies at its heart.

The Willeys' choice in moving to Crawford Notch shows that they thought no differently about land than do today's urban speculators. Both treat land—regardless of its state of development—as if it were a new frontier. Looking at land that way allows speculators to tell a brand-new story about it.

CHAPTER THREE

The Golden Age
of Tourism

THE GOLDEN AGE of White Mountain tourism began precisely on 4 July 1851—seventy-five years after Independence and twenty-five years after the Willey slide. On that day, the first train to the White Mountains pulled into the station at Gorham, New Hampshire, eight miles northeast of Mount Washington. This event heralded several big changes. Tourists from Boston, New York, and other northeastern cities could now get to the White Mountains in a matter of hours rather than days. The convenience and comfort of the new railroad meant that an avalanche of travelers would descend on the mountains each summer. The hotels that accommodated them would become much larger and more luxuriously furnished. To build and run them would require such large amounts of capital that big business would squeeze out local owners. Finally, the White Mountains would no longer belong to adventurous bachelors such as Hawthorne and Parkman; the mountains instead became a chic resort for the leisure class.

Nevertheless, this visible alteration in the landscape simply fulfilled the possibilities first imagined by Ethan Allen Crawford. He tried to centralize control of all aspects of the tourist business and failed. Almost immediately after the railroad came, however, big business formed a kind of syndicate that combined transportation, lodging, publicity, and access to tourist sights. By the mid-1850s, passengers getting off the train in Gorham could stay there at the Alpine House, a railroad-owned hotel, or be carried right away by coach to the Glen due east of Mount Washington, where the manager of the Alpine House owned another hotel. From there a coach would take tourists up to the top of Mount Washington to two more hotels owned by a Boston publisher who produced White Mountain travel books containing railroad timetables. This syndicate functioned much as an Atlantic City casino does today. Each is set up to keep customers within the bounds of one enterprise so that the largest possible portion of the money spent during an excursion goes only to the single enterprise.

A change in sensibility accompanied the exponential leap in the size and complexity of the tourist industry. Late nineteenth-century tourists generally viewed the White Mountains as less wild or dangerous than did Thomas Cole and N. P. Rogers. Indeed, paintings done after 1851 depict a tamer, more idyllic landscape than do Cole's works. A number of things contributed to this change. For one, the domesticated landscapes of midcentury European art strongly influenced American tastes. For another, the public became increasingly aware of the Rocky Mountains, whose extent, elevation, and remoteness outdid the White Mountains. But something even deeper affected the tourist's vision. The ease and convenience of travel to the mountains, combined with big business's near total domination, translated into a controlled environment for the tourist, who felt safer as a result. That sense of security tended to domesticate the landscape in people's minds. Thus, aesthetic perceptions during the late nineteenth century reflect the economic domestication of the White Mountains. The tourism business had finally mastered the commodity that Ethan Crawford first produced in 1819.

The Railroads

If the White Mountains in the early nineteenth century lay out on the margin of the American economy, their status changed significantly and became more complicated after the railroad's arrival. Thanks to the railroad, the region sustained economic activities of widely varying intensity. On the one hand, the mountains developed a large logging industry. On the other hand, the railroad allowed farmers to sell fresh dairy products in Boston.[1] Thus, the White Mountains were simultaneously near to the eastern cities and far away. Tourism remade itself to capitalize on these conditions: The White Mountains became America's "most accessible wilderness." The railroad turned a region that had been settled for three generations back into wilderness and, paradoxically, brought it within easy reach of urban dwellers. By cutting travel time from several days to a matter of hours, the railroad changed the nature of White Mountain tourism. Many of those who went to the mountains by rail for the summer season would not have wanted to bounce along in a stagecoach or trudge dirt roads for days at a time, as earlier visitors had had to do. The sensibility that drew a Nathaniel Hawthorne or a Thomas Cole to the White Mountains would not have characterized those who rode in Pullmans.

Although stagecoaches and improved roads made travel to the mountains easier, in the 1840s it still took days to cover the distance from Portland,

Boston, or New York City. Later in the century railroads advertised express trains to the mountains, but earlier travelers generally took their time and stopped to explore towns and scenery along the way. In *Travels in New England and New York*, Timothy Dwight, the president of Yale, described a 1797 journey of 280 miles to the White Mountains.[2] Leaving New Haven on September 18, he arrived at the Notch fifteen days later on October 3. Thomas Cole took about six days to travel the ninety miles from Concord, New Hampshire, in 1828.[3] In 1839, Thoreau went from Concord, Massachusetts, to the Notch in seven days.[4] A vigorous, young Francis Parkman traveled to the Notch from Boston in five days in 1841.[5] And Benjamin Brown French, a New Hampshire native and federal officeholder, visited the mountains in 1845. Using steamboats, trains, and horses, he went from Washington, D.C., to the Notch in seventeen days. French's experience is typical because along the way he visited friends in a few towns—stopping five days in Exeter, New Hampshire—and took time out to go "trouting."[6] Although this kind of travel must have been exhausting, it cost relatively little. French reported that, when he and his companion stayed overnight at a "very democratic" inn full of "pedlars, . . . our bill for 2 suppers, lodgings, breakfasts & horse keeping was 134 cents!"[7]

The railroad made traveling much faster and more comfortable but also more expensive. The original 1856 edition of Benjamin Willey's *Incidents in White Mountain History* includes a travel schedule.[8] Published just five years after the Atlantic and St. Lawrence Railroad (later the Grand Trunk Railroad) came to the White Mountains, it shows how dramatically things had improved. A passenger could leave Boston at 7:30 A.M., change trains in Portland, and arrive by 5:30 at Gorham, within eight miles of Mount Washington. The 202-mile, ten-hour trip cost four dollars. For $3.50 a tourist could take an overnight ferry from Boston to Portland and then the morning train to Gorham, a travel time of sixteen and a half hours. Paying a fare of $10.05, a New Yorker could cover the 350 miles to the Notch by train in twenty-seven hours. Later on, when other railroads were servicing the White Mountains, train travel became almost twice as fast. In the 1887 edition of his guidebook, Moses Sweetser reported that the Boston and Maine Railroad went from Boston to North Conway in just six hours. The train from New York City to near the Notch took just twelve hours.[9]

More striking than the speed of train travel was the new attitude toward White Mountain tourism fostered by the railroads. The speed of travel made a trip to the mountains more casual. Ironically, this very casualness led to the deaths of visitors who took climbing the mountains too lightly: The first fatalities among tourists in the White Mountains occurred only *after* the railroad's arrival.[10] The case of Benjamin L. Ball, a Boston doctor, illustrates how the convenience of travel during the railroad era blinded tourists to the dangers. Ball had planned to take a trip to the White Mountains in the summer of 1855 but had to postpone it until October. Although afraid that it was too late in the season, Ball resolved to go on October 24, weather permitting. When he woke on the twenty-fourth, the weather was fine, so he went to the station and boarded the Eastern Railroad's train for Portland. He planned to visit friends on the way in Portsmouth, but the train schedule did not allow it. In Portland, he boarded the Atlantic and St. Lawrence for Gorham and got off there at the Alpine House, where he inquired the best way to Mount Washington. He then took the stage eight miles south to the Glen House. The landlord, J. M. Thompson, explained that the low clouds that day obscured any view of the mountain. But Ball wanted to get as close to the peak as he could. As it was still daylight, he walked up to the Camp House, which served the workers building the new carriage road. He spent the night there with the foreman, J. D. Myers. The next day, against Myers's advice, he wandered up the mountain without gloves or hat but carrying an umbrella. He got lost in a two-day ice storm and blizzard.

Ball soon lost sight of the way back down the mountain and discovered that, because of the ice that coated everything, he could easily fall hundreds of feet down the mountain slopes if he tried to descend. Twice he tried climbing upward to reach shelter in the summit hotels, but the ice covering Mount Washington's band of dwarf vegetation formed an insurmountable barrier. He was forced to spend two nights in a shallow cave whose opening he closed up imperfectly with his umbrella and snow. Despite sixty hours of exposure to subzero cold, hurricane-force winds, hunger, dehydration, and lack of sleep, Ball survived.[11] Henry David Thoreau, the consummate walker, read Ball's book and remarked, "Of course, I do not wonder that he was lost." Thoreau went on to list the minimum gear *he* would take on such a hike: India-rubber outerwear, a tent, a map and compass, salt pork and bread, fishhooks, a jackknife, matches in a watertight vial, string, and paper.[12] But Thoreau also disdained train travel. His list and superior tone only serve to demonstrate the new reality that the railroad created by speeding up time. The blizzard surprised Ball, in part, because the quickened pace of travel implanted the feeling that he could always go a little farther and do a little more. After all, the trip that had taken Parkman five days Ball accomplished just in the daylight hours of one day in late October.

When the carriage road was finished a few years after Ball's adventure, people could travel from the farthest United States to Mount Washington's peak and scarcely put a foot on the ground. The railroad did not simply provide transportation; it sold a whole new sensibility about travel, which it fostered by offering complete travel packages. The railroad distributed literature about the mountains, offered special fares, and ran big hotels. This packaging allowed railroads to get the most profit out of every segment of the business because it appealed above all to the high-end customer who paid a premium for the luxury and refinement of White Mountain travel. In his history of the Boston, Concord and Montreal Railroad, Edgar T. Mead described what drew the typical traveler at the end of the century.

> Like its B[oston] & L[owell] predecessor, C[oncord] & M[ontreal] added to the flood of summer-vacation literature. Pictures of placid lakes alternated with views of misty mountains. Special excursion round-trip tickets tempted the travel-prone.
>
> Wealthy families chartered private cars from the Wagner or Pullman Palace Car companies. During the high season, members of the fleet [of locomotives] such as *Grasmere, Wanderer, Iolanthe,* or *Pickwick* could be seen parked at Fabyans. Mann Boudoir Cars were attached to the 1 P.M. train from Boston, arriving at Fabyans at 8:25 P.M.
>
> A typical bargain excursion special would start from Boston and run up the B[oston] & M[aine] "Seashore Route," then up the steep Maine Central line *via* Bartlett to Crawford Notch and Fabyans, back *via* Plymouth and Concord to Boston, all for $12.00.[13]

Invoking English pastoralism, the names of the locomotives indicate the direction that tourism had taken. Culture and elegance supplanted the rusticity that earlier travelers had found in the White Mountains. Wilderness and luxury went hand in hand during the late nineteenth century's Golden Age of tourism.

This unlikely combination of selling points reflects the larger contradiction in the region's economic status after midcentury. While the White Mountains remained isolated from the main flow of American commerce and industry, they sustained buildings of great size—the grand hotels—that normally do not exist, even today, outside big cities. Beginning with the railroad's arrival, the mountains always had several hotels that held hundreds of guests, and one or two, like Fabyan's, held four hundred.[14] In fact, by the early 1900s there were at least nine hotels with a capacity of three hundred or more guests.[15] The transportation revolution made possible this amazing density, but still more interesting is the way the tourist industry exploited the unusual juxtaposition of urban and upcountry geographies. Neither vision of the White Mountains, as wilderness or as readily accessible to the city, by itself made the landscape valuable. It could become valuable only when the two visions coincided and the difference between them could be exploited.

The railroad had created this contradictory situation by transporting Midwestern grain to the east. This development placed the White Mountains in a strange position. Just when the railroads brought the region very close to the eastern cities, its agriculture experienced a reversal of fortune. The market pressure that had led farmers in the 1820s to grow wheat on the intervales relaxed, and there was no longer a need for such extensive land use. If cultivated land represents the standard by which to judge a region's progress, as popular sentiment maintained, the White Mountains seemed *less* settled after the railroad than before. This was the condition of the landscape that Henry James found but could not explain (see chap. 1). In any case, along with better railroad service, the last half of the nineteenth century brought with it an increasing sense that the White Mountains were a wilderness. Tourism was the perfect scheme to exploit this paradox, to make valuable a landscape that had lost its value by normal standards.

The Hotel in the Garden

Although the railroad and the grand hotel needed each other to sustain their businesses, they developed a closer symbiosis than the mere dovetailing of interests could have produced. They represented two halves of a coordinated effort by big business to refashion the White Mountains into an attractive commodity for America's urban elite. The grand hotel enabled the tourist industry to package and sell the landscape to the mass of consumers which the railroad was delivering, and it accomplished this in two ways. First, the grand hotel offered a standardized room, something the Willeys and the Crawfords could never do with their cramped houses. The hotel room was a unit easy to replicate and readily salable; owners could increase profits simply by building hotels with more rooms, as many as their capital allowed. The Mount Washington Hotel, for instance, opened in 1902 with 650 rooms. Equally important, however, was that the grand hotel virtually monopolized guests' pocketbooks by rendering every conceivable service—from pickup at the train station to rides out to White Mountain attractions to meals, newspapers, and telephone service in the hotel itself. Together, hotel and railroad made the mountains into a virtual extension of the city, the railroad by providing swift, comfortable transportation and the hotel by providing all the modern conveniences and refinements.

In addition, the White Mountain grand hotel represented the outflow of capital and sophisticated business practices from city to countryside. Indeed, throughout the United States, the hotel was often an instrument of economic development that complemented other forms of investment. Dona Brown explained: "Hotels . . . played a key role in the economic development of sur-rounding regions. Typically, tourist hotels formed part of an interlocking development process that combined extractive industries, farming, land spec-ulation, manufacturing, and tourism. Through hotels and their related busi-nesses, the tourist industry brought capitalism into the countryside in con-junction with other industries—sometimes even before any other industries."[16] Of course, the White Mountain hotel did not foster development; that would have gone against its own interests. Still, it was an engine of capitalism equally as sophisticated as the railroad.

The grand hotel and the railroad arrived in the White Mountains at the same instant. The Atlantic and St. Lawrence Railroad made sure that it fin-ished building the Alpine House in Gorham before the first passengers to the region stepped off the train on 4 July 1851. Within two years, six big hotels had already sprung up.[17] Construction of the Atlantic and St. Lawrence (to run between northern Vermont and Portland, Maine) had begun in 1846, so men such as Horace Fabyan, who built the first grand hotel, had a few years to prepare for the railroad's coming.[18] From the beginning, the railroad itself strongly supported tourism as a way to build traffic in the middle of its route. R. Stuart Wallace described the "intimate relationship" between railroads and hotels: "The hotels needed the railroad to bring tourists, supplies, and the mail. They responded by building their own railroad stations, where hotel employees would meet incoming guests in elegant hotel coaches. Railroads, for their part, printed White Mountain maps, guidebooks, and collections of scenic photographs of favorite tourist attractions. In some cases, railroads di-rectly invested in White Mountain tourism by building hotels."[19] As the grand hotel had sprung to life simultaneously with the railroad's arrival, it died out in the early twentieth century when automobiles made traveling freer and more egalitarian.

In its most developed form, the grand hotel less resembled the Willeys' and Crawfords' humble inns than it did today's suburban shopping mall or gam-bling casino. Like its twentieth-century counterparts, the grand hotel acted as a self-enclosed substitute for the city.

> Providing luxury and good service within the hotels was costly but necessary. Employees of the summer resorts were well-mannered college students from Dartmouth, Bates, and some of the teacher colleges and seminaries in New Hampshire and Maine. Much of the food came from the local area, with some hotels owning their own farms. The remainder of the food came by train, and in-voices from some of the hotels indicate that exotic foods were not uncommon. Along with good food and service, hotels often had their own post office, a bar-ber shop, and a hotel store. The effort was to make the hotel a small city unto itself.[20]

Surrounded by its own farms and importing goods by train, the grand hotel's thoroughly controlled environment recreated a city's sophistication and wealth but excluded the problems of urban life, such as poverty. Like boutique retailers in an upscale mall, hotels took care that even the servants spared guests an unpleasant exposure to the lower classes. "The polite young gentleman who attends to your wants at table," William H. Rideing reassured the travelers of 1877, "bringing you a dish of fresh eggs and a glass of creamy milk . . . is a Sophomore at Harvard, and he is not the victim of any bitter reverse in life, as you may be inclined to think."[21] Owners made certain that the wealthy felt comfortable spending money at their hotels.

Grand hotels went to great lengths to attract Thorstein Veblen's "leisure class," an elite that identified itself with a fusion of culture, leisure, and wealth. Even before the Civil War, when tourism was more democratic, the richest travelers set the tone in the White Mountains and "gave the trade an increasingly cosmopolitan flavor."[22] Nathaniel Noyes, a proprietor of the hotels on Mount Washington's summit in the 1850s, recalled that "people from all parts of the country, and travelers from foreign lands as well, came up the mountain . . . One noon there were representatives of 13 different nations at dinner."[23] The amenities in the White Mountains surprised European visitors, many of whom had read about the crudity of American life in such books as Frances Trollope's *Domestic Manners of the Americans* (1828) and Charles Dickens's *American Notes* (1842). When Frances's son, English novelist Anthony Trollope, visited in the fall of 1861, he confessed, "That there was a district of New England containing mountain scenery superior to much that is yearly crowded by tourists in Europe, that this is to be reached with ease by railways and stagecoaches, and that it is dotted with huge hotels almost as thickly as they lie in Switzerland, I had no idea."[24]

Almost overnight, the tone of the White Mountains had altered dramatically: The grand hotels quickly replaced Crawford's tin horn and menagerie with culture and refinement. For food, the grand hotels did not just serve guests salt pork, baked beans, or whatever else happened to be in the house; the railroad brought to the hotels the best America had to offer. "Yesterday I ate sweet potatoes at dinner," reported Amelia Matilda Murray in August 1855 to a correspondent back home in England; "they taste very like chestnuts. Such things are not grown here, but come from the South. I find extreme civility and attention from the waiters and attendants in the White Mountain hotels. On the whole, my impression of the American people has been hitherto far more agreeable than I expected."[25] Murray's approbation really meant something. As a lady-in-waiting to Queen Victoria, she belonged to the English social elite envied by even the most privileged Americans. A few days later, Murray described life in the Flume House located in Franconia Notch (about twenty miles southeast of Mount Washington): "The larger drawing-room in this hotel, is filled with every comfort, and there is an excellent piano. The evening party was large, perhaps from forty to fifty; an elephant well manufactured out of two bipeds walked in to amuse the children; one of the house-attendants played quadrilles very fairly on the violin; two sets were made up for dancing; some young ladies also sang in tune and very sweetly together."[26] After the Civil War, the grand hotels offered still more high culture. Many hired some of the nation's best landscape painters to live in residence for the summer and to offer guests lessons and critiques (see chap. 4). In the 1870s, guests at the Twin Mountain House, who refined their aesthetic sensibility by viewing White Mountain scenery, could refresh themselves spiritually by listening to the renowned Henry Ward Beecher's sermons.[27]

Late nineteenth-century tourists gladly paid a premium for participating in the White Mountains' culture of wealth. In the 1880s, according to Sweetser's guidebook, the best and newest hotels, such as the Fabyan House and the Twin Mountain House, rented rooms for $4.50 a day, $21.00 to $25.00 per week. At this time, the best-paid, most highly skilled laborer made no more than $4.00 a day, and even a first-class hotel in New York City cost only $2.50 a day.[28] For their money, guests had access to a "telegraph and post offices, billiard and bowling rooms, a news-stand" and gas lighting.[29] A day in the mountains could be very expensive, indeed, especially to visit a big attraction like Mount Washington.

> To "do" the White Mountains fashionably means an expenditure of fifteen or twenty dollars a day, for the charges of the leading hotels, high as they are, form only a small item compared to the grand total of "extras," incurred for guides, drives, and other inevitables. The [cog] railway fare up Mount Washington is three dollars, and the fare down Mount Washington is an equal amount, an additional sum being charged for any bag or bundle that cannot be carried in the hand. The mildest drink costs twenty-five cents. Nearly as much is asked for carriage hire as would buy a respectable horse and buggy. And while the rate for board is four or five dollars a day below the summit, the price at the summit is six dollars a day.[30]

Fifteen dollars in 1877 is roughly equal to five hundred dollars today.[31] And it must be kept in mind that the deflation of American currency after the Civil War meant that each dollar was often worth a third more than before the war. As a typical tourist's outlay, then, these prices represent a vast increase—perhaps forty times—from the $1.34 that Benjamin Brown French and his companion had spent on a day's hospitality thirty years before. But the White Mountains' sophistication and style were excellent, and America's "unostentatious representatives of wealth and intellect" eagerly paid up. Rideing explained the tourist's psychology, which proved so lucrative for the grand hotel: "The society is so select, and the accommodations are so excellent . . . that no one who can afford it will complain of the cost."[32] Arcadia turned out to be a terrific product to sell—high volume and high margin.

The phenomenon of the grand hotel reflected its origin in fast-moving capitalism. White Mountain hotels had none of the solidity and architectural value of the chateaux and manor houses where the European aristocracy customarily spent its summers. The life cycle of these wood-frame structures was typically short. They went up practically overnight, they enjoyed tremendous success for a few years, and then they quickly perished through fire or changing fashion. Yet they remained highly profitable for those who could afford to build them, as shown by the fact that construction of hotels did not stop throughout the last half of the nineteenth century. If one hotel was destroyed or went out of business, another soon took its place. After the Crawford House burned to the ground on 30 April 1859, it took only sixty days to build a bigger replacement, even though all the lumber had to be hauled by horses from seventeen miles away. The new hotel served one hundred guests on the Fourth of July.[33]

Hotels had little permanence but were transitory phenomena, structures thrown together to exploit an opportunity that the railroad created. Open just three or four months a year, the grand hotel more closely resembled a theme park than the civilized institution it pretended to be. It was simply a mechanism for turning consumers' interest in the White Mountains into money. Building a grand hotel required a large initial outlay, but hotel receipts repaid the investment rapidly.[34] The early hotels did little to mask their utilitarian design. Like a skyscraper turned on its side, the grand hotel grew by the simple replication of its boxlike units. No longer a part of the innkeeper's own home, the "room" was now a mass-produced commodity, each one indistinguishable from all the others.

However much it projected itself as a haven of culture, a hotel operated only because the arithmetic worked: The average room generated more income than per-unit expenses. Adding rooms multiplied profits. For these reasons, the size of hotels and capital investments tended to grow over time. Already in the first decade of grand hotel construction, the 1850s, start-up costs exceeded what a Jacksonian individualist like Crawford could afford. According to Bulkley:

The Alpine House in Gorham cost about $30,000 to build in 1851 while the Conway House, also built in the same year, cost $25,000. The Crawford House [near the Gate of the Notch], which was built in 1851 and burned to the ground on April 30, 1859, was valued at $21,000: $13,000 for the physical structure and $8,000 for the furnishings. Therefore, it cost somewhere between $20,000 and $30,000 to construct one of these "Grand" hotels of the 1850's; Fabyan's Mount Washington House, although built between 1846–1848, was probably worth $25,000 and perhaps even more because of its choice location.[35]

Hotels grew even larger in size and expense later on. When the original Glen House in Mount Washington's eastern valley burned in 1884, it was immediately replaced by a hotel three hundred feet long and worth about $250,000. Fire destroyed the new Glen House only eight years later. The largest White Mountain hotel of all, the Mount Washington Hotel, incorporated the latest building technology—a steel frame with fireproof sheathing.[36] It cost $1,500,000.[37]

Hotels quickly and generously repaid these investments. Bulkley estimated that even Ethan Allen Crawford's inn, which accommodated just fifty guests and operated year-round, was producing a gross income of three thousand dollars when Fabyan took it over in 1837.[38] The bigger hotels returned much more money even though their season lasted only from midsummer to early fall. Bulkley cited an 1858 financial report from a company that operated two hotels in Franconia Notch, including the one Amelia Murray found very agreeable:

The Flume House and the Profile House each possessed 100 rooms and could accommodate 200 guests each per day. Earned gross income for 1858, according to the report, was $28,642 of which $16,041 was paid out in operating expenses, leaving a net profit of $12,601 for the 1858 season which was considered to be an excellent tourist year (which was true for the decade [as a whole]). Given a daily room and board rate of $2.50, to be divided into the total gross income of $28,642, it can be determined that both hotels accommodated 11,444 guests within the ninety day season. Were these results to be divided equally between the Flume House and the Profile House in order to determine what an individual hotel might have earned, one could generalize that the typical grand hotel of the 1850's took in about 5,722 guests during the season and that its gross earnings were $14,300, of which $8,000 would be paid in operating expenses, leaving a net profit of over $6,000 for the season. On this basis, a hotel costing between $20,000 and $30,000 could have been fully amortized in as little as a four to five year period. In short, thanks to the rail developments of the 1850's, such a heavy tourist trade evolved that the operation of the early "Grand Hotel" was practically a guaranteed success and a most lucrative and profitable business.[39]

If Bulkley's estimates are correct, the typical White Mountain hotel over the first five years of operation yielded an average annual return on investment of around 25 percent. There is no wonder why they sprang up so fast after 1851.

The Consumers of Arcadia

White Mountain tourism projected a high-culture appeal that freed it from the taint of vulgarity ordinarily attached to business. Of course, now and then, someone deplored the materialism of the Golden Age. For example, when Swedish novelist Fredrika Bremer, a friend of Emerson, visited in 1853, she thought that the ethos of the grand hotels detracted from what was truly edifying about the White Mountains:

> [The region overflows] with noisy, unquiet company, who do not seem to understand any other mode of enjoying nature than in talking, laughing, eating, drinking, and by all other kinds of noisy pleasures. They pass up the mountain laughing at full gallop, and come down again at a full gallop. Champagne corks fly about at the hotels, gentlemen sit and play cards in the middle of the day, and ladies talk about dress-makers and fashions. How unlike is this thoughtless life to that of nature, where the clouds come down as if to converse with the mountain.[40]

Yet it is surprising how seldom people voiced such criticism as Bremer's. Despite some reservations about the summer people, even Henry James thought the White Mountains could quite possibly incubate permanent social forms. For the most part, visitors upheld the illusion of the high-minded culture of the grand hotels.

Nevertheless, the phenomena of Golden Age tourism that both critics and supporters describe appear most comprehensible if the White Mountains are understood to have constituted a frontier similar to the industrial frontiers of the Far West, such as mining and ranching. Like its more celebrated counterparts, the tourist industry used the latest technology (railroad and grand hotel) to exploit land for profit. Yet two differences mask the fact that the White Mountain economy depended on resource extraction. First, instead of shipping its products to eastern markets, the White Mountain railroads brought tourist-consumers right to the source. Second, what makes White Mountain tourism particularly interesting as a frontier is that its products were not material—cattle, grain, minerals, lumber—but *imaginative*. The White Mountain frontier sold the sights and associations of its own landscape. In the tourist's mind, the hotel room or the train ride to the top of Mount Washington simply represented a convenient means to gain access to the White Mountains' rich store of things to see.

Like a typical luxury goods business, tourism appealed to the imagination to raise itself above the merely utilitarian. "The nation's tourist attractions," according to John Sears, "were consumer products, promoted by the railroads which carried the tourists to them and organized to satisfy the customers who had the leisure to enjoy them, but their role as products was often marked by religious rhetoric or behavior."[41] Or, as Robert McGrath put it, tourism is "the application to life of lessons learned from art."[42] Visitors to the White Mountains demonstrated a glib proficiency in reading its attractions as texts: romances, textbooks, and sermons. Although mystery hid the causes of the Willey disaster, for example, preachers immediately seemed to know that it betokened God's unutterable power over humankind. Immediately after the slide, Samuel Hazeltine from Bartlett had suggested as much by citing Isaiah 40:12: "Who has . . . weighed the mountains in scales and the hills in a balance?" This became a common reference to express the sublimity of many features of the White Mountain landscape. Dartmouth's Erastus Everett, for example, quoted it in 1836 after a trip to Mount Washington's summit.[43]

Early in the nineteenth century, men such as Theodore Dwight Jr. (Timothy Dwight's nephew) recommended travel as an important supplement to education. In his *Sketches of Scenery and Manners in the United States* (1829), Dwight argued that American landscape contains vivid associations with history and culture which make it an ideal textbook. "The White Mountains represent the sublime center of this geography both in a natural and political sense," wrote John Sears in his introduction to the reprint edition. "There the ruins left by the flooding and avalanching that tore up the Saco River valley in 1826, fifty years after the Declaration of Independence, become images of the violence of the Revolution."[44] Later on, Thomas Starr King, a Boston clergyman, found that the landscape evoked sentiments best expressed by romantic poetry. Accordingly, his volume *The White Hills* (1859) contains long quotations from English, continental, and American poets, few of whom had ever seen the mountains.[45] Nineteenth-century tourists considered it the region's best guidebook, nonetheless. In a similar way, tourists throughout the nineteenth century believed landscape to be virtually interchangeable with literature and the other arts, and they found it hard to think of travel except as a form of high culture.

This conflation of life and art played to the vanity of tourists, who welcomed narratives that let them participate in the landscape's history. The extent to which tourists identified with the landscape appears clearly in the only book-length treatment of the Willey disaster. In *Soltaire: A Romance of the Willey Slide and the White Mountains* (1902), George Franklyn Willey (the relation is unclear) grafted a story about turn-of-the-century hotel culture onto an account of the slide.[46] In the first part of this cliché-ridden story, a reclusive mountain man named Soltaire rescues ten-year-old Martha Willey (one of the three children whose bodies were never found) from the 1826 avalanche and carries her to a remote cave where he lives. Remembering nothing before the rescue because of amnesia, Martha is raised by Soltaire as his daughter until a wealthy, young tourist discovers her by chance and takes her off to civilization as his bride.

The story then leaps to 1901 and a White Mountain resort hotel, where young Louise Freenoble and Chicagoan Arthur Garland are spending the summer out of the city. Rumors that an old hag has been haunting the mountains prompt Louise, Arthur, and their friends to mount a search party. Their excursion is really just an excuse for fun—sightseeing, a picnic, some hunting. Shooting at what he thinks is an eagle, Garland recognizes the old woman as she falls and fears that he hit her. Unwounded but knocked unconscious by the fall, she turns out to be Louise's grandmother, who had disappeared unaccountably months before. The old woman also reveals herself to be Martha Willey: She regresses to the night of the avalanche and repeats the frightened, confused words she had spoken to her sister Mary as they stumbled about in the night hand in hand. A search of Soltaire's cave turns up the hermit's diary, which shows his true name to be Mark Garland; he is Arthur Garland's great-grandfather. Soltaire went to live in the White Mountains to watch his true-love from afar. Polly Hilton had believed that he had died on a sea voyage and so had married another man, Samuel Willey. These discoveries inspire the marriage of Louise and Arthur, direct descendants of these White Mountain "pioneers."

Soltaire embodies the tourist's fantasy. The story captures the boredom of summer-long guests staying in the comfortable, controlled environment of the grand hotels. Many must have dreamed of living out such a romance as Louise's and Arthur's, and *Soltaire* presents the typical nineteenth-century reading of the White Mountains as the potential setting for a romance. Thus, the improbable seventy-five-year gap does not keep George Willey from trying to give a sense of the trauma that the Willey family faced when the mountains were supposedly wild and dangerous. In addition, travelers probably thought that *Soltaire* expressed an important truth, despite its dime-novel simplicity. The urban aristocrats, Louise and Arthur, demonstrate the legitimacy of their social rank by tracing their ancestry back to high-minded pioneers. In the same way, the tourist industry helped visitors to enact a myth of aboriginal connection to the American soil. "The supreme raison d'être of the hotel trade's imagery," wrote Bulkley, "was its function as a haven in pristine nature where the city dweller could escape the ravage of urban materialism and find resuscitation."[47] Imaginative participation in the landscape's history and grandeur offered spiritual renewal to those who faced vulgar urban realities in their daily lives.

While proclaiming itself antimaterialistic, the tourism frontier depended entirely on urban consumers. After midcentury, tourism lost most of its local qualities and took on the cosmopolitan character of the city itself. Even in the very first years of the grand hotel, the White Mountains attracted overwhelming numbers of tourists from big cities. Bulkley analyzed the 1853 and 1854 guest registers of the Tip-Top House, located on Mount Washington's summit, to learn the demographic characteristics of the tourist trade immediately after the railroad's arrival. "If the hotel trade was anything," Bulkley concluded, "it was predominantly urban, with two-thirds of all tourists originating from cities of 10,000 population or greater" (153). The tourist industry targeted urban consumers as its market, and they in turn imagined the landscape in ways that addressed their own concerns.

As an extension of America's city-centered economy, late nineteenth-century tourism reflected America's accelerating industrialization. Although the Tip-Top House registers show a democratic variety in the status and wealth of visitors, Bulkley thought that tourism was already dominated by the newly created white collar "occupational elite" of managers, clerks, and professionals.

> These far-flung (and even lesser-flung) occupational elite, whether from St. Louis or Sandusky, New Orleans or New York, gave the trade an increasingly cosmopolitan coloration. They, in turn, were products of a process of explosive urban growth and commercialization which was both cause and effect to a transportation revolution which integrated cities into systems, generated an expanding urban market place, and multiplied the essential middle class components into a duplicative structure of white collar counterparts nationally. The White Mountain summer trade was increasingly defined by these broad economic and national forces (154).

This mirroring of national trends shows how completely the city had colonized the region. Although the White Mountains attracted a sizable number of farmers and locals from northern New England, tourism responded primarily to the needs of city-dwellers.

Changes in the sights that interested visitors reflect this demographic shift. Whereas earlier visitors, such as Cole and Parkman, came to see nature at its rawest, later visitors merged the sublimity of natural phenomena with the White Mountains' own version of the "technological sublime." In Moses Sweetser's *Views in the White Mountains* (1878), for instance, which contains photographs of attractions along with brief descriptions, railroads and hotels get equal billing with mountain vistas.[48] The book includes a traditional picture of the Willey House taken from the road looking north through the Notch. And it also includes shots of grand hotels—the Fabyan House, the Glen House, and the Profile House. In the past, travelers had considered the narrow opening and towering walls of the Gate of the Notch to be a natural wonder. Sweetser's photograph of the Gate of the Notch shows it excavated and widened to allow passage of the newly laid tracks of the Portland and Ogdensburg Railroad, which followed the route of the Tenth New Hampshire Turnpike through Crawford Notch.

More than almost any other sight in the mountains, however, travel writers celebrated an engineering feat, the cog railway to the summit of Mount Washington. Backed by New Hampshire native Sylvester Marsh, who had made a fortune in Chicago meat-packing and grain trading, the cog railway took three years to build, opening in 1869.[49] After a mediocre start, it eventually became one of the biggest concessions in the region. Sixty thousand tourists rode it during the first eight years.[50] According to F. Allen Burt, the railway made a profit of over eighteen thousand dollars in 1882, its best year.[51] Riders paid "three dollars up the mountain, three dollars down, or four dollars up and down on the same train."[52] That extraordinary price was about equal to the whole fare from Boston to the mountains, but only part of it was for the convenience of a faster, more comfortable ride to the top of Mount Washington. The other part represented the thrill of experiencing a technological marvel at first hand. Writers cited facts and figures to explain the cog railway's magnificence. It cost $139,500 to build the three-and-a-third-mile road, which ascended thirty-seven hundred feet to the summit. The ride up took seventy minutes. The most spectacular feature of the railroad was Jacob's Ladder, a trestle hundreds of feet long and twenty-three feet high, rising at a sharp thirty-three-degree angle (fig. 6).[53] As the litany of statistics suggests, the sublimity of engineering had begun to displace the sublimity of Mount Washington's forbidding dimensions. And the fact that tourists welcomed this exhibition indicates how much the White Mountains owed to the urban marketplace, with its commitment to technological innovation.

Land Values

Visitors to Mount Washington on 4 July 1851 saw a curious spectacle. A religious fanatic named John Coffin Nazro had erected toll gates on all the paths up the mountain and was trying to collect a dollar from everyone going to the top. Nazro wanted the money to build a temple on the summit. He had ear-

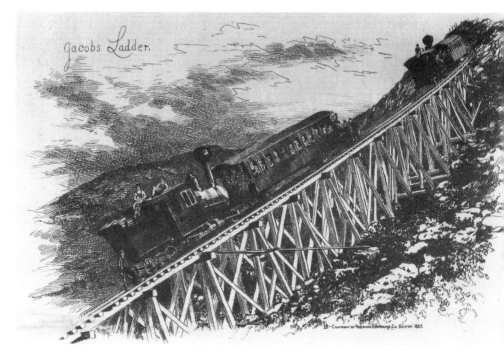

Fig. 6. *Jacobs Ladder* (Robinson Engraving Co., 1887). This steepest incline of
the Mount Washington cog railway became a popular attraction in itself.
Courtesy, Dartmouth College Library.

lier issued a grandiose proclamation inviting everyone to attend the dedication: "There will be a solemn congregation upon Trinity Height, or Summit
of Mount Washington, on the Fourth Day of July, A.D. 1851, and 1st year
of the Theocracy, or Jewish Christianity, to dedicate to the coming of the
Ancient of Days, in the glory of his Kingdom, and to the marriage of the
Lamb . . ."[54]

Nazro's claim to the summit of Mount Washington came about as a practical joke. Thomas Crawford had conveyed it to him by a deed, which Nazro
took to the courthouse and registered. Crawford and the older generation of
innkeepers laughed at the idea of selling a national landmark.[55] But the joke
was on them because Mount Washington had already been sold; David Pingree from Salem, Massachusetts, had bought it in 1846. For the summit of
Mount Washington and twenty thousand acres around it, Pingree had paid
$140.26.[56] Pingree's investment paid off that same July 4 while Nazro was try-
ing to collect tolls. This happened to be the day the first trains from Portland
started arriving at Gorham. Now thousands of tourists yearly would want to

visit Pingree's few hundred acres on the top of Mount Washington to see its spectacular views and to worship nature.[57] But these tourists needed a hotel to stay in, not a temple. It was raining, and no one was paying his toll, so Nazro gave up and went off and joined the navy.

Tourism's commodification of the landscape capped off eighty years of speculative interest in the White Mountains. Records show that speculation had begun with the first land grants before the Revolution and continued up to the coming of hotels and railroads. Although a fire in the Coos County courthouse in 1869 destroyed most of the deeds, enough have survived to sketch out a history of land values in the area. The great majority of deeds record very low prices for land, often not much more than one dollar per acre, even for tracts that had already had several owners. The White Mountains' ruggedness simply made the land worthless for conventional uses. Yet this very worthlessness invited speculation because a relatively small increase in per-acre price meant a substantial return on investment. The clearest opportunities came in the two periods of original land grants, the 1770s and the 1830s, when the government gave away large tracts for little or nothing. In the late 1840s, anticipation of the railroad and of the possibilities of tourism induced large-scale speculation, but, unlike the earlier opportunities, this one offered no sure-fire way to cash out at the end. The successful speculator would have to acquire land that was both in limited supply and in great demand, and only the summit of Mount Washington really fit the bill.

Over the long term, isolation and marginal fertility suppressed demand for land in the White Mountain region. Records of sales show that, with few exceptions, land prices remained low from first settlement into the grand hotel era. In the late 1790s, for example, Giles Richards, a Boston cart maker, bought several thousand acres in the White Mountain area for slightly less than one dollar per acre. In 1802 John Davis sold one hundred acres in Nash and Sawyer's Location to Eleazer Rosebrook for one hundred dollars. In the 1830s large tracts around Mount Washington went for one dollar an acre. But sometimes land sold for much less. For instance, in 1797 Richard Hart sold one hundred acres each to Abel Crawford and Charles Hanson for one dollar. In 1844 Samuel Thompson bought two thousand acres along the turnpike east of Mount Washington for $250. And, although land sometimes sold for two dollars, three dollars, or more per acre (as in 1851, when Joseph Cotton bought one hundred acres around Mount Washington for two hundred dollars), trading in land that was not freshly granted seldom yielded much profit. Cotton had to sell his land for the same amount five years later.

Buyers did little to improve their land in the seventy years between settlement and the tourism boom. The lack of investment is shown by the fact that, despite low values, the county frequently auctioned off land for nominal amounts to cover unpaid taxes. For $26.64 George P. Meserve bought half of Wentworth, Rogers, and Treadwell's Location at auction in 1847. The White Mountains never experienced the rise in land values that farming normally caused. Prices seldom matched even the modest seven dollars an acre that the Willeys' old farm in Lower Bartlett fetched in 1848.

Against this background of cheap land, speculative efforts stand out much more distinctly. As with the rest of America during the colonial period and beyond, speculation subverted the intent of original land grants in the White Mountains. In 1779 Daniel Rindge and Daniel Pierce sold 5,114 acres in an isolated area ten miles south of the Willey House for £5,369. Having received the land from the crown under the same conditions as Wentworth, Rogers, and Treadwell received theirs, Rindge and Pierce likewise did nothing with it during the seven years they held it. For service in the French and Indian Wars, Thomas Chadbourne received Crawford Notch. He sold it almost immediately for three hundred pounds to Richard Hart, after whom the land is named Hart's Location.[58] Starting in 1773, Joseph Whipple erected a manor house in Dartmouth (later called Jefferson) and tried to establish a proprietary estate along traditional English lines. He ended up practicing speculation in the American fashion, however. Whipple spent over twenty years in buying the town's entire twenty-six thousand acres for a total of about $4,200, or fifteen cents an acre. After dividing the land into one-hundred-acre lots, he lured settlers with gifts of fifty acres, selling them the other fifty later on for one hundred dollars.[59]

By the 1830s Coos County still had vast tracts of ungranted land with little obvious use. In 1831 the state appointed James Willey (apparently no relation) New Hampshire land commissioner and gave him the task of selling off the surplus land, probably just for the revenue. Over the next few years, Willey authorized the sale of thousands of acres at very low rates. The cheap prices, combined with the national speculation craze of the 1830s, speeded the pace of land trading in the White Mountains. To acquire the land through which his trail to the top of Mount Washington ran, Ethan Allen Crawford and two partners from Conway spent fifty dollars for 5,712 acres on the mountain's western slope. Henry G. Hadley picked up 8,371 acres next to Crawford Notch. Jeremiah Chandler bought ten thousand acres below Crawford's Purchase for three hundred dollars. George P. Meserve and Samuel W. Thompson paid five hundred dollars for twelve thousand acres on the northern slope of Mount Washington.[60]

Jacob Sargent of Thornton, New Hampshire, and four partners took best advantage of the opportunity. In May 1832 they bought twenty-five thousand acres on Mount Washington's south side for three thousand dollars, that is, for twelve cents an acre.[61] They began to sell off parcels right away. Whereas records show relatively little buying and selling of land in other grants, there were dozens of transactions in Sargent's Purchase. Thus, in December 1832 Sargent and the others sold 4,115 acres to Samuel Alexander for one thousand dollars—a 100 percent return despite the modest price. Sargent sold 658 acres to Elbridge Howe in 1836 for seven hundred dollars. In 1834 Samuel P. Mc-Question bought one thousand acres from Sargent for one thousand dollars; McQuestion resold three hundred acres within a month for three hundred dollars. Another measure of activity in Sargent's Purchase is the fact that land changed hands so frequently. For example, one parcel had had eight separate owners when Wright Stratten bought it in 1859! The four hundred acres that Alfred Garfield bought in January 1857 had belonged to four different owners by 1839, and he himself was the seventh. This volume of activity suggests that Sargent and his partners knew exactly how to go about disposing of their land. Their enterprise is the clearest example of pure speculation in White Mountain history.

The interest in Sargent's Purchase, which had no industrial or agricultural use, arose because it apparently included the summit of Mount Washington. By the 1830s Mount Washington, then thought to be the tallest peak in the eastern United States, had become the region's best-known attraction. Its fame was in part due to its own beauty, but it was especially noted for its splendid, panoramic views, encompassing much of northern New England from the ocean to the Green Mountains. Despite the mountain's ruggedness, dense undergrowth, and unpredictable weather, more and more visitors came to climb Mount Washington every summer. The summit represented virtually the only tract in the mountains where high demand from tourists, coupled with restricted space, pushed land values to extraordinary levels. The owner of Sargent's Purchase could derive a large income from the summit—if he held undisputed title. But the original land grant was vague, and the owners of Thompson and Meserve's Location just to the north also claimed the summit. The court battles that followed reveal both the value of the land and the way the tourist industry exploited it.

As soon as the proposed Atlantic and St. Lawrence Railroad won government approval in Maine in 1845, speculators snapped up the area around Mount Washington. Even before a foot of track had been laid, David Pingree, the president of the Jackson Iron Manufacturing Company, started buying up parcels of land along the turnpike leading south from Gorham, where the railroad was to stop, to the eastern base of Mount Washington. In September 1846, Pingree also bought about twenty thousand acres in Sargent's Purchase

Fig. 7. The Glen House, in Moses Sweetser, *View of the White Mountains* (1879).
The Glen House typified the structure of grand hotels, which resembled skyscrapers laid
sideways. Most hotels had farms to supply fresh food.
Courtesy, Dartmouth College Library.

(including the summit) for $140.26, but he did nothing to improve Mount
Washington for visitors. Perhaps he knew that he did not have to do anything;
he just had to wait.

John Bellows from Exeter, New Hampshire, got more involved. He partic-
ipated in a plan that eventually linked Portland directly to the summit of
Mount Washington. In January 1848 he bought half of Thompson and
Meserve's Location (six thousand acres) for $20.71. He later acquired the
other half. But Bellows had also recently purchased Martin's Location,
Green's Grant, and Pinkham's Grant in Mount Washington's eastern valley,
and these, too, cost him little. In 1851, the same year the railroad reached
Gorham, Bellows built a small hotel on the turnpike eight miles south from
Gorham at the base of the mountain. The next year he sold the hotel and
seven hundred surrounding acres to Joseph Thompson for eleven thousand

dollars, making an extraordinary profit. Thompson enlarged the hotel into what soon became one of the best-known grand hotels in the region, the Glen House, and remained its proprietor for seventeen years (fig. 7).[62] Thompson and the Glen House were at the center of the tourism boom. The Glen House probably owed much of its success to an agreement with the railroad, which may have backed Thompson. In any case, eight months after he bought it from Bellows, Thompson sold the land surrounding the hotel to the Atlantic and St. Lawrence for three thousand dollars.

Thompson also got involved with the two hotels that were built on the top of Mount Washington and with the carriage road that led from the Glen House to the summit. The difficulty of building big hotels on the summit—elevated forty-five hundred feet above the valley and suffering hurricane-force winds—indicates how powerfully tourism appealed to businessmen. The Summit House opened in 1852. "All the lumber for the sheathing and roof," explained Kilbourne, "had to be carried upon horses from a sawmill near Jefferson Highlands [over 20 miles away]. A chain hung over the horse's back and one end of each board was run through a loop at the end of the chain, two boards being carried on each side of the horse."[63] That same year Joseph Hall, the principal owner, sold a half interest to Nathaniel Noyes, a Boston publisher. Materials for the Tip-Top House, which was built by John H. Spaulding and others in 1853, came up from the Glen House. The proprietors paid rent to John Bellows as owner of Thompson and Meserve's Location with a claim on the summit.[64] The next year, Hall and Spaulding combined their ownership of the two hotels, which could accommodate about one hundred guests each.[65]

The Atlantic and St. Lawrence may even have had an interest in the Summit and Tip-Top Houses because J. R. Hitchcock, who ran both from 1862 to 1872, managed the railroad-owned Alpine House in Gorham in the mid-1850s.[66] In any case, while Hitchcock was working for the railroad, he and Spaulding both became directors in the Mount Washington Road Company when it was organized in 1853 at the Alpine House. Starting with fifty thousand dollars in capital, the company planned to build a macadamized road so that carriages could ride from the Glen House all the way to the summit. In 1856, when the road reached the halfway point, the funds gave out and construction stopped. The enterprise was reconstituted by early 1859 as the Mount Washington Summit Road Company, and the road opened in 1861. Joseph Thompson of the Glen House rode the first vehicle to the top.[67]

The railroad may have had a direct investment in every part of the operation. But, at the very least, the businessmen knew enough to cooperate with one another. The Atlantic and St. Lawrence brought tourists to Gorham, where they could stay at the Alpine House or go straight to the Glen House by carriage. From the Glen House another carriage ride brought visitors to the top of Mount Washington, where they could stay at the Summit or Tip-Top House. A small group of men controlled the entire route. But their reach extended even further. In 1855, with road construction apparently well under way, Nathaniel Noyes, part owner of the summit hotels, published in Boston the *Historical Relics of the White Mountains*, written by co-owner John H. Spaulding. The book is more a guidebook than a history, and it went through three editions in four years. Its 118 short sections include descriptions of White Mountain attractions along with historical vignettes. Spaulding did not omit details about the Glen, Summit, and Tip-Top Houses or the carriage road. The 1862 edition contains a list of routes from Boston to the White Mountains and ends with an advertisement for Hitchcock's Tip-Top and Summit Houses. Noyes followed the *Historical Relics* in 1856 with a little sensationalism in Benjamin Ball's *Three Days on the White Mountains*. He also published Benjamin Willey's *Incidents*, which included a route table and hotel advertisements. Thus, within four years after the railroad's arrival, one syndicate held combined ownership of all the components of tourism—transportation, accommodations, attractions, and publicity.

Things would have looked very promising to Spaulding and his partners except that David Pingree sued the Mount Washington Summit Road Company for building on his land without compensation. Pingree maintained that the summit properly belonged in Sargent's Purchase and not in Thompson and Meserve's Location, owned by John Bellows. In May 1859 the County Court agreed with Pingree. In exchange for giving up his claims *on the road alone* (while keeping the summit), Pingree received fifty thousand dollars from the road company. The land he had purchased thirteen years earlier for fractions of a cent per acre now seemed worth hundreds of dollars an acre.

In the 1860s Hitchcock had to pay two thousand dollars a year in rent to operate his hotels on the top of Mount Washington for the three or four months of the summer season.[68] The land further increased in value when the cog railway came to the summit. The cog railway company had bought the Summit House in 1872 to house its passengers. The original structure was pulled down, and a bigger one was erected for almost seventy thousand dollars.[69] The new hotel was too big, in fact, because the railway needed to lease a little more space from the estate of the now-deceased Pingree at three thousand dollars a year. This rent burden led to another lawsuit, which ended in 1894 with the cog railway company buying forty-nine acres on the summit for fifty-six thousand dollars. An acre of Pingree's land was now worth more than one thousand dollars.[70]

The Hotel-Spirit

The full history of the business that Ethan Allen Crawford started in 1819 would have appalled Henry James, had he known it. After all, it was the entrepreneur who had generated James's own idealized image of the landscape: The landscape had been invented for the sake of the hotel, not the other way around. Indeed, James could easily have made the connection because he understood the culture of the American hotel. After inspecting New York City's Waldorf-Astoria, the Breakers in Palm Beach, and other resorts, James concluded that hotels offered Americans the chance to try on new identities. The hotel epitomized American civilization for James because the hotel converted images into money. Unlike a railroad or a steel mill, a resort does not need machinery, an elaborate organization, or apologists. Even the hotel's large service staff can mislead one about its true nature, since the business transaction occurs on a very basic level, that of narrative and image. These are what the patron really buys, and James knew it.[71]

The Waldorf-Astoria proved to James that the public had accepted the skyscraper's values as its own. "Here was a world whose relation to its form and medium was practically imperturbable," he wrote of hotel life; "here was a conception of publicity *as* the vital medium."[72] Like the skyscraper, the Astoria's underlying condition was one of social blankness, in which everyone felt equally at home. People of diverse backgrounds, interests, and status mingled freely in the hotel's many corridors and public rooms. They carried on different kinds of activities in its facilities, connected by no deeper principle of order than convenience and proximity. Unrestrained by a permanent social rule, any guest could try out new identities or roles. Nobody cared about establishing a "correct" standard. The hotel's "rare beauty," James stated, "was that it was, for a 'mixed' social manifestation, blissfully exempt from any principle or possibility of disaccord with itself" (104). The hotel did not create this democratic milieu out of benevolence but in order to attract as many customers as possible.

As Ross Posnock noted, the hotel "neither opposes nor represses individuality and freedom, two 'American ideals,' but rather the hotel-spirit *produces* them."[73] And it sells them. The hotel did not just offer opportunities to spend money; it created an ethical climate in which spending money is the only pursuit or value that everyone shares. The sole feature common to all the different groups in the hotel, James found, was "the comparative ability to spend and purchase; the ability to spend with freedom being, as one made out, a positive consistent with all sorts of negatives."[74] Buying things made up for the absence of real social intercourse.

James makes this assertion while describing Florida's "hotel-civilization" and after analyzing all the big cities between Miami and Portsmouth. The last chapter in *The American Scene*, "Florida," stands as James's final judgment about America as a whole.[75] He concludes with the realization that the hotel ethic pervaded everything in America. It was not limited to New York and other cities or to a single class. The hotel was set up to convince guests that there was no other reality: "It is difficult to render the intensity with which one felt the great sphere of the hotel close round one, covering one in as with high, shining crystal walls, stretching beneath one's feet an immeasurable polished level, revealing itself in short as, the very form, the only one, of the habitable world."[76] And the hotel made itself into the standard by which to judge the outside world. "For the light of the hotel-spirit really beat upon everything; it was the only torch held up for the view or the sense of anything else" (443).

Thus, the hotel's significance reached beyond mere symbolism. James feared that it represented the upper limit of the nation's aspirations, that it was the chief result of 130 years of American striving and idealism. An incredulous note sounds in this epiphany at the Waldorf-Astoria: "The moral in question, the high interest of the tale, is that you are in presence of a revelation of the possibilities of the hotel—for which the American spirit has found so unprecedented a use and value; leading it on to express so social, indeed positively an aesthetic ideal . . . one is verily tempted to ask if the hotel-spirit may not just *be* the American spirit most seeking and most finding itself" (102). Like the Astoria, America offered the mere imitation of manners, society, and values. Commerce had defeated the slow accumulation of precedent and real taste. And history in America extended no farther back than a hotel stay.

James might have easily located the heart of American capitalism in the White Mountains instead of in Manhattan. He could have chosen as his main exhibit, say, the modern and expensive Mount Washington Hotel—open for just two years in 1904. After all, what James said about the Astoria was also true of any White Mountain grand hotel. But for all his fretting about America's lack of history, James neglected to learn the history of tourism and how it affected the meaning of landscape. Perhaps he would have viewed the hotel differently if he had known more about the White Mountains. He would have found out that earlier generations did not think of them as "delicately Arcadian" but as a massive, formless obstruction. He would have learned that Ethan Crawford, "the rude forefather," had reimagined the mountains more to James's taste. And he would have seen the Willeys choose between declining agriculture and rising tourism. But these inventors of tourism did not have to decide between money and society, as James implies. Their choice was poverty or risk.

CHAPTER FOUR

Tourism and Landscape Painting

I have had grand dreams, but they have been only dreams, because I have lived—and that, too, by my own choice—among poor and mean realities.
—Nathaniel Hawthorne, "The Great Stone Face"

As a natural disaster, the Willey slide received unprecedented attention, especially from intellectuals. Right after it occurred, scientists, artists, and writers began traveling to Crawford Notch to view the scene; their extensive descriptions appeared in books, newspapers, and professional journals throughout America and even in Europe. Before the nineteenth century, the causes and consequences of natural disasters simply did not interest intellectuals very much, as English geologist Charles Lyell noted in 1830. "All naturalists who have searched into the memorials of the past, for records of physical events," he marveled, "must have been surprised at the indifference with which the most memorable natural occurrences are often passed by, in the works of writers of enlightened periods."[1] As Lyell discovered, whole cities had been destroyed and parts of the earth submerged under the sea and then raised back up without contemporaries recording it. At most, natural disasters occasioned moralizing. For example, the famous Lisbon earthquake of 1755 stirred profound metaphysical doubts in Voltaire, yet his poems about the event include amazingly few details of what happened. It is truly remarkable, therefore, that artists, writers, and scientists found the Willey slide worth their attention.

As much as any other event, the Willey slide initiated a new order of consciousness about landscape in America. The disaster marks a point when Americans began to invent narratives that could properly explain the pathologies of their landscape—that is, why it deviated so catastrophically from the rational course the agrarians predicted. By itself, the catastrophic does not distinguish the new imagination of landscape, since catastrophe enjoyed a vogue in England, too, in the early nineteenth century.[2] For Americans, however, catastrophe was more than a fashion. It offered a way to describe the dynamics of the landscape, whose anomalous habit of changing suddenly and unexpectedly contradicted the theories of Locke and Jefferson. Catastrophe served an aesthetic function in Europe, but American artists, scientists, and writers grabbed at it for whatever explanatory power it held; they wanted to understand how landscape works as an autonomous environment. This new awareness of landscape affected nineteenth-century artists most strongly. Starting with Thomas Cole, American painters carefully imagined landscapes in fine detail, including such features as rock layers and identifiable plant species. In Europe, this kind of empiricism is rarely found outside the work of scientific specialists; in European landscape painting, detail is usually sacrificed to broader impressions. Thomas Cole's landscape of desolation manifests a new empiricism that enables him to imagine more vividly the precise relation between Man and Nature in America.

However, interest in catastrophes such as the Willey disaster signified more than just a concern for the natural environment. Catastrophe also offered a potent symbol for the sudden changes in the status of landscape caused by speculation. The dramatic slide in Crawford Notch resonated in public consciousness because it echoed the revolution in the White Mountains' status wrought just a few years before by the Crawfords and the Willeys. Speculation, too, contradicted agrarian precepts about land. The new environmental imagination expressed anxiety over the effects of speculation on the nation's moral and material well-being. Americans needed a symbolic language to express this anxiety because they were not ready to understand how far speculation pervaded their attitudes and behavior. The unconscious participation of Thomas Cole and other artists in the culture of speculation added much richness to these new landscape symbols.

Thomas Cole's New Landscape

Events such as the Willey disaster showed that landscape obeys laws of its own, independent of human values. Interest in the catastrophe reflected a broader cultural awareness, which Perry Miller identified in an essay title, "The Insecurity of Nature." Nature began to seem frightening, irrational, misproportioned, and outsized once the sense of balance implied in agrarianism was upset. But the insecurity went beyond agrarianism. Nineteenth-century Americans tried hard to sustain the belief that the material universe corroborated traditional moral values. The moral structure of Christianity was supposed to be inherent in nature and recoverable through reason. Neverthe-less, the Willey disaster supported a new idea—that Nature lacked moral con-tent. "The old confidence in meaning had fallen into meaninglessness," Miller explained, "not because nature had become an unknowable [entity] but because, of and by itself, it had proved inhuman."[3]

Thomas Cole made his reputation by depicting American landscape as in-human. His early works startled contemporaries and greatly influenced not just the painters of the Hudson River School, of which he is the originator, but also writers and scientists. Of all his paintings, none depicted nature so starkly and without human reference as his portrayal of the Willey slide: *Dis-tant View of the Slides That Destroyed the Whilley Family, the White Mountains* [sic] (1828). This painting (now lost but available through a lithograph by An-thony Imbert) shows Crawford Notch as a place of desolation, not sustenance (fig. 8). In other "operatic" landscapes, Cole tried to dramatize the enormous power of nature through use of the vista, monumental rock formations, and terrible storm damage—typically, trees blasted by lightning. A small human or animal figure often demonstrates the huge scale of the natural landscape. In *Distant View*, however, the environment is harsher still. The picture shows no evidence of human presence, and the terrain is simply a tangle of ruin. Un-like most writers whose accounts of the disaster appeared in the popular press, Cole made the *landscape* his primary subject, not the Willeys. The very insta-bility that he depicted asks for a redefinition of human society's relationship with nature.

In *Distant View*, Cole placed the viewer so that the Willey House—the main point of interest in Crawford Notch—cannot be seen at all. Absent, too, are the washed-out bridges and flooded farms whose damage had been tallied by local writers such as Benjamin Willey and Lucy Crawford. According to Robert McGrath, Cole "aligned the precipitous slopes of Mount Willey ('the great destroyer') obliquely to the picture plane and eliminated the signs of human habitation . . . Nature and its processes become the core subjects of the work, in which associations are of less importance than the evocation of the indefinable power of natural forces."[4] Of course, the viewer knows that the Willeys died in the slide, but he is positioned to see momentarily from na-ture's perspective. The viewer realizes that the Willeys matter little in a land-scape where such immense forces operate.

Distant View represents in purest form what critics have long called Cole's *wild* or *wilderness* scenery. When Cole was about to go abroad in 1829, William Cullen Bryant, afraid that Europe would tame his art, publicly ad-monished him to "keep that earlier, wilder image bright." After returning,

Fig. 8. Thomas Cole, *Distant View of the Slides That Destroyed the Whilley Family,
White Mountains*, engraved by Anthony Imbert. Lacking all human reference,
except for a small patch of road, this is Cole's starkest image of nature.
*Used with permission, collection of the Albany Institute of History and Art, Albany,
New York. Gift of Mrs. Howard Silberstein.*

Cole himself declared that "the most distinctive, and perhaps the most impressive, characteristic of American scenery is its wildness."[5] Looking back in
1900, White Mountain artist Benjamin Champney called Cole's early paintings "more thoroughly American than any landscape work perhaps yet accomplished."[6] And critic Edward Nygren, who insists on the importance of
American landscape painters before Cole, still "places him in the forefront of
artists who were inspired by and gave new meaning to the wilder aspects of
American scenery."[7] Nygren claims that Cole's originality was that he "captured the essence of American wilderness." However, if *wilderness* means a
landscape uncontaminated by humans (or even just Europeans), Cole proba-

bly never saw a wilderness, nor had his audience. As Nygren admits, "true wilderness had been experienced by only a few of the people who saw such images. The emotions aroused on viewing a picture were therefore triggered by associations with an aesthetic ideal [i.e., the picturesque], not with a particular place" (75). Most viewers, who learned aesthetics from English precedents, already knew what picturesque art looked like. They responded with special enthusiasm to Cole because he had expressed in compelling symbols Americans' unconscious attitude toward land.[8] The polite conventions of agrarianism and the picturesque began to drop away in operatic landscape paintings such as *Distant View*.

Of course, Cole uses the techniques of the picturesque. According to its English advocates, such as William Gilpin (a critic who wrote advice books for tourists), the picturesque lies between the aesthetic poles laid down by Edmund Burke in *Origin of Our Ideas of the Sublime and Beautiful* (1757). The picturesque combines the roughness of sublime images with the order of beautiful images. Gilpin said that "smoothness" makes objects beautiful but visually uninteresting.[9] For the landscape painter, "*Variety* too is equally necessary in his composition: so is *contrast* . . . From *rough* objects also he seeks the *effect of light and shade*" (56). Cole plainly followed Gilpin's instructions in *Distant View*, as in most of his early paintings. The overall impression is rough—from the mountains' scarred surfaces to the jagged tree trunks. In the sky, sunlight breaks strongly through storm clouds. One face of Mount Willey is brightly lit, but the dark shoulder of Mount Webster cuts across it sharply. The play of light across the terrain highlights its textures, and in the foreground the jumbled refuse from the storm invites the eye to linger and absorb details.

Despite this studied approach, however, Cole managed to present a stark, dynamic landscape; *Distant View* lacks the charm that Europeans customarily admired in picturesque landscapes.[10] Cole placed the viewer in the position of a traveler going through the Notch just after the storm of 28 August 1826. Time had not softened the horror of the disaster, nor nature begun to reclaim the damaged landscape; a boulder or two may still be falling from Mount Webster on the right. Stripped of leaves and branches, the trunks of uprooted trees stand out harshly in the foreground. These and other debris quickly swallow the small patch of clear road visible directly in front of the traveler and block his way. Slides have razed several wide swaths of trees from the mountainside; these scars lead one's eye and curiosity into the valley beyond. The viewer realizes that the storm has proved fatal to an entire household of nine people and that one could see their deserted house if allowed to go just a little farther. Still, civilization is far away, and help will be long in coming. Alone in the wilderness, the viewer-traveler is exposed to nature's immense power, just as the Willeys were. Such immediacy makes Cole's *Distant View* perhaps the nineteenth century's most compelling narrative of the disaster.

Of course, the real history of the mountains and the Willeys' own purpose in living in the Notch do not appear in *Distant View*. Nevertheless, tourism has determined Cole's vision. After all, Cole himself saw the White Mountains as a tourist at least three times. In October 1828, on his second trip, he traveled through the Notch, staying one night with Abel Crawford and two nights with Ethan Allen Crawford. He made sketches that he would later use in painting the *Distant View*. Cole also had an excellent tour guide. His traveling companion, Henry Cheever Pratt, had stayed with Ethan Crawford during the last week in August 1826 and was among the first to travel through the Notch after the slide.[11] In addition, just before Cole's trip, another powerful storm had caused the Saco River to flood and had damaged the road and bridges through the Notch. Thus, Cole would have received a vivid impression of how the Notch must have looked two years before. Pratt described their twelve-mile walk from Abel to Ethan Crawford's on 6 October 1828: "[W]e set out with our Baggage on our backs—our boots over on [top] of our Pantaloons and our caps tied fast under our chins . . . The passage of the Notch is nearly as difficult as it was after the great storm of 1826—we were obliged in some places to get a tree across the stream before we could pass— we arrived safe at E. Crawford's at sunsetting."[12]

Cole's own diary of the trip does not suffer from Pratt's matter-of-factness. Like any good tourist, Cole allowed his imagination to leap the two-year gulf separating him from the day of the fatal slide. Still, much of Cole's experience seems formed from what he brought with him to the White Mountains; he knew too well what he wanted to find. For example, three days before traveling through the Notch, Cole and Pratt ascended Mount Chocorua and looked down at the "[l]akes, mountains, streams, forests, villages and farms" below. "The view was sublime," Cole noted, "but not the scene for the canvass—too much like a map. It was not for pictures I ascended the mountain but for ideas of grandeur, for conceptions and for these this was the region."[13] Although Cole wrote expressively of Crawford Notch, his experience of it owes perhaps as much to his education in sublime aesthetics as to the land itself. A reader familiar with the Alps or the Rockies would scarcely expect the following to apply to hills less than forty-five hundred feet high: "We now entered the Notch and felt awestruck as we passed between the bare and rifted mountains that rose on either side thousands of feet above. The clouds had by this time partially abandoned the mountains but some were yet whirling round and round the sky-nursed pinnacles. The sun shone brilliantly and the clouds and shadows moving swiftly over the sides of the mountain contributed much to the grandeur of the scene" (325). Likewise, Cole's remarks on seeing the Willey House probably express what most tourists thought and felt. Strong words—*deluged, dread, horrors*—do not disguise the generic quality of his sentiments:

> The sight of that deserted dwelling (the Willey house) standing in a little patch of green in the midst of that dread wilderness of desolation called to mind the horrors of that night the 28th of August 1826 when these mountains were deluged and rocks and trees were hurled from their high places down the steep channelled sides of the mountains. The whole family perished and yet had they remained in the house they would have been saved[;] though the slides rushed on either side they avoided it as though it had been a sacred place. A strange mystery hangs over the events of that night. We walked among the rocks and felt as though we were but worms, insignificant and feeble, for as worms a falling rock would crush us. We looked up at the pinnacle above and measured ourselves and found ourselves as nothing (326–7).

Distant View portrays this scene more compellingly because of its detail and staging. Nevertheless, Cole remained as detached—indeed, distant—in the painting as he did in the journal, when he stepped back to take in the Notch with one sweeping gaze and to compare himself to a worm. In *Distant View* Cole explored the observer's feelings rather than the slide itself. Tourist and artist are inseparable in Cole; both relish the "mystery" of the slide too much to want to explain it away.

Like any tourist, Cole subtracted from his imagination of the scene any artifacts that diluted what he felt the landscape must have looked like when the decisive event occurred. Whereas other artists depicted the inn, road, stagecoaches, and tourists, Cole erased them from his picture. It is a favorite technique of Cole to pretend that the apparatus of tourism is not there. Alan Wallach explained that Cole used a similar approach in his depictions of Kaaterskill Falls. Cole eliminated "the wooden tower that allowed visitors to look down into the cave behind the falls, the steps, the handrail running along the inside of the cave, and so forth. Instead, the artist pictured the falls as he imagined it might have appeared before the advent of white settlement, with a solitary figure of a Native American placed at the very center of the composition certifying the falls' legendary status. He worked a similar transformation in dozens of other landscapes."[14] Cole treated landscape *as if* it were wild. Through the technique of subtraction, Cole portrayed, in *Distant View* and elsewhere, not the wilderness itself, but the idea of wilderness. In short, Cole assumed the perspective dictated by the entrepreneurs of tourism, who had reinvented the White Mountains as an untamed wilderness.

In such early paintings as *Distant View*, then, Cole's depiction of a harsher vision of the environment sublimated America's speculative relation to land. After all, the wild landscapes that captured the imagination of Bryant and Cole's other admirers lay well within any line of settlement. Regions that particularly attracted Cole in the 1820s were the White Mountains, from which "Cole had produced some of his finest pictures," according to Elwood Parry, and the Catskills, which inspired many of his best-known works.[15] When Cole toured the White Mountains in the 1820s, the area had only recently become a "wilderness" through the efforts of the Crawfords and Willeys to attract tourists. The Catskills had an even better-developed tourist industry. The Catskill Mountain House, designed specifically to serve tourists, opened in 1825 and offered the finest accommodations.[16] Thus, a picture such as *Distant View* represents not the literal wilderness but a symbolic wilderness of speculation, whose uncontrolled, unconscious force brought on catastrophic changes in the landscape.

Catastrophe and Speculation

Cole is key to understanding the hidden relationship between landscape painting and land speculation in nineteenth-century America. In a real sense, land speculation made Thomas Cole. The art world's "discovery" of this poor youth from Ohio and Pennsylvania served the interests of many important people—among them land developers. It happened in New York City almost on the very day that the Willey family moved to Crawford Notch, late in October 1825. John Trumbull, America's leading painter and president of the American Academy of Fine Arts, along with Asher B. Durand and two other painters, went to an art dealer's shop, where they found three of Cole's recent landscapes.[17] They bought them all on the spot, arranged to meet the artist, gave him commissions, and introduced him to other patrons.[18] One early Cole patron was "George William Featherstonhaugh . . . an English-born land speculator, geologist, explorer, and writer, whose estate overlooked the Schoharie River at Duanesburg, southwest of Albany" (28). In 1826, Cole painted four views of Featherston Park, which Featherstonhaugh wanted to take with him on a trip to England. He "intended to use the paintings of Featherston Park to promote foreign investment in developing his land holdings near Duanesburg" (34). Art can be really useful.

Cole's discovery illustrates two key points about the relationship between land and culture in nineteenth-century America. First, the speculator is the controlling force behind landscape images, since he puts them to the most decisive use. Land developers such as Featherstonhaugh and Stephen Van Rensselaer III were among the very earliest to recognize the value of Cole's art. Few patrons exploited landscape paintings as blatantly as Featherstonhaugh did; nevertheless, it is often hard to tell art from advertisement. Cole's *Distant View* probably made many wish they could see the White Mountains for themselves. Second, no clear lines divide the businessman from the man of culture. Featherstonhaugh's multiple roles were typical for the age. Art patron, writer, geologist, speculator—all of these roles derived from a common attitude toward the landscape. Moreover, Cole himself profited from business's use of the landscape. Most of Cole's works were of landscapes, including the White Mountains, that tourism first promoted and made known to his buyers. Thus, nineteenth-century artists were also in part speculators.

Yet painters such as Cole remained largely unconscious of their participation in America's culture of speculation, so the subject often appears in their work in disguise. Catastrophe and ruins symbolized speculation's effect on the landscape. Like Henry James, Cole saw speculation in America most clearly after a long sojourn in Europe, where he studied and traveled from 1829 to 1832. Cole returned to America impressed most, perhaps, by the ruins of ancient temples and monuments in Italy and Sicily. Though picturesque, they yielded a dark message. Like America, ancient Rome boasted that its greatness came from small farmers, who brought to the legions the toughness developed in wresting a living out of Italy's grudging soil. While the ruins testified to Rome's greatness, they also signified its decline and fall, its excesses and decadence. Cole feared that America had entered upon the same inexorable course that Rome had followed. Through its own excesses, he suspected, American civilization would end catastrophically.

Cole meditated upon this issue in his five-panel masterpiece *The Course of Empire* (1833–36), which compares ancient Rome with America (figs. 9–13). In panel 3—the large centerpiece—magnificent buildings surrounded by purposeful activity represent the "consummation" of the efforts depicted in panel 1 (a hunter chasing his prey) and panel 2 (a herdsman and a farmer tilling the soil). In short, the modest and virtuous activities of earlier generations lay the foundation upon which a great civilization rests. When people start living off of accumulated wealth (panel 4), however, the monuments of that virtue crumble into ruins (panel 5).

For Cole, economics almost gave his scenario the inevitability of a law of nature. Cole's work incorporated the agrarian theory of economic progress; that is, civilization improves to the extent that the land is improved and developed. Nineteenth-century Americans often imagined this idea in terms of a series of historical epochs marked by increasingly intensive uses of land. Conventional wisdom held that land use followed a predictable order: hunting and gathering, pasturing, farming, and finally commerce and other city-based activities.[19] *The Course of Empire* repeats this sequence while highlighting the transitions from one epoch to the next. Thus, in panel 1, entitled "The Savage State," Cole depicted hunters along with the beginning of a permanent settlement (fig. 9). In panel 2, "The Pastoral or Arcadian State," the shepherd and his flock dominate, but tucked discretely into the middleground left is a ploughman (fig. 10). In panel 3, the scene of a military triumph (celebrated with great pomp as under the Roman Empire) implies commercial activity through the boats in the harbor and the sumptuous furnishings (fig. 11). Cole chose such imagery because he feared that a mania for material wealth was bringing America to the same state of excess.

The lesson could have come straight from François Quesnay, founder of the Physiocrats, or Economists, whose theories about farming shaped Thomas Jefferson's agrarianism. In *Tableau Économique* (1756), Quesnay attacked practices that left French agriculture backward, including restrictions on internal trade and the feudal customs that kept peasants from owning their own land. The U.S. Constitution provided for both free domestic trade and liberal property rights. Eighteenth-century America did not need to act against another vice peculiar to the *ancien régime;* Quesnay had also warned against "spoliation" of capital by "excess of luxury."[20] By the 1830s, however, Americans made rich by commerce and manufacturing put on vulgar displays of wealth, according to Cole and many others. In *The Course of Empire*, Cole predicted ruin if America continued to flout Quesnay's economic law in this way. Like the court at Versailles, America's new rich threatened to despoil the honest wealth gained from agriculture.

Cole painted the work during the speculative mania and ballooning of real estate prices leading to the Panic of 1837. Convinced that land prices in the fast-growing nation could only go up, many people borrowed against homes and farms and signed promissory notes in order to play the real estate market. Banks accepted land assessed at inflated values as collateral for mortgages. People amassed paper fortunes overnight, only to lose them just as quickly. It was in this overheated atmosphere that someone offered Ethan Crawford twelve thousand dollars for his inn, which fetched just three hundred dollars a year later. To ensure that market prices were backed by something of real value, a nervous Congress passed the 1836 Species Circular, ordering that land be paid for with gold, not paper. Real estate collapsed within months, and America entered a seven-year recession, one of the hardest and longest in its history. Finishing *The Course of Empire* while the speculative frenzy was reaching its height, Cole gave Americans some old-fashioned advice: The way to wealth was through hard work and steady savings.

Fig. 9. Thomas Cole, *The Course of Empire: The Savage State*, 1834, oil on canvas. In the first scene of his five-part meditation on how history is shaped by agrarian economic laws, Cole shows humans chasing after the unrestrained energies of Nature. A hunter with a bow is on the path just to the *right* of the large tree in the *left foreground*. Three people run across the outcropping in the *center*, and a tepee village is seen at the *right*. Used with permission, © Collection of *The New-York Historical Society*.

Fig. 10. Thomas Cole, *The Course of Empire: The Pastoral or Arcadian State*, 1834, oil on canvas. Cole here shows humankind just starting to win control of Nature. In the *center*, a shepherd minds his flock and a construction of standing stones sits atop a plateau. *Used with permission,* © *Collection of The New-York Historical Society.*

Fig. 11. Thomas Cole, *The Course of Empire: The Consummation of Empire*, 1835–1836, oil on canvas. Though very successful at harnessing Nature's power, civilization and its monuments nearly blot Nature out of the landscape. *Used with permission,* © *Collection of The New-York Historical Society.*

Fig. 12. Thomas Cole, *The Course of Empire: Destruction*, 1836, oil on canvas. Having forgotten about Nature—the origin of all wealth—civilization destroys itself by living off of accumulated riches. *Used with permission,* © *Collection of The New-York Historical Society.*

Fig. 13. Thomas Cole, *The Course of Empire: Desolation*, 1836, oil on canvas. Nature reasserts itself, with only ruins to remind people of how civilizations rise and fall. *Used with permission,* © *Collection of The New-York Historical Society.*

Although many viewers must have felt its truth, Cole's epochal series did not reflect the complexity of America's treatment of land. The Willeys, for instance, did not fit within the conceptual framework assumed by Thomas Cole and his contemporaries. To apply Cole's terms, it must have seemed as if the Willeys—with their dilapidated house and handful of animals—had scarcely reclaimed the Notch from hunters and trappers when the land unaccountably skipped over three epochs of civilization—growth, maturity, decline—and went straight to the final stage, ruins. At least one poet imagined the disaster in this way. In "The American School of Catastrophe," Curtis Dahl explained that "Grenville Mellen in 'Buried Valley' (1833) tells the story of the destruction of happy homes by the terrible Willey slide in Crawford Notch, New Hampshire. Pictorially this mood is represented by numerous pictures of classical ruins, among them Washington Allston's painting of the ruins of Paestum and Trumbull's of the ruins of the Temple of the Sun at Palmyra."[21] Of course, the Notch did not contain the remains of monumental architecture any more than America contained the gleaming marble buildings that Cole shows in *The Consummation of Empire* (fig. 11). But ruins were the most accurate symbol then available to express the Notch's lack of the societal epochs that led from primitivism to desolation.

Speculation works in the same way. The speculator purposely omits the middle term, thereby causing a sudden shift in the narrative by which the land is imagined. The Crawfords and Willeys had changed the White Mountains from a backward agricultural region into Arcadia. And the slide itself simply enhanced the new image by adding the romantic notion of "the ruins of nature." Unaware of the family's speculative purpose, the public translated the change in narrative which the Willeys helped bring about into a tale of how nature's unexpected fury wrought disaster. This sublimation of the Willeys' story owed much to epochal thinking, which offered a limited number of "types" to describe landscape's economic history—wilderness, farm, city. The types rationalize Man's place in the world by asserting clear, simple relationships to Nature. But speculation works on a higher narrative level by envisioning the landscape in two or more ways simultaneously.[22]

Environmentalism

Cole balanced his pessimism about America's future with a certain amount of hope. After all, if hard work brought lasting wealth, American civilization promised to be the greatest ever because building it required the largest effort. Moreover, America's vast tracts of raw land also contained a larger quantity of the earth's "spontaneous energies" than almost any other nation possessed. The grand vistas that are the hallmark of Cole's landscapes symbolize America's potential, which needed to be developed properly, through patient, honest labor and no short cuts. If Americans would only act accordingly, Cole believed, they would gain moral wealth along with material prosperity. Just as James later did, Cole hoped that the grandeur of American landscape would impress itself upon the character of its inhabitants.[23] Thus, he professed a kind of environmentalism to correct America's speculative consciousness.

Cole articulated a notion of the environment's moral influence later shared by many nineteenth-century intellectuals. Henry David Thoreau, for example, offered a similar view of the grandeur of American landscape in "Walking" (1850–52). Here Thoreau tells of going to see two panoramas—extremely large, wide-angle views of landscapes designed to give the viewer a firsthand sense of what a place or journey was like.[24] The first was of the Rhine, the second of the Mississippi.[25] Like Cole's Italy, the Rhine's old cities and ruined castles recalled greatness past. "I floated along under the spell of enchantment," Thoreau wrote, "as if I had been transported to an heroic age."[26] Along the Mississippi, however, a comparable history seemed ready for enactment. "I saw that this was a Rhine stream of a different kind; that the foundations of castles were yet to be laid, and the famous bridges were yet to be thrown over the river; and I felt that *this was the heroic age itself*, though we know it not, for the hero is commonly the simplest and obscurest of men" (274–5). Thoreau could easily have pointed to the hunter or ploughman from *The Course of Empire* to illustrate his meaning.

Like Cole, Thoreau believed that America's future depended on the hardihood with which it took on the frontier. He continued with this famous passage: "The West of which I speak is but another name for the Wild; and what I have been preparing to say is, that in wildness is the preservation of the World. Every tree sends its fibres forth in search of the Wild. The cities import it at any price. Men plough and sail for it. From the forest and wilderness come the tonics and barks which brace mankind. Our ancestors were savages" (274). *Wildness* here is a more poetic version of those "spontaneous energies of the earth" which Jefferson and Quesnay had invoked. Thoreau's epochal imagination of the frontier agreed with Cole's; both extrapolated grand futures for America based on an implicit belief in the virtue of farming. That a skeptic such as Thoreau could feel such optimism demonstrates how powerfully the progressive, historical outlook shaped economic thinking at the time. Common-sense thinking about labor and productivity, inherited from the eighteenth century, made Cole and Thoreau confident that they knew how civilizations evolved—hard work invested in the land produced national wealth, which could be accumulated steadily or squandered.

To this environmental imagination, a natural catastrophe such as the Willey slide proved the immorality of America's way of making a living. It crystallized fears that Americans' eagerness to make quick money whenever they could was irrevocably damaging the land, the only source of wealth. James Fenimore Cooper's *The Pioneers* (1823), published just three years before the Willey slide, offers a classic example of how the environmental crisis was imagined. According to Cooper, settlers eradicate the land's aboriginal creatures and replace their authentic relation to nature with selfish opportunism. The dispossession of the Native Americans is one part of the problem, but environmental destruction is perhaps a greater threat. In the novel, Richard Jones entertains the settlement of Templeton by firing a cannon loaded with birdshot simply to see how many pigeons it could kill. Jones did not need the birds himself; he did not think of how his stunt would deplete the birds' population, nor did he consider that he was depriving others of the resource. Thus, he "purchased pleasure at the price of misery to others." Behind Cooper's anxiety over the landscape's ecological transformation lurks speculation. *The Pioneers* relates the "catastrophic" effects of land dealing by Cooper's father in central New York State.[27]

This concern with the environment served to bring the minute details of landscape into consciousness in a way that had no European precedent. As in the Leatherstocking tales, preoccupation with the land's "natural" state often took a nostalgic turn. Natty Bumppo himself might have expressed the regrets of local historian James W. Weeks, who deplored the heedless destruction of wildlife in Coos: "Pigeons came in reduced numbers till within a few years, but they are now gone with the other game animals and birds; and Coos, from being the finest sporting ground in the world, is now about the poorest."[28] In response to the sense of loss, Weeks recorded the variety of natural phenomena contained in the landscape before settlement. Pigeons, trout, salmon, beaver, otters, sables, bears, deer: Weeks listed them, explained their ranges, and estimated when they reached their population peak and why they declined. This kind of scientific envisioning of the landscape had earlier appeared in the work of Thomas Cole and his followers.[29]

Thus, a by-product of America's rampant speculation was widespread devotion to the close observation of nature. Like most pictures of the Notch, the foreground of Cole's *Distant View* is filled with the sharp outlines of boulders and trees together with much other detail. Similarly, accounts of trips to the Notch in scientific journals include descriptions of plants and rocks as well as mention of unusual phenomena, such as the report that the Connecticut River turned "a semi-fluid mass, of a light *brick red*" from the runoff of the 1826 storm.[30] This rage for significant detail on the part of artists and scientists hardly springs from a dispassionate commitment to a literal depiction of landscape. After all, as a painter Cole freely selected certain features, added others, and changed proportions and shading to heighten his effect. What brings artist and scientist together, however, is the desire to *imagine* the American landscape minutely and to conjecture its laws of operation. In this way, nineteenth-century intellectuals hoped to restore meaningfulness to nature, which speculation helped to mystify.

Cole's Influence

As he applied it to American landscape in such paintings as *Distant View*, Cole's environmentalism transformed the picturesque into a powerfully expressive aesthetic. From the first, American painters saw that Cole's originality stood out most clearly in this early vision and not in the ambitious, multicanvas works, such as *The Course of Empire* and *The Voyage of Life*, into which he put most of his energy after returning from Europe. Cole wanted the serials' high-toned allegory to make landscape painting as prestigious a genre as history painting, but his fellow artists were less interested in Cole's grand ideas than in his way of *seeing* the landscape. Although Cole had adopted the picturesque style, he inverted the relationship between art and nature that Gilpin had assumed. The most admirable natural scenery, Gilpin had told tourists, is that which most closely resembles the art of masters like Claude Lorrain and Salvator Rosa. Accordingly, in pursuit of picturesque images, tourists often carried "Claude glasses," small frames which, when held before the eyes, turned nature into a little painting.[31]

But for Cole, the picturesque led back out into nature. Faced with the troubling phenomena of American landscape, Cole used picturesque techniques to visualize it with greater resolution of detail. "Nature now is not so much seen through pictures (i.e., the picturesque)," Barbara Novak shrewdly observed, "but rather pictures instruct on how to see nature for itself."[32] "The *picturesque*," wrote Paul Shepard, "was fundamental to the intellectual preparation of leaders in the arts and sciences who examined with the greatest pleasure rough rocks in their minutest detail."[33] Thus, Gilpin's rules of roughness, contrast, variety, and strong shading induced in Cole a more empirical, or scientific, imagination of nature. This empiricism is Cole's contribution to Americans' imagination of landscape.[34]

Cole made the painter into a kind of scientist whose task was to lay bare landscape's laws of operation.[35] This implied that painting should be ahistorical, which dovetailed with Americans' sense that their landscape lacked the ennobling historical associations possessed by Europe in abundance. Cole

Fig. 14. Asher B. Durand, *Rocky Cliff*, 1860, oil on canvas. With his superb naturalism, Durand surpassed Thomas Cole, who had inspired the painters of the Hudson River School to portray landscape phenomena accurately. *Used with permission, Reynolda House, Museum of American Art, Winston-Salem, North Carolina.*

himself seems not to have grasped fully this implication, since he used allegory in the serial paintings to give landscape historical movement. But almost all the painters who followed him adopted the scientific, antiassociationist approach he discovered (fig. 14).[36] This had become old news by the time the Hudson River School's second generation began work. Worthington Whittredge recounted a conversation with Sanford Gifford when both were studying art in Germany in the 1850s. Gifford's notion of the painter's obligation might have come straight from Isaac Newton. "If I remember rightly, he said in general terms that no historical or legendary interest attached to landscape could help the landscape painter, that he must go behind all this to nature as it had been formed by the Creator and find something there which was superior to man's work, and to this he must learn to give intelligible expression. These ideas were not new or wonderful, but he impressed me as a man earnestly looking into a problem, as in truth he was."[37] American artists saw that Cole had produced a new kind of landscape. Although Europeans had begun to paint nature more faithfully around 1800, they lacked the scientist's cold eye. John Constable, whom Cole met in England in 1829, produced realistic landscapes, but their comfortable rural settings, with farmhouses and herds, recall the old German *landschaft* (fig. 15).[38] German romantic artist Caspar David Friedrich painted scenes of rugged mountain grandeur but frequently obscured the details with cloud layers.[39] By comparison, Cole depicted the landscape's hard edges.

Cole turned to science itself to make his art more empirical. He was the first American painter to study geology, then a new and popular science. He knew America's leading geologist, Benjamin Silliman, through Silliman's brother-in-law and Cole's own patron Daniel Wadsworth.[40] Silliman and Wadsworth often traveled together in New England. Wadsworth visited Crawford Notch right after the Willey disaster, and some of his sketches of the slides survive. It was he who encouraged Cole to visit for himself. Early

Fig. 15. John Constable, *Stour Valley and Dedham Church*, ca. 1815, oil on canvas. Though he used many of the same picturesque techniques as American painters, Constable revealed a much more domesticated landscape. *Used with permission, Warren Collection. Courtesy, Museum of Fine Arts, Boston.*

on, Cole began to incorporate in his paintings geologic phenomena that he had seen described in Silliman's *American Journal of Science and Art*.[41] Nevertheless, geology remained for Cole primarily a source of interesting forms to represent and not a reality to imitate. "In practice," explained Rebecca Bedell, "this means that his rocks look the same from painting to painting, whether he was depicting the granites of the White Mountains . . . or the sedimentary formations of the Genesee region."[42]

Geology played a more intimate role in the art of Cole's successors. For Asher Durand, Frederic Church, John Kensett, Sanford Gifford, and many others, geology "informed both their eyes and their hands," according to Bedell. "Studying the science heightened their perception of geologic features, helping them to see more, and more clearly, than they had before. At the same time, it guided their hands, enabling them to record what they saw with greater clarity and precision."[43] Yet even this understates the significance of artists' interest in geology because they sought neither to copy landscapes with photographic precision nor to make symbolic landscapes more realistic and convincing. Instead, Hudson River School painters tried to record their perception of landscape as an autonomous phenomenon. When they talked of this, they usually resorted to religious language. In his 1855 *Letters on Landscape Painting*, Durand echoed Sanford Gifford by declaring that "the true province of Landscape Art is the representation of the work of God in the visible creation, independent of man, or not dependent on human action."[44] American painters imagined a God who was not at all like the deist's watchmaker because he had made no mere machine but a creation teeming with organic complexity and beauty.[45]

Scientific discovery was one paradigm for the work of American landscape painters, and science, especially geology, often supplied the narrative for artists' visions of the landscape. "Their work was panoramic and detailed," wrote Paul Shepard, "not necessarily because they had set out to document the beauty of [regions such as] New England, or because of vague naturalistic philosophies slavishly followed, but rather because the aesthetic impulse as they felt it was inseparable from the discovery of nature as it constitutes the visible landscape."[46] Besides empirical observation, then, Hudson River School paintings depicted geologic processes, such as erosion by water, which slowly shape the visible landscape over long stretches of time. This scientific awareness led to a subtle, yet decisive, change in what landscapes signified. "Mountains were no longer everlasting. The process instead—the mountain brook—goes on forever, rendering Time . . . most strikingly real" (37–8). Mountain scenery had belonged to the pastoral tradition's iconography for a place of meeting with the everliving gods, immune from the passage of history. American artists and scientists saw mountains as the representatives of vast changes still in progress on the earth's surface. During tourism's golden age, this view filtered down to ordinary White Mountain visitors, for whom awareness of natural history made the landscape more enjoyable.

Regions such as the White Mountains and the Catskills drew painters who were interested, for example, in how the Ice Age had scarred hillsides, carved out valleys, and left behind rubble. John F. Kensett, who would have heard the latest theories from the geologists he met at the Century Association in New York City, took up permanent summer residence in the White Mountains in 1851.[47] According to Shepard, Kensett's painting of North Conway's rock cliffs (across the valley from where Samuel Willey grew up) updated the architectural ruins that Cole and others had used, a generation before, to gloss American landscape. The cliffs

> offset America's paucity of castles and cathedrals . . . John Kensett's *North Conway, New Hampshire* is of the nearby Cathedral Ledges. It is perhaps unfair to suppose that such tabernacular rocks were only salve for the wounds in our national cultural pride. Men of any nation have found them equally architecturally appealing. Nearer specifically to the heart of the early nineteenth century Anglo-American was the antiquity and the condition of such time-worn edifices. Present dilapidation compounded former magnificence.[48]

Kensett did not choose the scene for its superficial resemblance to European monuments. Rather, his painting presents a new order of sublimity, one far older and subtler than Gothic architecture.

Louis Agassiz, the famous scientist who had emigrated to the United States from Switzerland in 1847, expressed a similar conceit when he titled one popular essay on geology "America the Old World."[49] Agassiz meant that American nature trumped European history by any measure of size and time. Likewise, Kensett displayed geologic processes to greatest advantage. The most sublime view is also the most accurate: "The mass wasting of the Cathedral Ledges is most clearly seen from just Kensett's position. The acid-stained cliffs, with their newly broken and old exposed surfaces, taluses, the evidence of frost and water, and the incessant mouldering lichens, are the wounds of time. The sharp angles and blocky fracture pattern of this granite, together with the knowledge that granite was a building material, firmly impressed the beholder with the delightful illusion of an inexorably decaying pile."[50] A painter such as Friedrich might allude to geologic theory, but only American artists depicted the landscape with such particularity.[51] The earth they imagined is changing beneath our feet, but geologic processes move so slowly that their powerful effects appear only in the fine details.

Fig. 16. Asher B. Durand, *Kindred Spirits*, 1849, oil on canvas. In this tribute to Cole (on the *right*, shown with William Cullen Bryant), Durand featured the sensibility toward landscape that the former had discovered; however, Durand painted with greater fidelity to such features as rock layers. *Used with permission, Collection of The New York Public Library, Astor, Lenox and Tilden Foundations.*

The painters of the Hudson River School knew they had learned this lesson from Cole. When Durand wanted to pay homage to Cole after his death, he chose a landscape made famous by Cole's art. However, Durand made visible features that Cole had taught others to see yet had never quite realized for himself (fig. 16). Of all New England landforms, the waterfall perhaps best dramatizes the earth's perpetual decay:

> Asher B. Durand, who immortalized William Cullen Bryant and his friend, the artist, Thomas Cole, in *Kindred Spirits*, one of the most widely known paintings of the period, chose such a landscape for its setting. This painting, from the Kaaterskill Clove in the Catskill escarpment near Palenville, shows the stream deeply incised in sandstone, its abraided chasm walls, pot holes, and typical ovate limestone fragments from upstream. In sedimentaries successive layers of rock offer differing resistance to the downcutting stream, developing stair-steps and waterfalls . . . It was exactly in this geomorphic setting that the actual process of mountain decay was most evident and the agencies of weathering and abrasion most easily determined.[52]

The image of desolation which first attracted Cole to a detailed representation of American landscape survived in the work of his successors, though in a less obvious form. Cole's rhetoric of wildness transformed the latent, catastrophic effects of speculation in the Catskills and White Mountains into a violent, Gothic environmentalism. Starting with Durand, Cole's followers refined his vision into less operatic images of landscape. Even so, their dramatizations of geologic processes express an equally dynamic environment. Like Cole's depiction of Crawford Notch in *Distant View*, the landscapes of Durand, Church, Kensett, and others argue for nature's being in constant motion. Hudson River School artists introduced an unprecedented amount of detail into landscape painting to try to capture these movements. But this new technique did not arise merely from a sudden affection for the wilderness. Instead, painters went to wilderness to find an adequate symbol for a landscape already known to be in constant flux. Cole's empiricism provided the most intelligible way to describe the inexplicable changes native to American landscape because of speculation.

The Art of Tourism

Benjamin Champney, who testified to Thomas Cole's influence, and John F. Kensett first came to sketch and paint in the White Mountains in 1850 (fig. 17). Like good entrepreneurs, these artists were just slightly ahead of the curve when it came to making money there. The year 1851 marked the arrival

Fig. 17. Benjamin Champney, *Mount Chocorua, New Hampshire,* 1858, oil on canvas.
Champney and Kensett were entrepreneurs of White Mountain art who saw that
picturesque scenes like this would appeal to wealthy summer travelers. *Used with
permission, Bequest of Maxim Karolik. Courtesy, Museum of Fine Arts, Boston.*

of the railroad, the Alpine House, and John Coffin Nazro. That was the year
when businessmen with hard heads and deep pockets finally realized on the
schemes first dreamed up by the Crawfords, Willeys, and Fabyans. Starting in
1851, the White Mountains became the destination for growing thousands
of well-heeled vacationers, and these tourists had the wealth and taste to appreciate good landscape paintings, too. Having visited the year before,
Champney and Kensett would already have had a stock of finished work for
tourist-patrons to buy.[53] Art and tourism were not at all separate in the White
Mountains.

The links between the two realms were much closer than even the opportunism of Champney and Kensett suggests. The truth is that artists and businessmen served each others' interests perfectly. On the one hand, White
Mountain tourists naturally formed a pool of potential buyers for landscape
paintings. It made good sense for artists to paint scenes with which their customers were already familiar. On the other hand, the railroads and hotel own-

ers welcomed artists because their work helped to publicize the area and give it chic. For this reason, the tourist business actively recruited painters to work in the White Mountains and even to take up residence in the hotels. Moreover, art trained the sensibilities of tourists to appreciate the landscapes that they visited. At bottom, then, the artist and the hotel owner cooperated in pursuing the exact same business—selling the landscape.

The story of how Champney and Kensett came to the White Mountains illustrates how perfectly the interests of art and business coincided. The two painters had been recruited by Samuel W. Thompson, an innkeeper and mail carrier from North Conway. Thompson belonged to Horace Fabyan's generation, and like Fabyan he first opened his inn in the 1830s when the tourist business was already established but not yet mature. At this time, the stage-coach line that carried tourists to Crawford Notch did not stop in North Conway. Barbara MacAdam explained how "Thompson eventually succeeded in establishing a competing line that passed through North Conway. He was also instrumental in the formation of a line running through the Pinkham Notch to the Glen House [in Mount Washington's eastern valley]."[54] Thompson was interested in the latter because he had bought up a three-mile stretch of the Pinkham Notch turnpike in 1844 for twelve and a half cents an acre. The purchase proved either very lucky or very shrewd. It occurred just the year before the Atlantic and St. Lawrence Railroad was chartered in Maine. Tourists getting off in Gorham and staying at the Glen House would have to pass over Thompson's road to get to Crawford Notch, which they routinely did.

Thompson participated in ambitious schemes to build up area tourism. Along with other local businessmen, he helped to transform North Conway from an insignificant village into the Gateway to the White Mountains, an obligatory jumping-off place for visitors—an impressive accomplishment. After all, among its rivals, Bartlett was closer to the mountains, Conway was larger, and Gorham had the train station. But none of them became as popular as North Conway in the quarter century after 1851. The town had one of the region's highest concentrations of grand hotels. And North Conway owed its popularity, above all, to art.

Thompson demonstrated as much shrewdness in attracting artists to the town as he did attracting stagecoach lines. MacAdam explained his scheme: "According to one local history, Thompson had met Champney and Kensett on Sebago Lake in Maine in 1850 and persuaded them to come to North Conway later that season, making an arrangement with them whereby he would 'board them for a low price, carry their dinners to them, and they were to put "North Conway" on their sketches.'"[55] The White Mountains never saw a more effective promotional scheme. "After his first season in the White

Fig. 18. Jasper F. Cropsey, *An Indian Summer Morning in the White Mountains*, 1857, oil on canvas. Cropsey was one of dozens of artists who followed Champney and Kensett to the White Mountains. *Used with permission, The Currier Gallery of Art, Manchester, New Hampshire; 1962.17.*

Fig. 19. Thomas Hill, *Crawford Notch*, 1872, oil on canvas. Like many painters, Hill was artist-in-residence at a grand hotel, yet Hill here ignores the hotel that Horace Fabyan built onto the Willey House in 1845. *Used with permission, New Hampshire Historical Society, no. 118.*

Mountains," MacAdam continued, "he [Champney] returned to Boston and immediately began to promote the region's virtues" among his friends (23). Two summers later, North Conway was hosting forty painters, including Jasper Cropsey (fig. 18). Of course, many of them boarded at Thompson's.[56] Robert McGrath called them "the first important American artist's colony."[57] By 1853, the guidebook for the traveling public published by the Boston, Concord and Montreal Railroad (which approached the White Mountains on the southwest) identified North Conway as an artists' hangout. Thus, thousands of ordinary tourists began coming to the town to see the scenery that impressed the painters, to watch them sketch, and to bask in the cultural aura they created.

The nature of tourism made this close bond with art inevitable. Indeed, the nineteenth century regarded tourism itself as a kind of art, and McGrath described tourism as "the application to life of lessons learned from art" (see chap. 3, n. 42). As in Europe, tourism in the White Mountains largely meant viewing the landscape as if it were a painting. Thus, ordinary visitors to North Conway would perhaps have admired its artists for being master tourists who were highly skilled in seeing landscape correctly. Moreover, one common occupation for the tourists themselves was to sketch and paint the scenery, and hotels catered to them. "Many large hotels," MacAdam explained, "hosted resident artists for whom they would supply a studio. For his or her part, the artists generally offered instruction to visitors and contributed to the cultural life of the hotel by judging parades or other 'artistic' expressions, designing menus, and entertaining guests." Painters of some note, including Frank H. Shapleigh, Edward Hill, and Thomas Hill (fig. 19), spent many summers as resident artists in grand hotels.[58] Their presence shows how far art and the artist's sensibility dominated tourism.

But tourism influenced art, too. William Gilpin developed his theory of the picturesque as a result of writing how-to manuals for tourists. This major aesthetic category, which Thomas Cole adapted for his own painting, was in fact tourism's aesthetic. Not surprisingly, North Conway became famous for its picturesqueness. "In terms of pictorial structure," wrote MacAdam, "the picturesque . . . was generally characterized by a rough and broken foreground, a gentle middle ground, and a distant vista of grand mountains. The view of Mount Washington and its surrounding peaks from the Intervale in North Conway came to be recognized as a 'classic' of this genre."[59] That view—with the stony Saco in the foreground and Mount Washington looming behind—occurs more than any other among paintings of the White Mountains. Though less prevalent, the view looking down Crawford Notch and often including the Willey House offered a similar kind of image.

Fig. 20. John F. Kensett, *Mount Washington from the Valley of Conway*, 1851, oil on canvas.
Widely copied by other artists, this most famous of all nineteenth-century American
paintings defined the Saco River valley as the epitome of picturesque landscape.
*Used with permission, Davis Museum and Cultural Center, Wellesley College, Wellesley,
Massachusetts; gift of Mr. and Mrs. James B. Munn (Ruth C. Hanford, Class of 1909) in the
name of the Class of 1909; 1977.37.*

In the pivotal year of 1851, John F. Kensett painted what became by far the
most popular version of the Saco-and-Mount Washington type—indeed, the
most popular American landscape painting of the whole century (fig. 20).
"The most celebrated and widely disseminated vision of natural sublimity in
nineteenth-century America," wrote McGrath, "Kensett's *The White Mountains—Mt. Washington* is an inspired reprise of the most enduring landscape
model in western art . . . Engraved by the American Art-Union and reissued
by Currier and Ives under a similar title in 1860, Kensett's view of the Intervale became a virtual icon of native landscape art during the Romantic period,
visible on the walls of thousands of American homes."[60] The Art-Union chose
Kensett's painting to be the prize in its annual lottery and, in addition, distributed engravings of the work to all its members. The painting was also engraved for the public several times in the last half of the century. Perhaps
tourism as much as artistic merit explains the popularity of Kensett's image of

the White Mountains. After all, North Conway promoted itself on the basis of its picturesqueness, and its fame as a tourist destination generated nationwide public awareness of the scenery. No doubt, many of those who visited North Conway—or wished they could visit—bought copies of Kensett's work.

In North Conway and in the White Mountains as a whole, then, art and tourism created each other. The ease with which high art served tourism's purposes indicates how nearly identical had become their needs and outlooks. Artists of Kensett's caliber helped establish certain views of the mountains as standard, and these standard views appeared not only in the work of lesser artists but also in mass-produced images. For example, Alfred T. Bricher, a minor Hudson River School painter, copied Kensett's *The White Mountains—Mt. Washington* in his own work. Then, around 1870, Louis Prang of Boston began selling chromolithographs of Bricher's painting for six dollars.

No real boundaries separated businessmen from artists—or from tourists, writers, and scientists. Hotel operators toured the attractions and wrote about them. Tourists sketched and practiced botany as part of their vacations. Artists incorporated the latest scientific theories in their paintings while acting as entrepreneurs to peddle them to visitors. Writers sought to exploit the White Mountains' popularity and described the landscape from the tourist's perspective. Scientists were taught to look at the landscape by artists and included accounts of scenery in their reports. All belonged to a single tourist culture at whose center lay speculation. Whether they sold paintings or hotel rooms, they made money off the landscape.

CHAPTER FIVE

The Literature
of the White Mountains

THE WORST literary work to come out of the Willey disaster has to be Franklin Leavitt's poem (1885):

> Eighteen hundred and twenty six
>   The Willey mountain down did slip,
> It missed the house and hit the barn
>   If they'd all staid in they'd met no harm.
>
> It being in the dark of night
>   The Willey family took a fright
> And out of the house they all did run
>   And on to them the mountains come.
>
> It buried them all up so deep
>   They did not find them for three weeks,
> And three of them were never found
>   They were buried there so deep in the ground.[1]

Bad as it is, the poem is more than a curiosity. It belongs to a series of poems on the White Mountains which Leavitt, a longtime mountain guide, published in broadsides and sold to summer visitors. His poems are the literary equivalent of folk art paintings, and the tourists who bought them must have liked their quaintness. He thus tried to make money off the landscape through literature just as artists made money with paintings. Furthermore, the poem summarizes the weakness of nineteenth-century literary depictions of the landscape. Although Nathaniel Hawthorne and others wrote about the Willeys and the White Mountains with greater skill, their work scarcely reveals more about the landscape itself than does Leavitt's poem. Indeed, they imagined the subject in the same terms as Leavitt and did not probe beneath the stereotypes offered by the tourist culture.

Writers saw the Willeys as helpless victims and never dealt with their entrepreneurial spirit. The disaster itself usually just furnished writers with an occasion to express trite sentiments about hearth and home. Thus, poems and stories about the Willeys seem empty rhetorical displays when read against the historical record. Even from a literary perspective, writers failed to do justice to the portentousness of the event because it occurred for them in a vacuum. Unlike Europe, where battles, kings, and poets had hallowed almost every spot, here the landscape was essentially free of historical associations. (Henry James might have said that the White Mountains had succumbed to America's habit of erasing what was already there in order to put in something new.) For a location that had no usable past, writers had to adopt Ethan Crawford's strategy: They imported ready-made—and sometimes comically inappropriate—stories from the outside so they could do business with the landscape.

While writers followed tourism's strategy for cashing in on the Willeys' fame, they were largely unconscious of tourism's influence and accepted as a given the vision of the landscape which it projected. Writers show almost no awareness of how tourism shaped perceptions of the landscape, although most had gone to the mountains and seen tourism's importance firsthand. In Grenville Mellen's "Buried Valley," for example, the narrator is a traveler through the Notch who tells about the Willey slide as an eyewitness. Hawthorne's "The Ambitious Guest" is told from the point of view of a casual traveler who wanders past the Willeys' inn at sunset and decides to stay the night. These ploys replicate the tourist's fantasy of gaining direct knowledge of the events that have drawn him to the landscape. In a sense, writers had little choice; after all, tourism worked only because it convinced people that its vision of the landscape was authentic. Writers also were limited by their vocabulary. They brought to the White Mountains the language of the sublime and picturesque to describe what they saw and felt. Europeans had invented these terms to explain what one should feel upon seeing the Alps and other grand natural sites, and Americans uncritically applied the same aesthetics to the White Mountains. Travel writers often did not sketch the White Mountains directly; they simply quoted Byron on the Alps. For most, the high-toned language of tourism mattered more than actual experience.

Aesthetic Blindness

Deliberate disregard of the landscape's particulars could be taken to absurd lengths. For example, in 1833 travel writer Nathan Hale published *Notes Made During an Excursion to the Highlands of New Hampshire*. Signed "by a gentleman of Boston," the book has 184 pages, yet it contains almost no concrete references to the actual place Hale claims to have toured for seventeen days— no dates, no people, no place names, no physical descriptions, no story.[2] The tour is largely an excuse to frame his opinions on art, education, society, history, oratory, and so on. Though an extreme case, Hale's book shows how far indifference to location could be carried, and this indifference afflicted better minds than his.

This remarkable phenomenon separates literary and artistic depictions of the White Mountains.[3] Although painters and writers employed the same aesthetic theories, they represented landscape in different ways. Cole adapted the category of the picturesque to help him render the landscape with greater resolution of physical detail. In this way the picturesque led to greater empirical study of landscape by artists and scientists. However, the picturesque also blinded writers to what was actually in the landscape. Writers deliberately avoided empirical representation because they felt that it would detract from higher moral purposes. Representing the landscape itself, they felt, interfered with the presentation of aesthetic ideals. And the degree of blindness from which a writer suffered was directly proportional to his faith in European models.

Byron's *Childe Harold's Pilgrimage* (1818) influenced White Mountain writers the most. Childe Harold, the main character of this book-length poem, has lived a sensual and privileged life in England but grows bored and travels on the continent seeking a larger meaning. In four books, Harold tours Portugal and Spain; Albania, Greece, and Constantinople; the Rhine and the Alps; and Italy. Each place he visits has notable buildings and monuments, striking natural scenery, or associations with famous people and important events. He draws out morals from these associations and applies them to his own life. The more Harold sees, the deeper his character supposedly becomes. *Childe Harold's Pilgrimage*, then, contains more philosophizing than description or narration. But readers in both Europe and America prized the book for just this reason. The whole point of travel, they thought, was that it improved the tourist's moral, intellectual, and aesthetic faculties. Moreover, readers believed that Byron had transcribed his own experiences in Harold's story, and they likewise sought to reenact the poem in their own travels. They kept the book in their pockets as the ideal guide to touring.

Childe Harold's Pilgrimage did not just give people a form into which they could pour their own ideas and experiences of landscape. It told people what they should feel and think. Harold's visit to Rome in book 4 gave to Cole's *Course of Empire* its main gloss on the cycle of history: "There is the moral of all human tales; / 'Tis but the same rehearsal of the past, / First Freedom, and

then Glory—when that fails / Wealth, vice, corruption—barbarism at last."[4]
Lesser minds than Cole's simply allowed Byron to speak for them. For example, the chapter of *Incidents in White Mountain History* in which Benjamin Willey speculated on the family's movements before the fatal slide—and on the
terror they must have felt—ends with Byron's description of a thunderstorm
in the Alps:

> Far along,
> From peak to peak, the rattling crags among,
> Leaps the live thunder! Not from one lone cloud,
> But every mountain now hath found a tongue,
> And Jura answers, through her misty shroud,
> Back to the joyous Alps, who call to her aloud.[5]
> (3, 92)

Willey felt inadequate to convey the power of the fatal storm, "one of the
most terrible ever transpiring," so he borrowed the poet's more "correct" sentiments. Nevertheless, the description can voice only approximately Willey's
feelings because Byron's personification of landscape masks the impersonal
terror of a real catastrophe, with which Willey was struggling.

Willey also knew that his readers would thoroughly approve of his taste,
demonstrated by his quoting of Byron to express his feelings. After all, he was
doing just what tourists did when they hiked to a waterfall or some other
scenic spot, pulled out a little volume of poetry, and read from it. They
wanted to foster the correct frame of mind for viewing the sublime or picturesque. Travel writers cited the romantic poets when they wanted to stress
a scene's excellence. To cap off his descriptions of scenery, guidebook writer
Thomas Starr King quoted stanza after stanza of Byron, Wordsworth,
Goethe, Longfellow, Emerson, and other poets—most of whom had never
seen the White Mountains. Well over four hundred pages long, King's *The
White Hills: Their Legends, Landscape, and Poetry* (1859) was considered the
most tasteful and ennobling guidebook. Even scientists, with a professional
interest in detail, often used poetry's rhetoric to express a scene's larger meaning. Those who did not like romanticism used the Bible to describe the
mountains. As one minister claimed shortly afterward, prodigious events such
as the Willey disaster "not only teach a lesson strikingly accordant with the
instructions of inspired truth, but are often most accurately described in the
very language of the bible."[6] Whatever text was used by writers and tourists,
it served to hide the reality of the landscape.

Tourists who bought King's book no doubt had forgotten why they should
quote Byron rather than look for themselves. But aesthetic blindness had long

roots. Hidden inside the sublime and the picturesque lay a prejudice against the empirical. "These eighteenth-century aesthetic discourses," explained Elizabeth Bohls, "all display a pattern of excluding or rejecting material particularity in favor of abstract or formal considerations."[7] Bohls noted that English landscape painter Joshua Reynolds called details "deformed," by which he meant both ugly and formless. Artists should reach toward ideal forms, Reynolds taught, by creating generalized images that eliminate idiosyncratic details (19). And that is just what a tourist did when viewing landscape through the lens of romantic verse. Moreover, the viewer or tourist must look at a thing with "disinterested contemplation" and not have "any practical stake in the existence of the object" (16). In other words, good viewers cannot be mercenary. Thus, aesthetic blindness to particulars was antimaterial in two senses: It led the viewer to despise both the physical world and the world of profit.

Certainly, most nineteenth-century Americans considered tourism antithetical to moneymaking, but the notion required outright denial of the obvious. Perry Miller described this curious denial of economics as a broad trend in America. Although America expanded enormously in both size and wealth, most writers spoke of this in terms of spiritual progress. "But the amazing fact about this gigantic material thrust of the early nineteenth century," Miller wrote,

> is how few Americans would any longer venture, aside from their boasts, to explain, let alone to justify, the expansion of civilization in any language that could remotely be called that of utility. The most utilitarian conquest known to history had somehow to be viewed not as inspired by a calculus of rising land values and investments but (despite the orgies of speculation) as an immense exertion of the spirit. Those who made articulate the meaning of this drama found their frames of reference not in political economy but in Scott and Byron, in visions of "sublimity."[8]

Spiritual ideals were intended to correct materialism's excesses as well as to conceal its disturbing effects. Few noticed that high culture itself had a powerful commercial use, especially in tourism.

Aesthetic blindness, then, meant not just ignoring the physical landscape but also refusing to admit even the most obvious cases of economic interest into one's understanding of the landscape. Most writers adopted the naive tourist's view that art and money had nothing whatever to do with each other. Thus, in accounts of the White Mountains, writers and tourists alike casually placed the sublime and the mundane side by side—to comic effect. The following passage, for example, appears in Ethan Crawford's visitors' album for 1827. It records a trip probably made by a legislative committee to assess the damage done to the turnpike in 1826. The most striking feature of this description of the slide is how generalized and literary it is. It could have been written before the trip itself:

> Sep 10 The Hon. Henry Hubbard of Charlestown, speaker of the [New Hampshire] House of Representatives, visited the notch of the white mountains and the desolations of the notch House & looked on the graves of those buried by the enormous Slides of earth & rocks & trees mingled by the passions of tempests in one common mass—On arriving at the notch hill we all became satisfied that no rain could have torn the immense rocks from their native lands & rolled them like little playthings down the narrow pass & piled 100's of tons in huge masses at the verry head of the Saco where it now ripples a small brook—we were further of opinion that 5 or 6 000 dollars would fully repair the road. After enjoying the sublime yet dreary views we returned and dined nobly on roast Beef.[9]

Roast beef and exaltation, tragedy and transportation funds. The combination was typical—not just of vulgar state legislators, but also of writers of refined sensibility. The pragmatic and the sublime lay beside each other, and no one noticed that they were the inseparable components of a single speculative enterprise.

Empty Associations

Even the firmest believers in the duty of high culture and tourism to correct materialism often found the actual experience of landscape unsettling. Their aesthetic idealism suggests a certain anxiety over the actual way in which the Willeys and Crawfords had exploited the land. Writers came closest to naming what bothered them when they expressed disdain for the "utilitarian." Yet the Willeys had practiced an exploitation of landscape that was not utilitarian so much as speculative. When nineteenth-century writers came to Crawford Notch, they did not find a pattern of use that fit a recognized category, whether agrarian or utilitarian. Writers assumed that nature here was pristine, but the land also seemed void or formless. It could never be more than a store of raw materials unless given a noble form. Therefore, writers set out to shape the landscape conceptually (much as Crawford had done), but they imported images and narratives from Europe which, if tasteful, were also incongruous.

For example, Theodore Dwight Jr. tried to link landscape with elevated thoughts in *Sketches of Scenery and Manners in the United States*, which described his trip from Connecticut to northern New England, across New York State, and into Canada. Dwight wanted to instruct others on "Travelling to Good Purpose," as he titled the last chapter. "Dwight's book," according to

John Sears (in his introduction), "was aimed at families and was designed to help them discover the Christian and republican values he wished to promote in the landscape they encountered. By teaching them to read the landscape in this religious and patriotic fashion, he hoped to bind the American 'social and family circle' more closely to the land."[10] As did Nathan Hale, however, Dwight often sacrificed concrete detail to generalities and moral lessons.

The Willey House offered Dwight an opportunity to talk about the sublime, but his observations are predictable: "The more we approach to the centre of devastation, the more do we yield up to the feelings of astonishment which the scene so naturally inspires."[11] He said little more about what he himself saw and felt; even after stating this, Dwight had trouble articulating just how the landscape fit sublime criteria. Immanuel Kant described the sublime as a temporary check to one's vitality when confronted with something immense. Dwight echoed this idea and remarked that the sublime's intensity must be relieved from time to time:

> The feelings of sublimity become painful, after they have been long excited by the view of vast magnitudes, and useless extensions of height, depth, or level surface; but they are often relieved by our recurring to milder, calmer, and more encouraging objects, with which we generally find them intermingling. The comforts of a cottage, the pleasant aspect of a river's margin, the green nibbled turf under the shade of a grove, alternately administer to us a calm which alleviates the painful exertion we make in contemplating things too great for our powers (63).

This statement does not reflect what Dwight felt or even what theories of the sublime induced him to feel. The rugged scenery merely called to mind a school lesson on aesthetics, which he dutifully recited. Here is an astonishing gulf between Dwight's travel narrative and the actual landscape. In fact, the Notch was a poor specimen of the mixed landscape about which he wrote. The soothing "cottage," "turf," and "grove" came straight from Wordsworth's England. Certainly, the shabby, deserted Willey House and the deeply scarred mountain slope above it were not "green and pleasant" in 1829. Moreover, the rounded peaks of Crawford Notch are not especially high. They are mere foothills compared to the Alps, which Dwight had seen in 1818.

The word that carries true emotion is *useless*—"useless extensions of height, depth or level surface." What Dwight found "sublime"—that is, disturbing to his equanimity—was that the mountain landscape of the Notch seemed so prodigiously useless. Dwight saw dimly that the Notch defied the ideology of moral and material progress. Indeed, the word expressed his anxiety over American materialism generally, for, in its natural state, Dwight felt, landscape amounts to nothing more than a formless mass. It has to be given a higher use. If not, America's mountains would never be anything "but huge piles of earth and rocks, covered with blighted firs and fern," as Sarah Josepha Hale put it scornfully.[12] Dwight's *Sketches*, then, represents his attempt to improve landscape by linking it to finer ideas—aesthetic, literary, and historical. Whether they suited the location was beside the point.

Dwight was an associationist. Many in the early nineteenth century argued that landscape was a kind of living textbook in that its associations with significant events in American history reminded visitors of deep thoughts and noble deeds. This movement stemmed largely from the Scottish Common Sense philosopher Archibald Alison, William Gilpin's contemporary. "According to Alison," Sears explained, "the spectator's emotional response to the landscape arises from the associations evoked in the mind by objects in the landscape rather than from the physical properties and aesthetic qualities of those objects alone."[13] Alison's theory may have accurately described the situation already existing in Europe, with its long, memorable history and educated traveling public. But since most American places had little history, Dwight and others set out to *create* landscape associations, meaning that the idea changed radically in its American context. Although Alison merely extended Locke's materialist theory of perception, the invention of associations turned out to be quite antiempirical. Again, writers such as Dwight had to ignore the landscape itself in order to impose tasteful ideas on it.

The most common conceit of those who wrote about the White Mountains in an elevated style was to choose a tourist or traveler for the narrator. No doubt, *Childe Harold's Pilgrimage* suggested this ploy, but it has some advantages. Tourists have an emotional distance from landscape, which allows them to comprehend the larger significance of a scene while helping to underscore the power of landscape when it does move them. The tourist acts as a surrogate or eyewitness to give the reader a sense of direct connection to the landscape. However, the tourist-narrator did not live up to its promise in the White Mountains. A writer could not simply make up a history for the region because it would obviously not be true. The best he could do was suggest several images that described what such a landscape *should* be. As a result, poems and stories about the Willey slide often seem little more than a hodgepodge of clichés about mountains.

The best example is Grenville Mellen's "Buried Valley" (1833).[14] Over thirty pages long, this poem encapsulates most features found in the literature about the Willey slide. It recalls Lydia Sigourney's 1828 elegy on the Willeys (Mellen dedicated to her his volume of collected verse, for which "Buried Valley" is one of the two title poems) and anticipates George Willey's *Soltaire* (1902).[15] To a modern reader, the most noticeable feature of "Buried Valley" is that it contains few facts about Crawford Notch and Mount Washington, even though Mellen focused the poem on the landscape. It has two parts. The twelve pages of part 2 tell the Willeys' story in short lyric lines arranged as if they were a choral ode from a Greek tragedy. Part 1, which sets the scene of the disaster, runs for seventeen pages and has longer, more compact lines. Thus, the setting gets twice the attention that the story itself does, yet generalities make up almost all of this description, and Mellen places most details about Crawford Notch in endnotes.

What makes this more remarkable is that Mellen (unlike Lydia Sigourney) knew the place about which he was writing. Mellen had stayed at Abel Crawford's in August 1819 and was among the first to climb Mount Washington via the Crawfords' new bridle path.[16] Mellen invoked this trip by making his narrator a traveler who has returned with a companion to Crawford Notch some years after the disaster. On the narrator's earlier visit, the "valley had unbosom'd all / The countless beauties that enthral, / In their unutter'd mystery, / The painter's or the poet's eye."[17] Like a tourist, Mellen was interested in the Notch only to the extent that it could be read as a sample of romantic verse or painting. The narrator's main point, of course, is that such a landscape teaches a moral: "How strong this mountain-land!—how eloquent! / How large the living lesson that it reads!" (272).

In "Buried Valley," Mellen wove together disparate yet familiar ideas about landscape. For example, mountains represent the eternal and prove the impermanence of human institutions. Here Mellen stole from Byron the same gloomy thought that Thomas Cole took for *The Course of Empire:* "Change! change!—the fields are dotted o'er with graves, / And Man and Empires to their common fate / Have pass'd in silence" (271). But then again, mountains can reinvigorate people; their sounds win "back the spirit from its apathy" (273–4). On the one hand, the site of the Willey disaster shows it is "madness to forget, defy / The dread Omnipotence of earth and sky" (273). On the other hand, mountains are an "Emblem of FREEDOM" (275). At the Willey House, the narrator tells his companion to deduce from the wreckage left by the slide how indiscriminate and powerful nature can be. But he also recalls a scene from his earlier trip that would have pleased the Physiocrat Quesnay. He had looked "O'er bending grass and yellow grain / And his ear heard, in welcome peals / Of far-off cadence, from his fields / Man's voice in faint hallooings come, / Shouting his harvest cheerly home!" (277). Mellen drew all of these mountain images from Europe, and none was accurate. He apparently did not feel the need to resolve these obvious conflicts between the images in his poem.

His complacency extended to the relationship between Man and Nature.

Mellen followed Sigourney's lead in heightening the pathos of the story by making the Willeys out to be simple-minded peasants. The smallness of their lives is meant to contrast with the immensity of the mountain; their piety gives them no reason to suspect the giant calamity awaiting them. Sigourney herself wrote:

> In yon dell
> Once bright with emerald verdure,—was a home
> Of rural peace. There, in confiding love,
> The parents rear'd their babes,—as in some nest
> Of the far wilderness, the brooding birds
> Make their own little world,—nor dream how deep
> The solitude that wraps them. It was sweet
> To see the child its first weak steps essay,
> 'Neath the deep shade of those eternal hills,—
> Still looking up with wonder, as the name
> Of Him who made them all, was on the ear
> Press'd in a parent's tone.[18]

Mellen's poem touches the same notes. Samuel Willey "taught his children lessons high / Drawn from this broad immensity!"[19] Of course, this pious view of the Willeys' life offers a moral little different from the one James derived from the White Mountains seventy years later when he expressed the hope that unsullied Nature would teach vacationers humane values. Hawthorne, too, professed the same belief. In "The Great Stone Face" (1850), the Old Man of the Mountain instructs an untutored rustic in the simple, noble philosophy of faith, fellowship, and good works. Neither great writers nor small, then, felt the urge to understand the landscape on its own terms. Without such knowledge, they could only adopt a patronizing tone toward the Willeys.

For Mellen and Sigourney, the moral of the Willey disaster seems to be that we are all mere children when it comes to understanding Providence. In the face of such an astonishing catastrophe, this utter triteness suggests a lurking dissatisfaction with the view then prevailing that Nature reflects God's will. Only a small step divides Mellen's and Sigourney's empty sentiment from the idea of nature as inhumane, which Thomas Cole had rendered so effectively in his early paintings. For example, in a poem written quite late (about 1884), Emily Dickinson provides an analogue to Cole's image of nature in *Distant View*:

> Apparently with no surprise
> To any happy Flower
> The Frost beheads it at its play—

> In accidental power—
> The blonde Assassin passes on—
> The Sun proceeds unmoved
> To measure off another Day
> For an Approving God.[20]

One could easily imagine Dickinson having written this poem in response to a deadly natural catastrophe such as the Willey slide. She used the same homey images as Mellen and Sigourney, though with cutting irony. Likewise, in the Willey disaster, Mellen and other writers confronted a nature lacking particular concern for human life. Nature had unaccountably become a moral void, and early nineteenth-century writers could not imagine anything new with which to fill it.

Farmer Willey's Cottage; or, Death among the Lowly

The story that Mellen told follows well-established patterns, as do his landscape images. Interestingly, he listed and rejected possible genres for his story of the Willeys and the White Mountains until he found the one he liked best. They form a litany of the nineteenth century's sentimental and melodramatic tropes. Other writers eventually tried them all, but no one stepped outside the bounds laid down by Mellen and looked at the Willeys' story in an original way. Even Hawthorne's stories about the White Mountains—"The Ambitious Guest," "The Great Carbuncle," "Roger Malvin's Burial," and "The Great Stone Face"—stay within those limits.

The conventional nature of White Mountain literature indicates a failure of imagination on the part of nineteenth-century writers. This failure is plainest in works about the Willey disaster itself. Writers failed to imagine the slide and the nine deaths in such a way as to give meaning to the catastrophe. On the surface, the family lives intimately with nature, but the slide proves they are really disjoined from the landscape. Writers imagined the Willeys as simple country folk who have no fear of the mountain and are, therefore, surprised by the slide. Better dramatists would have depicted some tension between the tragedy's two principle actors. But it was not just prosaic minds that kept nineteenth-century writers from good work. Rather, they embraced the conventional because they could not imagine the relationship between the Willeys and the landscape in any other terms. Tourism promoted a romantic vision of the White Mountains, which writers—like the public itself—accepted as authentic and inevitable. Limited to this view, they could talk about the Willeys only in melancholy strains cribbed from Byron.

Through his list Mellen tacitly admitted that no genre exactly suited the tragedy that he and the others wanted to write. "It is no tale of mad Romance . . . No legend of young love" begins Mellen's list of genres. Yet Hawthorne and George Willey both imagined the Willeys' story this way. Similarly, Charles Dudley Warner set his romance *Their Pilgrimage* (1886) among upper-class tourists who wander in turn through the Northeast's best summer resorts.[21] Hero and heroine finally get together in the White Mountains, the climactic stop of both novel and tour (which included a stop at the Willey House, naturally).

It is "No story of some ruffian band," Mellen continued, yet several times the White Mountains served as the setting for stories about seedy frontier skirmishes. *Laconia; or, Legends of the White Mountains and Merry Meeting Bay* (1854), an anonymous novel, tells how the Indians of northern New England were cheated of their land.[22] In "Roger Malvin's Burial" (1832), Hawthorne wrote about a scalp-hunting expedition in 1725, which Americans later exalted in memory as an epic battle between marauding Indians and heroic settlers. Lovewell's Fight occurred about ten miles from Conway in Fryeburg, Maine, and White Mountain tourists often included the site in their itinerary. In 1845, Francis Parkman published a sketch called "The Scalp-Hunter," which drew upon his own adventure on Mount Willey in 1841.[23] In this story, an older white man chases an Indian into Crawford Notch to get the ten-pound bounty for his scalp. To elude pursuit, the Indian climbs up into the ravine carved by a landslide. The scalp-hunter follows and gets trapped in the ravine for two days until a sudden thunderstorm washes him down the mountain. The Indian escapes.[24]

Mellen's list continues: "No lines of warrior memory / Stain the reft granite . . . the weary tale / Of slighted hopes and friends that fail, / Of passion's pride—ambition's art."[25] Here Mellen recalled heroic battles that took place in mountain passes, such as the one in the medieval epic *The Song of Roland*. Roland commanded the rear guard of Charlemagne's army as it returned from a victory over the Saracens in Spain. Roland and his men were betrayed and attacked in a pass over the Pyrenees called Roncesvalles. Others imagined the same kind of story for Crawford Notch. In *Scenery of the White Mountains* (1848), William Oakes likened the Notch to the mountain pass at Thermopylae in Greece where Leonidas and three hundred Spartans held off an invading Persian army in 480 B.C.[26] In his 1828 diary, Thomas Cole wrote that "a hundred men might defend this pass against a thousand."[27] Samuel Adams Drake, the author of a popular White Mountain guidebook, also invoked Leonidas in a series written for *Harper's*. This time, Drake equated Lovewell's

Fight with Thermopylae.[28] The heroic tale was the least likely possibility of them all, since White Mountain history held no pretext for it. To writers under Byron's influence, though, the geography of Crawford Notch seemed grand enough that events of epic scope *should* have taken place there. Some wondered whether the expected events had occurred among Indian tribes in the forgotten past; others perhaps wondered whether they might occur in the future.

But the variety of ways in which writers imagined the Willeys and the White Mountains indicates why they found the landscape so hard to explain. Each genre implies a different geographical status for the region, and, by trying out different genres, writers were in part trying to fit the landscape into the right category. Thus, romances such as George Willey's *Soltaire* depict the White Mountains as an isolated, uninhabited wilderness. In the scalp-hunter stories, they form a porous boundary between Indian savagery and white civilization. And in the warrior epic, they act as a barrier between hostile nations. Of course, none of these categories reflects the reality of the White Mountains because they are too static. Above all, it was the *changes* caused by speculation (tourism) which defined the landscape.

The favorite genre for the Willeys' story was one that turned inside, away from the landscape. A simple, bittersweet, domestic tale is the way most chose to write it. "An inspiration purer—higher, / Has lur'd him to his humble lyre," Mellen wrote, "And woke the musing bard to fling / So rude a hand along its string— / A story of our children's time— / Simple—yet saddening and sublime!"[29] Like the other genres, this one led writers to suppress the truth about the Willeys and their relationship to the landscape. In this version, the Willeys turn into simple folk who have little formal education but learn life's morals directly, that is, from the Bible and nature. Mellen's Samuel Willey is "content" in his isolation and lacks worldly ambition. He is inevitably an "honest man," a devoted husband, and a cheerful father.

In literature, the Willeys become an idealized American family whose "innocence" is violated by the slide. One writer after another stressed the family's unaffected happiness before the disaster in order to gain the reader's sympathy. Joseph W. Turner sketched this image in "The Willey Family" (1877):

> Among the mountains, wild and drear,
>   A lone and solitary spot,
> Where father, mother, children dear,
>   Were dwellers in an humble cot,—
>
> There sunshine blest them day by day,
>   Contentment lingered round their home,

'Till Desolation's sad display
   Enwrapt them in her darkest gloom.[30]

The poem's most interesting aspect is what the author does *not* do with his images. They could have been used powerfully. The gloom in this poem, for instance, might have symbolized a flaw in America's blind faith in progress, much as the long mountain shadows in Vergil's *Eclogues* portend wrenching social change in Italy. But Turner would then have had to imagine the Willeys differently, as much more shrewd and aware of the environment in which they lived. As he and others presented them, the Willeys were completely unaware of the danger until it overwhelmed them.

For this reason, the outcome of most literary works about the Willeys is not the tragic hero's enlightenment but mere pathos. Creating pathos was virtually the only way nineteenth-century writers could tell the story. They were forced back on this effect because they did not understand the Willeys' complex relationship to the White Mountains. The Arcadian images promoted by tourism led most writers to set the family in an uncomplicated pastoral-agrarian landscape. A good example is Thomas W. Parsons's "The Willey House," published in *Putnam's* in 1855. In this poem the Willeys' story is told by an adult to some children who are berry picking in Crawford Notch. They see the house in the distance, but it is not the busy tourist attraction and hotel that Horace Fabyan built:

You see that cottage in the glen,
   Yon desolate forsaken shed—
Whose mouldering threshold, now and then,
   Only a few stray travelers tread.

No smoke is curling from its roof,
   At eve no cattle gather round,
No neighbor now, with dint of hoof,
   Prints his glad visit on the ground.

A happy home it was of yore:
   At morn the flocks went nibbling by,
And Farmer Willey, at his door,
   Oft made their reckoning with his eye.

Where yon rank alder trees have sprung,
   And birches cluster thick and tall,
Once the stout apple overhung,
   With his red gifts, the orchard wall.[31]

Parsons took most of these images from Horace's *Odes*—the curling smoke, the friendly neighbor, the orchard—but these do not accurately represent what Crawford Notch was like in 1855 or even in 1826. Writers such as Parsons simply did not recognize the complexity of American landscape the way Roman poets had theirs. What nineteenth-century writers left out was the influence of the city and market economy on areas such as the White Mountains.

One must remember that the market had not brought *visible* changes to the White Mountains so much as a change in their status. Thus, writers could feel they were stating eternal truths about rural life when they imitated ancient poets. After all, Horace went to his farm to escape Rome just as American tourists went to the Notch to find relief from Boston or New York City. But nineteenth-century writers did not see the fundamental difference: In the White Mountains, capitalism had come out from the city to fill tourists' needs. Without this awareness, the poems and stories themselves became simplistic. The ancients again offer a revealing comparison. The herdsmen of Vergil's *Eclogues* are uprooted by the reallocation of their land to veterans of Augustus's army and are forced out of the countryside and into the city. Vergil used the herdsmen's troubled simplicity to show the breadth of the social and economic changes then occurring. But the Willeys in Parsons's poem cannot yield deep insight because they do not feel any uneasiness with their surroundings. They lead a static, old-fashioned life up to the very end and are incapable of registering catastrophic change.

Literary portrayals exhibit no awareness of how tourism had influenced the Willeys. They do not serve tourists, much less help to direct the trade themselves. Of course, the family shows the proper hospitality to travelers, but this does not mean they are running a business. Rather, Mellen, like Turner, called their house a "humble cot," almost as if it had a thatched roof and stood far out in the English countryside:

> That humble cot!—'tis silent now!
> No smoke-wreath to the mountain's brow
> Curls from its low, o'er shadowed roof—
> No steed, with loud impatient hoof
> Calls to the girded traveller more
> To quit the hospitable door—[32]

The scene might have come from *Tom Jones*. The Willeys here could be peasants honored by the visit of a squire riding to London on business. His visit occurs by chance; there is no hint that he might have been lured there to see the mountains. Mellen also denied that the Willeys left behind a going concern. Several owners did run the inn after the slide, but, by saying the house

stands deserted, Mellen suggested that the family had occupied it only because they had wanted to live close to nature.

With this simplistic view of the Willeys' life, even the most skillful account
of the slide itself would seem anticlimactic. No matter how intimately a writer
imagined the final scene, it would seem purposeless. Benjamin Willey's account of the family's last hours in *Incidents* remains the best because he was at
least willing to imagine the tragedy's critical moment. Others gave up without
trying. In his 1846 docudrama *Avalanche of the White Hills*, for example, Isaac
McClellan lavished space on a sentimental portrait of the Willeys as a family
yet passed over the actual disaster in two or three sentences. The reason is not
a lack of fancy but ignorance of the landscape. The story might have begun,
"It was a dark and stormy night":

> "Listen, dear father!" cries little Eliza, the eldest of the children, "hark! how the
> rough wind roars up the chimney and whistles through the chinks of the door;
> and hear how the lashing rain pours against the casement . . . Will you not relate
> to us, in what manner our Notch through the Hills was first discovered. You
> promised to give us the story, on some leisure evening, and no time can be better
> than the present."
>
> "Yes, my children," said the kind father, "I will now relate to you the tale."[33]

The bedtime story takes up eighty lines, but the Willeys' own story is missing;
McClellan passed over it in a few vague phrases. For McClellan, landscape is
a mere backdrop to point up the fragility of family life; the slide became a
melodramatic way of saying, "It's a cruel world out there!"

To move beyond melodrama or voyeurism, writers should have tried to discover the real relation between Man and Nature in Crawford Notch. By contrast, Parsons and Mellen justified their attempts to imagine the Willeys' actual death on mere technical grounds; they reasoned that the slide would have
been visible because lightning flashes would have illuminated the mountainside. "A flash! O Christ!" wrote Parsons, "the lightning showed / The mountain moving from his seat! / Out! out into the slippery road! / Into the wet
with naked feet! / No time for dress—for life! for life! / No time for any word
but this."[34] And that is it. The Willeys exclaim a few syllables and then the
earth buries them. In *Soltaire*, all that Martha Willey (imagined as the lone
survivor) tells of the experience is a few clipped phrases shouted to her fleeing
family.[35]

Although Mellen's version seems less abrupt, it still tells little about the
Willeys themselves. In part 2 of "Buried Valley," the narrator recalls climbing
to the top of Mount Washington on the day of the slide and experiencing the
serenity of nature. "And when I upward gaz'd / As into some clear fount . . . /

It seem'd to bow and bathe the mount / In one transcendent hue!"[36] It is the calm before the storm. Clouds roll in. Thunder booms, and storm winds blast. The narrator runs headlong down the western slope toward Crawford Notch. The gigantic storm blackens the whole mountain as lightning flashes and rain pours down like rivers. One flash shows a precipice at his feet, from which he springs back. A landslide begins to drop from the precipice, and the horrified narrator sees, far below in the valley, a small house lying in its path. As he watches, "Forth from that little cabin sprung / A thing of life—and—suddenly—another! / A human form—and others round it clung. / O God! perhaps some frantic mother / Bow'd with her children!" (294–5). The Willeys' death scene occupies fewer than two of the thirty pages in Mellen's commemorative poem.

How strange that the Willey slide should have left normally verbose writers dumbstruck. Surely, the mystery of death did not induce them to speak in reverent undertones. They said little because the mystery of the Willeys' *life* baffled them. Without understanding their life, writers could not imagine any last-minute realization the Willeys might have had in Crawford Notch. Writers who did not know *why* the family had moved there could not have guessed that they might have regretted the pecuniary motives that had brought them to the Notch house.

Ambitious Guest, Slack Host

Nathaniel Hawthorne's short story "The Ambitious Guest" surpasses other literary treatments of the Willey slide, despite repeating many features that mar them.[37] The story's superiority stems from Hawthorne's skepticism about the tourist culture, which he observed during his 1832 trip through Crawford Notch and his stay with Ethan Crawford. Hawthorne satirized the tourists he saw in "The Notch of the White Mountains," a sketch he wrote to introduce "The Ambitious Guest." Tourists are not ideal, reverent viewers of landscape; rather, they are noisy and too self-absorbed to appreciate the White Mountains' grandeur. Likewise, "The Ambitious Guest" mocks the clichés that represented the popular view of the Willeys and that other writers used sincerely. With subtle psychology, Hawthorne analyzed how both tourists and the Willeys *fail* to read the landscape accurately. However, his portrayal of the Willeys does not move beyond Mellen's and Sigourney's characterization of them as naive, nor did he acknowledge their active participation in the tourist trade.

In plot, "The Ambitious Guest" is as melodramatic as Isaac McLellan's version of the Willey disaster. It opens with a youth of romantic sensibility traveling alone one evening through Crawford Notch and stopping at a lonely house for the night. The house belongs to the Willeys, although they go un-named. While the wind howls outside, a warm fire and the cosiness of the family circle lead the guest to open his heart. "The secret of the young man's character," wrote Hawthorne, "was a high and abstracted ambition. He could have borne to live an undistinguished life, but not to be forgotten in the grave. Yearning desire had been transformed to hope; and hope, long cherished, had become like certainty that, obscurely as he journeyed now, a glory was to beam on all his pathway—though not perhaps, while he was treading it." The whole family loosens up under the guest's influence, and they confess their own ambitions, some serious and some silly. For example, the grandmother would like someone to hold a hand mirror before her face when she is laid in her coffin so that she can "see whether all's right."

Finally, the guest and the seventeen-year-old daughter draw apart for a pri-vate chat. The sound of a slide coming down the mountain suddenly breaks in upon the household's revery. A shout goes up, "The slide! the slide!" which resounds like "the peal of the last trump," and they all rush outside to their deaths. "Who has not heard their name?" Hawthorne asked, knowing that his readers have indeed heard of the Willeys; his refusal to name them simply un-derlines their fame. The egotistic youth, though, remains forever anonymous, his ambition unrealized. Hawthorne implied that the Willeys deserved to be-come famous because their very simplicity—their modest lives, their happi-ness together, and their hospitality to strangers—made them exemplary.

The tale is not so simplistic, however. The central irony, of course, is that everyone dies because, at the crucial moment, they abandon the one safe spot—the home. The guest enters it from the larger world of striving and movement, and he uncovers the ambition latent in each family member. But along with the consciousness of ambition comes loneliness, so that the Wil-leys become more aware of their individuality and less secure in family ties. When the father muses on his own ambition, his wife, Esther, addresses him in the third person to acknowledge that ambition estranges him from his usual role: "Is the man thinking what he will do when he is a widower?" He can think of no more sincere expression of his fidelity to their relationship than to reassure her, "When I think of your death, Esther, I think of mine, too." This common wish not to survive a spouse is ultimately fulfilled. The Willeys abandon the literal house, but they do not entirely abandon what the home symbolizes. Hawthorne suggested that the Willeys died less bitterly than the lonely guest because they achieved something substantial by living and dying together. In contrast, the father decides, ambitions are "things, that are pretty certain never to come to pass." As if to clinch the argument, Hawthorne ended with this flourish: "Wo, for the high-souled youth, with his dream of

Earthly Immortality! His name and person utterly unknown; his history, his way of life, his plans, a mystery never to be solved; his death and his existence, equally a doubt! Whose was the agony of that death-moment?"

Nevertheless, the Willeys' approach to life is flawed. They deliberately ignore the world outside, with the result that they are left at its mercy. Heralded by "the peal of the last trump," the slide is apocalyptic because it suddenly reveals to the family a doom they have long expected yet never admitted. Early in the story, "the frank-hearted stranger had just drawn his chair to the fire when something like a heavy footstep was heard without, rushing down the steep side of the mountain, as with long and rapid strides, and taking such a leap in passing the cottage as to strike the opposite precipice. The family held their breath, because they knew the sound, and their guest held his by instinct. 'The old Mountain has thrown a stone at us, for fear we should forget him,' said the landlord, recovering himself." To maintain the routine of daily living in an environment so evidently dangerous as the Notch, the Willeys must bar from consciousness the realization of that danger. And part of their defensive strategy is to diminish Nature by speaking of it in familiar, human terms. Thus, their method for coping also keeps them from feeling the urgency to move away. The psychology is intriguing. And it makes Hawthorne the only one in the nineteenth century who attributed to the Willeys any real sensitivity to the landscape in which they dwelt. Even Benjamin Willey failed to do that.

Still, Hawthorne's Willey family chooses to suppress what it knows about the landscape—and about the world of affairs, too. As in Mellen and Parsons, Hawthorne's Willeys can be amazingly naive. When a wagon rolls up to the door and its passengers consider whether to stay the night or drive further, Mr. Willey reacts strangely for an innkeeper: "'Father,' said the girl, 'they are calling you by name.' But the good man doubted whether they had really called him, and was unwilling to show himself too solicitous of gain by inviting people to patronize his house. He therefore did not hurry to the door; and the lash being soon applied, the travelers plunged into the Notch." This lack of business instincts reverses the reality of the Willeys' life. In Hawthorne's story the family is isolated because its "honesty" relegates it to the margins of the economy; in fact, however, the Willeys accepted isolation as the price for moving a little closer to the center of the economy. Hawthorne surely realized the improbability of his portrayal and chose it anyway to point a contrast—the guest wants fame more than anything yet suffers anonymity; the travelers from the world at large know Mr. Willey's name, but his disbelief in that possibility demonstrates his humility or his poverty of spirit. Unlike Mellen, Hawthorne gave a psychological justification for the Willeys' simple-mindedness.

Despite this deep characterization, Hawthorne still arrived at the same moral about the Willey slide as would McLellan: It's a cruel world. Hawthorne was not so much artfully ambiguous about the disaster as genuinely divided in his thinking. The uncertainty reflects his contradictory relationship with tourism. On the one hand, as his extended trip in 1832 shows, he participated in tourism enthusiastically and even depended on it to fuel his writing. On the other hand, he satirized the tourist culture and wondered whether the intimate connection to landscape and history that tourism promises is possible. Because of this skepticism, Hawthorne could not imagine that the Willeys had any sort of a deep relationship to Crawford Notch.

Starting in his midtwenties, Hawthorne traveled regularly, but his 1832 trip was probably his longest until he went abroad in 1853. It was also his most deliberate tour and the most important to his literary career. He set out from Salem, Massachusetts, in early September, traveled north to the White Mountains, and then headed west across Vermont to Lake Champlain. He turned south to the Erie Canal, which he joined near Utica, New York, embarked on a boat headed west, and capped his journey by visiting Niagara Falls at the end of the month. Thus, Hawthorne followed a very common itinerary for early nineteenth-century tourists and saw many of the Northeast's most important attractions. Hawthorne used this trip to gather material for a book-length work called *The Storyteller*, never finished. *The Storyteller*'s premise was that a tourist (like Hawthorne himself) would visit famous sites and tell what he saw in a series of travel sketches. At the same time, he would relate stories that he picked up from the local people; "The Ambitious Guest" and "The Great Carbuncle," both set in the White Mountains, were to be two of them. By associating his stories with well-known places and events, such as the Willey slide, Hawthorne hoped to give his fiction popular appeal. He tried to make money from the White Mountains' national reputation just as did Franklin Leavitt, the painters, and the hotel operators.

Hawthorne took an associationist approach to American landscape, a philosophy he shared with Theodore Dwight. He chose associationism because it offered a serious method to an artist who wanted to produce high-quality literature that was distinctively American. Hawthorne learned about associationism from his philosophy professor at Maine's Bowdoin College, Thomas Upham. Curiously, on the day of the Willey slide, Upham happened to be in Crawford Notch climbing Mount Washington. He barely escaped off the mountain before flash floods wiped out his camp. Two years later, he sent a four-thousand-word report on the slide to the New Hampshire Historical Society.[38] "Individuals die, and are forgotten," wrote Upham, "whole families disappear from the face of the earth, and speedily no memorial of them remains. But it has seemed to me, that the remembrance of the recent sad events, in the remote solitude of the White Mountains, ought to be perpetu-ated."[39] In writing "The Ambitious Guest," Hawthorne followed Upham's hint. He tried to create an enduring literary work that would memorialize the virtue of a real American family. Hawthorne intended the story to be the lit-erary correlative of the Willey House, the visible remnant of the disaster in the landscape. Thus, the conception underlying "The Ambitious Guest" is analogous to that of a souvenir, which also kindles memory and reverence. Both are meant to curtail the emotional distance between past and present. In this way, Hawthorne's fiction parallels tourism.

Unlike Grenville Mellen, however, Hawthorne realized that nothing can erase the difference between an actual event and what the tourist-reader feels about it. Personality and past experience color one's perception. For this rea-son, Hawthorne avoided any simple narration of the Willeys' story; instead, he maintained an ironic distance from his characters and readers. Irony about tourism appears even in his most personal writing about his trip to the White Mountains. He described it in a letter to his mother written at Burlington, Vermont, a few days afterward:

> I passed through the White Hills and stayed two nights and part of three days in Ethan Crawford's house. Moreover, I mounted what the people called a "plaguey high-lifed crittur" and rode with four gentlemen and a guide six miles to the foot of Mount Washington. It was but four o'clock A.M. when we started, and a show-ery morning, and we had to ride through the very worst road that ever was seen, mud and mire, and several rivers to be forded, and trees to be jumped over (fallen trees, I mean) through all which I galloped and trotted and tript and stumbled, and arrived without breaking my neck at last. The other particulars, how I climbed three miles into the air, and how it snowed all the way, and how, when I got up the mountain on one side, the wind carried me a great distance off my feet and almost blew me down the other, and how the thermometer stood at twelve degrees below the freezing point, I shall have time enough to tell you when I return.[40]

Hawthorne did not gush with enthusiasm. He was not bursting to tell what sublime feelings the view from Mount Washington aroused, even though he did the same sightseeing that Mary Jane Thomas and her new husband had done the year before. Thomas implied that the bad weather, the long wait, and the poor accommodations had enhanced the experience of the summit when finally reached.[41] These only mobilize Hawthorne's sense of humor.

Hawthorne knew what he was supposed to feel on top of Mount Washing-ton, but the very knowledge kept him from feeling it. For him, the ordinary circumstances of travel deflated the idealized images of the landscape pro-moted by tourism. He underscored this theme in the sketch he wrote about

Niagara Falls for *The Storyteller.* The sheer anticipation of such a grand sight overwhelmed him; to savor it, he dawdled at his hotel for the better part of a day rather than going right out to the Falls. When he finally did go, they disappointed because they looked too commonplace. Of course, the actual Falls could never match the idea of them which the rhetoric of tourism and his own imagination conjured.

Hawthorne continued to explore this chasm between the sublime and the mundane in two White Mountain sketches that he intended for *The Storyteller.* He was forced to publish "The Notch" and "Our Evening Party among the Mountains" in *New-England Magazine* as "Sketches from Memory" (1835). If the afflatus of tourism could diminish for Hawthorne the world's most powerful waterfall, Crawford Notch may have disappointed him deeply. On most days, the rounded, wooded hills that form it do not look particularly dangerous or immense. Thus, Hawthorne fancied that the Notch was formed by a giant elbowing his way through the mountains. "Shame on me," he mocks in the next breath, "that I have attempted to describe it by so mean an image—feeling, as I do, that it is one of those symbolic scenes, which lead the mind to the sentiment, though not to the conception, of Omnipotence."[42] This sentence spoofs the empty judiciousness and grandiosity of Gilpin, Dwight, and other writers who gave advice on how to interpret landscape. At the same time, Hawthorne made fun of the average tourist, who substitutes "sentiment" for real thoughts and feelings. Tourists reduce Kant's sublime—the temporary check to one's vitality in the presence of immensity—to a fad. Their self-conscious aestheticism keeps them from experiencing landscape in a genuine way.

Hawthorne's tourists pursue travel with a casual attitude at odds with the sacramental function the associationists gave tourism. The narrator himself demonstrates the proper way to view landscape: He goes on foot and examines the Notch slowly to absorb its lesson fully. Then a stagecoach hurtles past carrying a load of tourists. They are an assortment of types:

> One was a mineralogist, a scientific, green-spectacled figure in black, bearing a heavy hammer, with which he did great damage to the precipices, and put the fragments in his pocket. Another was a well-dressed young man, who carried an opera-glass set in gold, and seemed to be making a quotation from some of Byron's rhapsodies on mountain scenery. There was also a trader, returning from Portland to the upper part of Vermont; and a fair young girl, with a very faint bloom, like one of those pale and delicate flowers, which sometimes occur among Alpine cliffs.[43]

Scientist, aesthete, trader, and storyteller: Only tourism could have brought these different types together. However, the fact that a different aspect of the landscape interests each one becomes an object for Hawthorne's satire—landscape cannot edify those whom private concerns enthrall.

Self-absorption gives tourists a materialistic, acquisitive attitude toward landscape, a theme Hawthorne explored in "The Great Carbuncle" (1837). An allegory of tourism, it draws upon Winthrop's account of the unsuccessful rush to the White Mountains for jewels after Darby Field's trip in 1642. However, Hawthorne made the object of the search a mythical red gem that shines of its own accord and has curative powers. The carbuncle legend appears in *Heinrich von Ofterdingen* (1802) by the German writer Novalis, whose romantic view of landscape influenced tourists in both Europe and America.[44] However, the most direct source for Hawthorne's tale is Ethan Crawford, who recalled that, when he was a child, some men reported glimpsing a carbuncle lodged high on a cliff on Mount Washington.[45] Crawford must have told the story hundreds of times to entertain guests sitting by the fire at night. Such a gathering appears in the sketch "Our Evening Party," written to introduce "The Great Carbuncle" in *The Storyteller.* In describing the urge to seek the carbuncle, Hawthorne also described what impels the tourist to visit a famous site: "They who had once beheld its splendor were enthralled with an unutterable yearning to possess it. But a spirit guarded that inestimable jewel, and bewildered the adventurer with a dark mist from the enchanted lake. Thus, life was worn away in the vain search for an unearthly treasure."[46] The carbuncle parallels such famous sights as Mount Washington or Crawford Notch. Like a carbuncle seeker, tourists already have in mind an image of the places they will visit; the tourist travels to acquire their value. Yet carbuncle and tourist attraction are just as illusory as the holy grail in that mere desire and the will to search do not lead one to the goal. Success depends on the viewer's *attitude*, and a true sight of the grail or the attraction—if ever granted—occurs as an unexpected revelation. Tourists who travel for vanity, self-improvement, fashion, or other selfish reasons will only disappoint and deceive themselves.

Thus, the treasure hunt in "The Great Carbuncle" is really a White Mountain tour. The search party on which the story focuses is diverse as only a collection of tourists could be; it recalls the group depicted in "The Notch." Each member has different motives for seeking the carbuncle and fails, or succeeds, because of them. One has spent his entire life looking for it. One is a scientist whose thirst for knowledge has made him miserable. One is a Boston merchant. One is an anonymous member of the public who wears rose-colored glasses. One is a sentimental poet and loner. One is a haughty English lord. Finally, there is a young married couple—Hannah and Matthew, "a young rustic"—who want to be together more than they want the carbuncle. They are the ones who find it, of course, but they agree to leave it behind because its wealth would only overshadow their happiness. Being granted a *sight* of the carbuncle implies that they approach the world with the correct attitude; they also properly refuse to *possess* the carbuncle. Thus, Hawthorne argued, with Joshua Reynolds, that only disinterested viewers may discover spiritual value in landscape, and he indicted the tourist culture for its materialism. Hawthorne still believed in landscape's aesthetic and spiritual value but doubted the average person's ability to perceive it.

"The Ambitious Guest" offers a darker version of this idea. The landscape contains danger, not a prize, and innocence does not save the Willeys as it did Hannah and Matthew. Indeed, domesticity blinds everyone to the landscape, including the guest. Like Goethe's Werther, the prototypical romantic hero, the guest values the simplicity to be found among the "lowly." And just as Werther feels inspired by Lotte in part because of her spontaneity among children, the guest is enchanted by the cozy family circle: "[A] prophetic sympathy impelled the refined and educated youth to pour out his heart before the simple mountaineers, and constrained them to answer him with the same free confidence." This growing intimacy accompanies a narrowing of attention that marks the story's development. Its focus spirals inward from the unsettled vastness of the Notch to the comfort of the inn to the warmth of the family circle to the heart-to-heart between the guest and the eldest daughter. After this inward drawing of attention, the shout "The Slide! The Slide!" sounds all the more panicked.

Hawthorne, too, focused his attention inward upon the guest and the family, not out at the landscape. He treated the landscape as mere backdrop for the drama rather than as something that needed to be understood in order to grasp the disaster's significance. Ironically, some of the factors that create intimacy indoors indicate the impersonal menace of the woodland environment. The firelight that "hovered about them fondly, and caressed them all" is fueled by "the driftwood of mountain streams, the dry cones of the pine, and the splintered ruins of great trees that had come crashing down the precipice." The wind whips past with "a sound of wailing and lamentation." These brief details suggest a churning, volatile landscape not fit for habitation; they seem to point to the environmental awareness pioneered by Cole. An environmentalist such as George P. Marsh would have seen the Willeys' fuel as evidence of the deforestation and erosion that perhaps caused the slide (see chap. 6). However, rational causes and natural processes are not at work in Hawthorne's landscape. The real slide occurred after an entire day of heavy rain, which loosened up the earth and trees on the slope above the house; in "The Ambitious Guest," rain does not fall, and the slide just happens without an apparent trigger. Moreover, Hawthorne retained a prescientific view of mountains as changeless masses that will pass away only with the second coming: "Mountains are Earth's undecaying monuments," he wrote in "The Notch." The purpose of the slide in "The Ambitious Guest" is not so much to provoke sublime thoughts as to dramatize the vanity of ambition.

Hawthorne portrayed the Willeys as the landscape's victims, not its shapers. His moral is that those passions are dangerous which lure one out of the home's safety and into the world—and that even the home is not very safe. The annihilating landslide offers a bleak view of the possibility for happiness in the world. The actual Willey family showed more optimism about life by moving to Crawford Notch. It took control of its future by leaving the farm in Lower Bartlett to pursue a better economic opportunity. But Hawthorne suggested that the Willeys live in the Notch because they have no option. The way in which Hawthorne's Mr. Willey describes his ambition suggests that poverty limits the family's choices: "But I was wishing we had a good farm in Bartlett, or Bethlehem, or Littleton, or some other township round the White Mountains; but not where they could tumble on our heads. I should want to stand well with my neighbors and be called Squire, and sent to General Court for a term or two; for a plain, honest man may do as much good there as a lawyer." Mr. Willey's sentiments are Jeffersonian. Success means owning a farm and enjoying a respectable position in the community. Therefore, to live in an isolated, dangerous place such as the Notch highlights the family's relative poverty.

The Willeys' simple, domestic virtues are meant to stand out against the hostile, capricious world outside, which can overwhelm anyone, however great his ambition. To point the contrast, Hawthorne deviated from the facts. "Hawthorne introduces a daughter of seventeen," B. Bernard Cohen writes, "'the image of young Happiness,' to whom the guest is immediately attracted, and also an aged grandmother, 'the image of Happiness grown old.' With these additions the family represents every important age of man; becoming a symbol of mankind itself."[47] If the world ran properly, Hawthorne seems to argue, a model family such as the Willeys would not have to live in jeopardy but could work a good farm and enjoy some prosperity.

The Notch is apparently not a place to make a lot of money. Although Hawthorne saw for himself how popular it was with tourists, tourism—a business the Willeys actively pursued—disappears behind stereotypes. "When the ambitious guest enters," said Sears, "he brings with him the striving of the commercial world that streams past the family's door, but in an idealized form."[48] Although Hawthorne acknowledged that "the Notch is a great artery, through which the lifeblood of internal commerce is continually throbbing," the Willeys remain isolated and innocent. Hawthorne portrayed them as simple, generous rustics of the sort one might find in Walter Scott. Like a way station on a pilgrimage route, the inn seems to exist for the traveler's benefit rather than to be a profit-maximizing business. "And here," wrote Hawthorne, "the teamster, on his way to Portland market, would put up for the night; and, if a bachelor, might sit an hour beyond the usual bedtime, and steal a kiss from the mountain maid at parting. It was one of those primitive taverns where the traveler pays only for food and lodging, but meets with a homely kindness beyond all price." The tourist who stays several nights and pays extra to be guided up the mountain is wholly absent.

The fact that the Willeys and other entrepreneurs created the landscape's value in the minds of the traveling public does not appear in "The Ambitious Guest." The depth of involvement in the landscape that this implies was beyond Hawthorne's imagination. Though cosmopolitan, tourism is shallow, he reasoned, and a local family such as the Willeys could hardly be more sophisticated. Hawthorne did not realize that the Willeys lived off of storytelling, too.

CHAPTER SIX

Science and Sightseeing

Henry David Thoreau's trip to the White Mountains in July 1858 had disappointing results. It inspired no great work, as had his visits to Maine and Cape Cod, his journey down the Concord and Merrimack Rivers, or his lengthy stay at Walden Pond. He left only a dull sixty-page journal record of his two weeks in the mountains. This transcendentalist, who found spiritual glory in nature, barely responded to the physical landscape that was then America's best example of natural sublimity.[1] For one thing, rain and thick clouds obscured his view of the landscape during much of the trip. Moreover, Thoreau badly sprained his ankle on Mount Washington and could not walk for a couple of days. Also, Thoreau scorned tourism because it shielded people from wild nature: "I heard that Crawford's House was lighted with gas, and had a large saloon, with its band of music, for dancing. But give me a spruce house made in the rain."[2]

Yet a deeper reason underlies Thoreau's failure to appreciate the White Mountains. He went there on vacation with Edward Hoar, a botanist. Before setting out, the two made a list of forty-six plant species found in the area, and then they spent their time plant hunting. (They managed to find forty-two.) Botany thus served as a kind of recreation. But their dedication to science prevented them from dwelling on the grand views that made the area so popular. Science obliged them to concentrate on the minutiae of the landscape, and the sheer variety of the plants, animals, and topography in the White Mountains overwhelmed them. "It is surprising," Thoreau remarked, "how much more bewildering is a mountain-top than a level area of the same extent. Its ridges and shelves and ravines add greatly to its apparent extent and diversity."[3] He then summarized his findings by identifying six bands of flora succeeding one another up the slopes of Mount Washington. The valley held plants typical of northern New England, while the peak had species normally found well above the Arctic Circle. The upper slopes also exhibited dwarf varieties of trees found nowhere else in the world. In short, Mount Washington contained a greater diversity of plant life than any other spot in the eastern United States. For such a science-minded traveler as Thoreau to do justice to it all, he almost had to ignore the White Mountains' vistas.

As Thoreau's experience suggests, a paradox marks the relation between science and White Mountain tourism. On the one hand, science contributed as much to tourism as did literature and art. After all, science influenced the way tourists looked at the landscape, too. They saw in the mountains not only aesthetic objects and literary associations but also natural wonders and clues to the earth's structure. Most guidebooks said something about the geology of the White Mountains, and some included long lists of the plants and animals found there. On the other hand, the empiricism of science—its reliance on minute observations—clashed with tourism's envisioning of the landscape on a grand scale. The closer scientists looked, the more detail they discovered. Facts and specimens multiplied endlessly. It was difficult to synthesize them all into an accurate, comprehensive picture. Faced with this demand, many scientists entirely rejected theory—science's form of the vista—and simply listed the facts they uncovered. Grappling with the profusion of species in the White Mountains may have driven one botanist, William Oakes, to suicide.[4]

Still, science needed an aesthetic. It needed the operatic imagination of tourism and art in order to organize the empirical landscape. Thoreau himself understood this. He concluded an early essay on ecology, "Natural History of Massachusetts" (1842), with an image of the ideal scientist. A good scientist should not just observe things dispassionately; he must feel and experience, too.

> The true man of science will know nature better by his finer organization; he will smell, taste, see, hear, feel, better than other men. His will be a deeper and finer experience. We do not learn by inference and deduction and the application of mathematics to philosophy, but by direct intercourse and sympathy. It is with science as with ethics,—we cannot know truth by contrivance and method; the Baconian is as false as any other, and with all the helps of machinery and the arts, the most scientific will still be the healthiest and friendliest man, and possess a more perfect Indian wisdom.[5]

Thoreau's scientist exhibits many of the same qualities that were in the ideal nineteenth-century tourist—refinement, sympathy, and moral attainment. Like the tourist, the ideal scientist experienced things firsthand. Baconian empiricism (that is, disinterested observation) tells little about a landscape's meaning. The scientist must measure it, not with numbers, but with the soul.

Perhaps Thoreau could practice this humane form of science within the cosy limits of Walden Pond, but the enormous natural variety of the White Mountains resisted such treatment. In fact, Hawthorne's depiction of the landscape in "The Ambitious Guest" had already shown the futility of applying the ideal of humane science to the White Mountains. Like Thoreau in *Walden* (1854), the Willeys lived in a small house surrounded by woods and tended to imagine nature in human terms. However, the slide proved that the landscape operated on a vastly greater scale than did humans. It was a tragic mistake to attribute human proportions to nature, which is what Thoreau implied with his transcendental scientist. George Perkins Marsh offered a better way to mediate between Man and Nature. He stopped thinking about humans individually and focused instead on humankind's aggregate effect on the environment. Whereas agrarians idolized "the farmer" for his honesty and productivity, Marsh the ecologist saw that "farming" often contributed to deforestation and erosion. In short, farming actually helped to *destroy* the soil's productive capacity. Here was an image of Man comparable in size to the earth he inhabited. By this method, Marsh documented the pathology of American land use.

Marsh's ecological perspective allowed him to blend a huge number of facts and figures into a coherent picture of the landscape. His book *Man and Nature* (1864) sorted masses of detail into a few categories according to the ways in which human activity degraded the environment. Marsh thereby solved the dilemma that Thoreau's visit to the White Mountains dramatized: At what scale should one envision the landscape? Stepping back from America's belief in progress and individual enterprise, Marsh showed how short-sighted opportunism caused ecological damage of proportions so large they escaped casual observation. For example, he connected the Willey slide to the economic exploitation of Crawford Notch. This view of the Willeys assumed that their life represented American attitudes and practices generally. Marsh did not sentimentalize the family and patronize them as isolated rustics. He thus became the only thinker in the nineteenth century who did not imagine the White Mountains in pastoral or agrarian terms.

From the Empirical to the Sublime

The sublime offered scientists a landscape aesthetic just as it did tourists and painters. It may have been even more essential to nineteenth-century science than to art. Sublimity was the object or effect that the landscape painter tried to create. It stood with the picturesque and the beautiful among the aesthetic modes open to the artist's choosing. By contrast, the sublime gave science its very rationale. Scientists had measured and observed the earth more thoroughly than ever before, and they needed both a justification for their work and a controlling image that would draw isolated facts together cohesively. Scientists claimed that their minute knowledge revealed the mind of God, nature's creator; through science one could glimpse the infinity lurking within observable phenomena. In other words, the ultimate goal of scientific endeavor was sublime experience. Not surprisingly, scientists were the first group to view the White Mountains as sublime.

The sublime also met a psychological need arising from the rigid empiricism of science, which rejected most other interpretations of nature. Nineteenth-century scholars advocated empiricism to correct the excesses of the preceding era. Earth science had suffered from systematizers such as Thomas Burnet, who traveled through the Alps in 1679 and wondered how the earth's crust had formed.[6] Burnet and many who followed tried to explain the earth's structure using simple, grand schemes backed by little evidence. About 1800, scientists turned away from theory altogether as being delusive. Instead, they adopted Francis Bacon's method, "the study of facts as opposed to idle speculation." (Thoreau was attacking this dichotomy when he mentioned Bacon.) When nineteenth-century scholars invoked Bacon, George Daniels noted, it meant three things: "First, and most evidently, 'Baconianism' meant 'empiricism,' in the sense that all science must somehow rest on observation . . . Secondly, it meant 'anti-theoretical,' in the sense of avoiding 'hypotheses' and not going beyond what could be directly observed . . . Third, and most radically, it was the identification of all science with taxonomy."[7] After gathering data, the only acceptable procedure was to arrange them in abstract categories. Scientists could not draw any inference, however simple and sound, nor could they formulate a hypothesis and then test it against the facts. Thus, early nineteenth-century science imagined the physical world in static ways and tended to ignore process.

Such a one-sided outlook often retarded scientific advances. For example, Daniels explained how Elias Loomis belatedly demonstrated that storms rotate counterclockwise. Loomis examined the tangle of tree trunks left after a tornado had struck an Ohio forest and reconstructed the direction of the storm winds from the fall pattern. At first sight, there was only "a mass of trees pointing in every direction," but, where trees had fallen on top of one another, Loomis found, "the bottom tree invariably pointed to the west and the top tree to the east." When Loomis published his findings in 1842, he was unaware that his conclusion amounted to a deduction from observed phenomena. In fact, Loomis had had enough data from earlier observations to have drawn the right inference six years before, but "Baconianism" kept him from looking for a pattern that was not immediately obvious.[8]

Botanist William Oakes took empiricism to its tragic extreme. Oakes devoted his career to developing a complete taxonomy of New England plants. The number of individual species to be described was so vast, however, that the completed whole eluded him. In 1848, right after buying ten pounds of lead shot, Oakes fell from a ferryboat in Boston harbor and drowned, a likely suicide. In an obituary, fellow botanist Asa Gray (later Darwin's chief American supporter) described Oakes's obsessive quest to collect specimens. Oakes

> had unweariedly amassed an immense store of materials, and if his premature death has left them in a state which shows little progress made towards their final elaboration, this is to be attributed not to any lack of industry or perseverance, but to a too fastidious taste, and an over anxious desire not merely to satisfy the ever increasing demands of the science, but to realize his own high standard of perfection . . . in consequence every piece of work that he undertook grew rapidly under his hands until it became well nigh impracticable.[9]

In 1842, Gray added, geologist Charles T. Jackson asked Oakes to write an essay on White Mountain plants for a state-commissioned survey eventually published as the *Final Report on the Geology and Mineralogy of the State of New Hampshire* (1844). Though already an expert, Oakes revisited the mountains every year until his death to look for more specimens. The project expanded from an essay to a book on the natural history of the White Mountains. "The Geology, Mineralogy and Zoology of the mountains claimed their share of attention," too, and so the essay that Jackson commissioned, its scope now hopelessly broad, never appeared. But the sheer quantity of natural phenomena left no escape for scientists such as Oakes. If they were to stay within the narrow limits of observation, then, logically, collecting samples of *all* species was the only way to complete or perfect a work.

Oakes did not allow himself to invent a theory to encompass the tremendous variety of phenomena that his scientist's eye differentiated. Oakes's backwardness appears in the one work he did manage to publish. *Scenery of the White Mountains* (1848), a folio volume with sixteen drawings of famous sights and explanatory text, came out the year of his death.[10] The drawings may have been part of the illustration work Oakes had commissioned for his natural history of the White Mountains. In the text accompanying Isaac Sprague's "The Notch of the White Mountains with the Willey House," Oakes turned to classical antiquity for his vision of the landscape (fig. 21). Although he had seen it "a day or two after" the Willey slide, Crawford Notch reminded him of Thermopylae, where three hundred Spartans had held back a whole Persian army. "The Notch is a mountain pass," he wrote, "like those in the old world, where often a few brave men, defending their liberties and native soil,

Fig. 21. Isaac Sprague, *The Notch of the White Mountains with the Willey House*, in William Oakes, *White Mountain Scenery* (Boston, 1848), plate 3. The endless detail shown by Sprague suggests how hard it was for scientists to document the profusion of forms and specimens in the White Mountains. *Courtesy, Dartmouth College Library.*

have driven back or destroyed invading armies, fighting hand to hand in the narrow passage." In the drawing, however, history does not dominate nature. The Willey House sits at the bottom of a bowl whose sides are the mountain slopes. Bald rock protrudes from Mount Willard in the center and Mount Webster on the right. On the left, boulders and detritus from the slide have made Mount Willey's base a wasteland. Only two lines of trees, one on either side, offer the picture relieving detail. Elsewhere the eye wanders over stretches of innumerable stones and banks of vegetation. The scene leaves the viewer agape at the minutiae of the landscape, which undermine its larger, picturesque composition.

With Thoreau's organic and transcendental approach forbidden, Baconian science needed a metaphysical rationale. And scientists assumed that "philosophy, revelation, natural theology and physical science, are united in perfect harmony, proclaiming with one voice that there is a God."[11] This belief made scientists complacent. For the most part, they measured, observed, and categorized material things—and worried little about what lay beyond. But whenever discussion called for a higher principle, scientists talked about the divine order, which their work supposedly clarified, in terms of the sublime.

Here science converged with art and tourism. Science did not simply appropriate the rhetoric of these other fields; it shared with them the whole philosophy of the sublime. Immanuel Kant's work on the sublime shows how close scientific observation was to aesthetic perception in the early nineteenth century. Kant's discussion incorporated most previous notions of the sublime, and so it proved to be rigorous and comprehensive. He placed his theory of the sublime within the framework of a larger work on material knowledge, *The Critique of Judgment* (1790). Kant realized that "aesthetic" and "scientific" perceptions of the world come blended together. "That which is purely subjective in the representation of an object . . . is its aesthetic quality. On the other hand, that which in such a representation serves, or is available, for the determination of the object (for the purpose of knowledge), is its logical validity."[12] He might have said "scientific validity." To describe the relation between the subjective and the objective in perception, Kant used aesthetic terms, the beautiful and the sublime.

"The beautiful" describes a circumstance in which one's feeling about an object precisely matches the truth (472). The pleasure called *beauty* comes from having intuited a complete understanding of the object. A beautiful object, then, is discrete and knowable. "The beautiful in nature," Kant explained, "is a question of the form of the object, and this consists in limitation, whereas the sublime is to be found in an object even devoid of form, so far as it immediately involves, or else by its presence provokes a representation of *limitlessness*, yet with a superadded thought of its totality" (495). A sublime view exhibits no controlling form, so "that it is rather in its chaos, or in its wildest and most irregular disorder and desolation, provided it gives signs of magnitude and power, that nature chiefly excites the ideas of the sublime" (496). The unorganized multiplicity of phenomena overwhelms the mind at first, until it makes a leap of imagination to God, who encompasses all things. Unlike beauty, "the feeling of the sublime is a pleasure that only arises indirectly, being brought about by the feeling of a momentary check to the vital forces followed at once by a discharge all the more powerful" (495). Beauty fosters life; the sublime threatens death.

The sublime capped off the experience of landscape for both tourists and scientists, who looked at nature in similar ways. Sublimity was felt by the tourist on Mount Washington's summit who, in one gaze, saw hundreds of peaks and thousands of square miles of territory spread out below. The terrifying thought of one's smallness in the midst of earth's immensity supposedly made way for a kind of pride that one's mind grew larger from this very perception.[13] Sublimity was likewise felt by scientists, staggered by the uncountable variety of objects revealed by their close observation of nature. They, too, felt proud that their discipline was expanding under this realization. But strict adherence to Baconianism must have put that consolation in doubt at times. The limitlessness of the sublime in nature must have overpowered many scientists, as it did William Oakes.

Time-seeing

Limitlessness also encouraged a holistic vision of the earth, which the more positivistic science of the late nineteenth century lost. This vision arose from geologists' realization that the earth was immense in age as well as in size. With the first volume of *Principles of Geology* in 1830, Charles Lyell demonstrated that the earth was inconceivably old. Rock layers, he pointed out, were created by slow natural processes, such as sedimentation, which took far longer to occur than human history could measure. In the absence of radiometric dating, no one could put a definite number to the earth's age. Instead, geologists came to resemble tourists of the earth's remote past as they traced "deep time" through sequences of souvenir-like images—fossils, for example. Thus, an impressionistic view of the earth's past dominated geology and stirred the popular imagination as well. Scientists interested in the White Mountains adopted Lyell's vision of the past and applied his methods. Geology also gave tourists a way to conceive of the mountains which complemented sublime aesthetics, while painters tried to achieve scientific accuracy in their work by including geologic details. In short, earth science added much that was new to the nineteenth-century imagination of landscape.

Today, with science thoroughly professionalized and divided among innumerable specialties, it is hard to appreciate the close links between earth science and popular culture in the nineteenth century. Scientists at the end of the twentieth century can scarcely pursue their professional interests as tourists, but through the mid nineteenth century, scientists readily combined research and pleasure. Like Benjamin Silliman, William Oakes, and Charles Lyell, many traveled to the White Mountains both because they offered great summer vacations and because they seemed a likely place to find answers to serious scientific questions. Thus, Silliman traveled to the site of the Willey slide to learn how much a sudden deluge could affect mountain formations. Moreover, the scientific conceptions of the earth that they developed also provided a context within which ordinary tourists could better understand the natural landscapes they viewed. The history of nineteenth-century earth science reveals a good deal about popular perceptions of landscape. For example, midcentury painters and educated tourists saw the White Mountains as exemplifying the geologic time scale, whose reality Lyell had been the first to demonstrate scientifically.

A few thinkers before Lyell had realized that the earth must be far older than recorded history. The difficulty lay in *imagining* geologic time, which was Lyell's contribution.[14] Until the nineteenth century, people were used to thinking about time within the limits set by *Genesis*—that is, about six thousand years. Since they knew no reason to object, scientists tacitly agreed. The Comte de Buffon, almost alone, argued that the earth was older. In 1744, Buffon suggested physical analogues for the six days of creation—cooling of the earth, precipitation, earthquakes, and so on. Stretching his imagination, Buffon thought the whole process might have taken as long as seventy-five thousand years.[15]

Buffon underestimated the earth's age by several orders of magnitude, but mere numbers meant nothing, anyway, to scientists who knew little about the earth's structure. A better way to imagine deep time occurred to Adam Smith's friend, James Hutton. Hutton proposed that the earth's crust had gotten its present form through an endless cycle of sedimentation and volcanic uplift. Rock layers formed when sediment sank to the ocean floor and hardened; these layers were then thrust up by volcanic forces to form dry land. The cycle repeated itself as wind and water eroded the rock and dumped it back in the ocean as sediment. To confirm his view, Hutton sailed along the Scottish coast, where high cliffs jut into the sea. He saw dozens of rock layers many feet thick, each of which represented to him the residue of an entire cycle of creation, a world like the one we dwell in now. Yet each must have taken an undreamed-of time to form, since the cycle within which we now live had made no perceptible advance within the whole span of history. Hutton had done away with the six-day creation and replaced it with something even more awe inspiring.[16]

But Hutton's discovery rested on a less obvious assumption. Stephen Jay Gould pointed out that Hutton did not think of time as flowing in one direction but as returning back on itself. This cyclical view implies that the earth is a self-sustaining environment. Hutton published his findings in *Theory of the Earth* (1788) and concluded with this thought: "But if the succession of worlds is established in the system of nature, it is vain to look for anything higher in the origin of the earth. The result, therefore, of our present enquiry is, that we find no vestige of a beginning,—no prospect of an end."[17] Hutton was perhaps the last of the systematizers. Like Thomas Burnet's, his theory proved too broad and simplistic to explain much about the earth's structural mechanics, and geology soon turned entirely to the concrete and particular. Nevertheless, Hutton provided an image of deep time which Lyell elaborated in *Principles of Geology.*

In this work's three volumes (1830–33), Lyell tried to integrate the ocean of data that geologists had collected in thirty years of dedicated observation. He thought geology was ready for a unifying theory, "uniformitarianism." Hutton provided some of its basic features: the immensity of time, the earth as an environment, and especially continuity between past and present. "Catastrophists" such as Silliman argued a competing theory. They believed that large features—ocean beds, mountains, and so on—must have been caused by sudden, global cataclysms that punctuated long periods of stasis. Indeed, the huge forces that had so obviously deformed the earth's crust made catastrophism quite plausible. However, inspired by Hutton, Lyell reasoned that, since the laws of nature never change, geologic processes visible today must have operated in the past at the same rate and in the same way, that is, uniformly. These forces were sufficient to produce all the earth's landforms, but they must have done their work over millions of years, not the brief span suggested by *Genesis* and the catastrophists.

Lyell gathered an impressive amount of evidence from around the world to support his views. His command of facts transformed Hutton's "idle speculation" into a fully developed theory that became the foundation of the modern discipline of geology. Most interesting is that Lyell imagined the geologic past in the form of dynamic images. He cited the Willey slide, for example, to show that even localized geologic events could yield gigantic effects. "The power which running water may exert, in the lapse of ages," Lyell writes, "in widening and deepening a valley, does not so much depend on the volume and velocity of the stream usually flowing in it, as on the number and magnitude of the obstructions which have, at different periods, opposed its free passage."[18] Slides like that of 1826 must have occurred in the Notch periodically, blocked the Saco's flow, caused it to flood, and thus carved out a much larger valley than might be expected from the river's smallness. Lyell's temerity in proposing a new geologic law connects the Willey slide, not just with the natural history of the White Mountain region, but with forces that shape landscapes worldwide. The specifics of a local event help validate a grand view of earth history.

Lyell's operatic imagination of landscape lasted through many different geologic theories. It persisted among geologists of all stripes despite continual change in the hypotheses that made it seem scientifically valid, a fact that testifies to its mythic power. Lyell's suggestion that landslides such as the Willeys' helped widen Crawford Notch was disproved in 1837 when Louis Agassiz demonstrated the existence of the Ice Age. Glaciers, not flash floods, had given valleys such as Crawford Notch their broad, rounded shape. When Lyell visited the Notch on his second trip to America in 1845, he wanted to see whether the evidence supported Agassiz. Agassiz maintained that the parallel lines often found carved in the rock of these valleys could only come from glaciers, which pick up stones and drag them slowly across hard surfaces. Lyell wondered whether landslides could make such lines. Old Abel Crawford led him up the channel carved by the Willey slide to a bare outcropping of rock. Lyell was disappointed.

> There is a small cataract at the spot, where a dyke of basalt and greenstone, four or five feet wide, traverses the granite, all the rocks being smoothed on the surface, and marked with some irregular and short scratches and grooves; but not such as resemble in continuity, straightness, or parallelism, those produced by a glacier, where hard stones, which grate along the bottom, have been firmly fixed in a heavy mass of ice, so that they can not be deflected from a rectilinear course.[19]

A dedicated scientist, Lyell easily accepted Agassiz's theory even though it superseded his own. The Ice Age was a more spectacular story, anyway. Still, Lyell's essential vision remained intact. It represented in empirical science something comparable to Thomas Cole's imagination of landscape as a dynamic environment. The slow working of storms, rivers, and glaciers over vast stretches of time once again demonstrated the inhumanity of nature.

Kant had anticipated this dynamic environmentalism by dividing sublime experience into two categories. "The estimation of magnitude by means of concepts of numbers (or their signs in algebra) is mathematical, but that in mere intuition (by the eye) is aesthetic" or dynamic.[20] Kant identified the mathematical sublime with reason and science and no doubt thought it higher because it mobilized higher faculties. Yet he admitted that the dynamically sublime affected the mind more powerfully because it was more concrete, more immediate. Nineteenth-century geologists imagined the sublime almost entirely in the dynamic mode. They abandoned mathematics for two reasons. First, the sheer size of newly discovered phenomena defied positive measurement. On this point Kant anticipated the problem Lyell faced in comprehending deep time: "Now in the aesthetic measurement of such an immeasurable whole, the sublime does not lie so much in the greatness of the number, as in the fact that in our onward advance we always arrive at proportionally greater units" (501). That is, certain ways of viewing nature overwhelm our capacity to gauge it with numbers or arrange it in logical categories. The sublime becomes a problem of *scale*, not of absolute quantity.[21] Lyell understood that deep time was like this and refused to express it numerically. Instead, he measured it through fossils. He examined each rock layer's fossilized plants and animals and determined the percentage of extinct species in it. The higher the percentage, the older the rock. Thus, fossils provided a visual gauge of deep time.

For Lyell this method was not just a stopgap until a good method of absolute dating became available. He believed that it gave a more vivid—and therefore more accurate—depiction of the geologic past. In choosing image over number, Lyell went against the spirit of empiricism that scientists cherish, yet he did so because he had a greater appreciation for the difficulties of learning about the geologic past than had most of his contemporaries. Lyell perceived that geologic forces would have destroyed most artifacts from the past and left very spotty evidence. Observations could never be complete or checked by controlled experiments, as with studies of the present. Thus, the scientist had to use imagination in reconstructing the past. As Hooykaas explained, "nobody witnessed the events, so that one can but write a '*roman de la nature*' which perhaps closely approaches the historical truth, but never offers complete certainty."[22] The historical geologist has to be a kind of novelist or tour guide.

The second reason earth scientists abandoned mathematics was that they began to think environmentally. They saw that a landscape is a complex system of interconnected elements; the relationships between things are more important to understand than the things themselves. Again, the static Baconianism practiced by William Oakes failed to reveal the processes of nature. George Perkins Marsh, Lyell's disciple, brought the geologist's holism to ecology. Marsh's biographer wrote that he "will be remembered for his masterful expositions of the round-robin character of natural resources, his comprehensive delineations of the symbiotic relations between man and his habitat, and his balanced consideration of social aims and physical needs, resources and responsibilities. Without neglecting details, he viewed problems in the large, which is the way they are posed in reality."[23] Only by viewing landscape as an integral system can a scientist see the importance of each part. Like Lyell, Marsh had an encyclopedic knowledge of facts and measurements but rejected numbers as the basis of earth science. "The introduction of mathematical method into physical science . . . has impeded the progress of . . . Geography by discouraging its pursuit as unworthy of cultivation because incapable of precise results."[24] Marsh and Lyell agreed that a number, an equation, or a syllogism cannot yield a complete understanding of landscape. That understanding can come only from a dynamic image.

Earth science, therefore, turned to the aesthetic sublime; as a result, the scientific and the popular imagination of landscape often coincided. Benjamin Willey and other writers of White Mountain guidebooks began their sketches with natural history, and they cited Lyell on the region's geology. Educated by science and art in how to view landscape, many tourists must have gaped at the vistas of time displayed in the geomorphology of the White Mountains. Lyell himself adopted the tourist's perspective. References to famous touring stops lend an irresistible urbanity to the argument of the *Principles of Geology*. Lyell also wrote travel literature, namely, two books about his trips to America; his tour of Crawford Notch appeared in *A Second Visit to the United States of North America* (1845). In this book, he devoted to history as much sensitivity as he brought to the geologic past. Directly following the White Mountains, Lyell visited Plymouth Rock and concluded that such artifacts make the best gauge of the past. "For we measure time," he explained, "not by the number of arithmetical figures representing years or centuries, but by the importance of a long series of events, which strike the imagination."[25] Lyell had in mind the method he invented for telling the age of rock layers. But this statement also summarized the philosophy of tourism, which taught history through concrete images, through the same mode of feeling and imagination.

The Scientist as Tourist

Nineteenth-century scientists, then, viewed the White Mountains very much as tourists did. Of course, scientists looked with greater discipline, focused more on certain kinds of phenomena, and were more reserved in stating their reactions. Nevertheless, scientific observation closely resembled sightseeing. Most scientific explorations of the White Mountains doubled as vacations so that it is hard to tell professional interest apart from common curiosity. Indeed, earth science and tourism mingled because the two had grown up together by the end of the previous century. Those who pursued botany or mineralogy formed a subset of ladies and gentlemen who traveled for pleasure.[26] In fact, science incorporated many of the tourist's skills in viewing landscape—sketching, for instance. Furthermore, many of the same objectives spurred the interest of scientists and the public in landscape. They wanted to know whether the landscape contained anything of practical value, and they felt that understanding landscape both aesthetically and scientifically brought one closer to Nature and to God. And again, scientists projected an operatic imagination of landscape that fired the public's interest. Far from being elite and inaccessible, earth science represented one facet of nineteenth-century tourist culture.

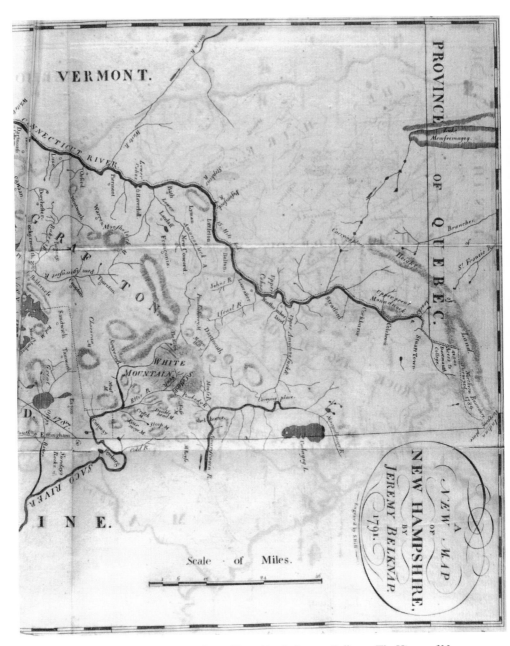

Fig. 22. Detail, *A New Map of New Hampshire*, in Jeremy Belknap, *The History of New Hampshire*, volume 2 (Boston, 1791). Drawn after Belknap's 1784 visit to the White Mountains, this map shows little visual appreciation of the landscape. Note how the mountains are represented by "molehills." *Courtesy, Homer Babbidge Library, University of Connecticut.*

One result of this close tie is that science derived from tourism and art a greater visual sensitivity to landscape. Before this habit took hold, scientific writing about the White Mountains included measurement and inventory but no portrayal of the broader landscape's appearance. Afterward, science more and more reflected the perspective of the sightseer. Martin Rudwick put the maturation of a "visual language for geology" at about 1830. Thus, Lyell's *Principles* was among the first geologic texts with sophisticated illustrations, but many others had them, too. Topographic maps, sections, diagrams, and so forth helped geologists to see a landscape in three dimensions. Rudwick argued that geology acquired this skill from the touring elite.

> The ability of most [early nineteenth-century geologists] to draw field sketches with reasonable competence . . . is probably related to the fashion for amateur drawing and watercolour painting, which was widespread in the social classes from which many of these geologists came, particularly in England . . . This widespread artistic skill points to the historical significance of a very general cultural trend at this period toward a greater degree of visual awareness, particularly of romantic subjects such as mountain scenery and intrinsically curious subjects such as fossils, among the leisured social classes.[27]

Perhaps William Gilpin and other touring professionals had indirectly taught geologists how to view landscape. Beginning in the 1820s, scientific descriptions of the White Mountains show that scientists eventually adopted the traveler's perspective. Their reports resemble accounts written by artists, writers, and ordinary tourists.

Earlier scientists wrote clumsily about the White Mountains as a spectacle. Their awkwardness stemmed from the lack of a sense of panorama, not from lack of interest. The fascination that drew treasure hunters there in the seventeenth century also seemed to allure scientists. The first scientific exploration of the White Mountains occurred in 1784. In the expedition were Jeremy Belknap, author of *The History of New Hampshire* (1789–92), and Manasseh Cutler, a Boston physician and scientist as well as head of the Ohio Company, the first real estate venture to buy public land from the U.S. government (fig. 22). They took as a guide Joseph Whipple, the White Mountain land developer. Belknap's report to the American Philosophical Society led the *Monthly Review* to expect great things: "These mountains seem to afford ample matter for the observation and examination of future philosophers; they may contain a vast fund of wealth, and be the source of immense riches to the country."[28] For his part, Cutler used a barometer to measure Mount Washington's elevation. He miscalculated by almost four thousand feet, putting the summit at 10,001 feet above sea level, and was sure the peak "must be placed in no inconsiderable rank among the highest mountains on the globe." He knew of only four taller.[29]

Yet Cutler could not translate his respect for the White Mountains into a convincing picture. The description in his journal is episodic, dry, and factual. Even unusual sights are understated. "When we were near the summit," he wrote, "we were highly amused with large and dense clouds moving along the mountain, perhaps a thousand feet below us. Over our heads there was a very rare haze, through which the sun shone very clear—it appeared high. We arrived at the summit 32 minutes after 11 o'clock."[30] It is hard to tell whether Cutler found the clouds enjoyable in themselves or just interesting meteorologically. Similarly, a homey comparison tamed the only vista Cutler described. The view from the summit, he said, "suggested the idea of viewing an extensive marsh from an eminence far above it, with numerous stacks and cocks of hay settled down and extending over a broad base." The vertigo and nausea that White Mountain vistas induced in later viewers did not threaten Cutler.

Cutler did not respond enthusiastically to such views because he had not been educated to sublime aesthetics and showed no sense of the landscape as a whole. In the journal, he moved from place to place and sight to sight with no awareness of where each fit into the larger context. On his Mount Washington trip, Thoreau remarked that a mountain, which displays a regular outline from a distance, presents such broken terrain to the climber that "you would have thought you saw the summit a dozen times before you did."[31] The mental image of the mountain's regularity was precisely what made Thoreau and other tourists comfortable enough to hike on Mount Washington. But Cutler did not have such an image in mind. He focused on the ground immediately under foot and wrote of Mount Washington's shoulders or outcroppings as if they were separate summits. After the expedition, in fact, Belknap told Cutler of doubts that the specific peak he had climbed and measured was really the highest.[32]

Jeremy Belknap knew more about the sublime, yet the potential for it in the White Mountains scared him. The 1784 expedition was the source for his account of the mountains in volume 3 of the *History of New Hampshire*. "Almost every thing in nature," he wrote, "which can be supposed capable of inspiring ideas of the sublime and beautiful, is here realized."[33] This is not a recommendation. Rather, Belknap, a Federalist and man of the Enlightenment, feared the uncontrolled emotion associated with the sublime. He issued a warning that the White Mountains might be too dynamic.

> Nature has, indeed, in that region, formed her works on a large scale . . . A person who is unacquainted with a mountainous country, cannot, upon his first com-

ing into it, make an adequate judgment of heights and distances; he will imagine every thing to be nearer and less than it really is . . . When amazement is excited by the grandeur and sublimity of the scenes presented to view, it is necessary to curb the imagination, and exercise judgment with mathematical precision; or the temptation to romance will be invincible (3:40–1).

Travelers should carry a compass to keep from getting lost in the White Mountains and a knowledge of math to keep from getting lost in their emotions. The empirical outlook is recommended as an antidote to the poison of sublimity. Belknap feared the very *roman de la nature* that Lyell and later scientists eagerly wrote.

Before 1820, then, scientists who explored the White Mountains disjoined fact and landscape. And they responded in this way even when they accepted the sublime. Botanist Jacob Bigelow surveyed Mount Washington in 1816 and mainly just listed the plant species he found at various elevations.[34] George Shattuk climbed the peak in 1807. He reported almost entirely on times and temperatures, botanical and mineralogical specimens, and so on. "The phenomenon which most attracted my attention, while upon the top of the mountain," he wrote, "was the rarity of the atmosphere. Sound was much more impeded than respiration."[35] Hardly a compelling experience. But Shattuk did mention the sublime once. He repeated a story he had heard from his guide (perhaps Eleazer Rosebrook), who had led two men up the year before. "While they were upon the very pinnacle," Shattuk related, "a severe thunder-storm came on, which, with a thick fog, completely obstructed their vision. While the lightnings were shooting, in every direction, beneath their feet, they were so completely enveloped in darkness, as to render their descent hazardous to them." Shattuk then confessed: "I sighed, in secret, for the repetition of the same scene, that I might once behold the truly sublime in nature" (32). For Shattuk, the sublime represented a wholly separate experience from scientific observation. Also, in the European fashion, he associated the sublime with obscurity rather than with the panoramic view from Mount Washington's summit, as in Ethan Crawford's time.

After 1820, earth science shared a great deal with tourism largely because science needed to prove itself worthy of public support and, therefore, needed to respond to popular concerns. Scientists argued that they contributed to national wealth by locating valuable minerals and doing helpful agricultural research. Furthermore, geologists suggested that understanding natural beauty was part of their discipline. Earth science was also at the developmental stage, and scientists had a relatively vague notion of what was of professional interest; some really believed they should investigate the natural features that tourists found aesthetically pleasing. One popular geology text reveals how elastic the field could be. In *The Wonders of Geology* (1845), Samuel Goodrich divided the science this way: "1. *Economical Geology*, or an account of rocks with reference to their pecuniary value, or immediate application to the wants of society; 2. *Scenographical Geology*, or an account of rocks as they exhibit themselves to the eye in their general outlines . . . 3. *Scientific Geology* . . . "[36] Here mining and natural scenery have a status equal to that of pure science.

Charles T. Jackson displayed a similar view of the field in his *Final Report* (to which William Oakes was asked to contribute his monograph on White Mountain plants). This book concluded a three-year effort to map geologic formations and to inventory New Hampshire's mineral wealth. It was the first complete geologic survey of the state. The state appropriated nine thousand dollars for the survey, which employed six people full time. A leader of such surveys in other states, Jackson repeatedly stressed the work's usefulness. Without geology, he argued, much mineral wealth would go undiscovered, and people would waste time mistaking worthless rocks for valuable ones.[37] The *Final Report* (1844) included all three of Goodrich's categories. Jackson began with an up-to-date summary of the science of geology, including the latest theories and discoveries. He carried on this interest in pure science with a detailed description of the state's geologic formations. In addition, the book records Jackson's investigation of the state's mineral resources. For instance, he reported on iron deposits in Bartlett and tin in the town of Jackson. Finally, Jackson noted geologic "wonders," such as the Old Man of the Mountain, of interest mainly for their popularity. He also included many illustrations of New Hampshire scenery, which would appeal to the curiosity of the state officials who commissioned the survey. Actually, the power of such scenery to draw tourists into New Hampshire made it just as valuable as ore deposits; both fell under the rubric of "natural resources."

The drawings by artist J. D. Whitney which accompanied the survey reflect science's new visual awareness of landscape. One drawing is "Slide at the Willey House, White Mts." (fig. 23). At first glance, the drawing seems an all-too-literal rendering: The atmosphere is still and clear; the house and barn stand up in sharp, rectilinear outlines. It lacks the sense of movement and drama that Cole would have given it. Still, sublime elements structure the drawing. On either side, the base of a mountain slopes upward at a steep forty-five-degree angle to frame the picture and to suggest the immensity not drawn. Whitney further emphasized the mountains' size by foreshortening the house and barn in the middle distance. In the foreground, a large boulder looms up right in front of the artist's perspective point and thereby implies his relative smallness. The drawing corresponds to the expedition's measurement

Fig. 23. J. D. Whitney, *Slide at the Willey House*, in Charles T. Jackson, *Final Report on the Geology and Mineralogy of the State of New Hampshire* (Concord, N.H., 1844), 78. The scientific survey for which Whitney worked was measuring the height of Mount Washington when he drew this. Art, science, and tourism worked closely together to derive value from the landscape. *Courtesy, Department of Rare Books and Special Collections, University of Rochester Library.*

of Mount Washington's elevation by comparing the difference in atmospheric pressure between summit and valley. While Jackson and Whitney climbed down into the Notch, two colleagues remained at the top. "They were directed to camp near the summit of the mountain," Jackson explained, "and to commence their observations during the next day, while we were engaged in making observations below, at the Notch House."[38] Thus, Whitney represents the experience of viewing the large features of the landscape as a correlative to scientific observation.

Scientists came to share the interests of artists and tourists for the dramatic. Scientists, too, made the great loop through the White Mountains to see the

Old Man of the Mountain, Mount Washington, and the Willey House. Though their profession shaped the language they used, they responded to these sights in similar ways. A disaster such as the Willey slide exhibited the sublime in nature, and the scientist wanted to discover its implications no less than did the painter or tourist. To the scientist, the slide gave a hint of processes that had shaped the earth's crust in the remote past. In May 1828, for example, Benjamin Silliman—a friend of Thomas Cole and Daniel Wadsworth —examined the site of the Willey slide for clues that might demonstrate the geologic mechanics of Noah's flood. Silliman was no Biblical literalist or scientific amateur. He was a professor at Yale and one of America's leading geologists. As a catastrophist, Silliman believed that a few cataclysmic events had shaped the earth's crust and caused the massive irregularities visible in it. The Genesis flood was simply a poetic version of a real episode from the geologic past. According to this theory, rock strata were originally deposited horizontally. At some point, these had broken apart, and reserves of water from below had roared out and overwhelmed the earth. Strata were bent and buckled out of the horizontal, and some even twisted past the perpendicular.

Silliman hoped to find evidence of this kind of structural damage when he visited Crawford Notch. His disappointment is plain as he reports only superficial disarray. "The avalanches were very numerous," he wrote his family; "they were not, however, ruptures of the main foundation rock of the mountain, but *slides*, from very steep declivities."[39] Silliman's disappointment indicates his eagerness to see the dramatic in nature. He wished to document scientifically the same catastrophic vision of the earth that Cole and others had imagined on canvas. But the Willey slide disappointed only in degree. It actually reaffirmed Silliman's basic belief. "This catastrophe," he concluded, "presents a very striking example of sudden diluvial action, and enables one to form some feeble conception of the universal effects of the vindictive deluge which once swept every mountain, and ravaged every plain and defile" (222). The matter-of-fact observations that make up the bulk of Silliman's report and that were the professional standard in scientific research serve to bolster an operatic vision of the earth, even if this vision is understated.

Science's newly found appreciation for the dramatic appeared in the pages of the *American Journal of Science and Arts*, founded by Silliman in 1818. Now known simply as *Science*, it is today the oldest scientific publication in America. During the nineteenth century, it was the premier journal for scientific publication, and George Daniels called it perhaps "the greatest single influence in the development of an American scientific community."[40] This quarterly published articles in every scientific field, including geology. It ran at least six articles on the White Mountains during a twenty-two-year span beginning in 1824. Professional scientists wrote some, amateur correspondents others; some contain more purely scientific observation, others more local color. But one striking feature is that they greatly resemble accounts of White Mountain travel written by ordinary tourists. Like Thomas Cole and Benjamin Brown French, the authors wrote chronologically. They reported on features in the order in which they came to them on their trips through the mountains. In some cases, these scientific reports were given in diary form, like Francis Parkman's and Timothy Dwight's accounts. In other words, nineteenth-century science followed tourism in how it narrated encounters with the landscape.

Just as the sublime's unanswerable majesty completed the tourist's endeavor, it also marked the end point of science. Through the sublime, Nature made its meaning self-evident. "My object is to record facts," stated Dartmouth professor Oliver Hubbard, beginning a report on his White Mountain trip, "and I am happy to say they are so numerous, and so decisive that we do not seem to be in the region of theory, when we infer at once the nature of those causes that have produced the sublime and beautiful scenery that adorns the greater part of this state."[41] Hubbard practiced science like a tourist: For both, seeing alone is sufficient. Direct aesthetic perception provides ultimate knowledge and not the scientific method of observation, hypothesis, and testing. Scientists must go and read Nature firsthand, just as one would read the Bible. Of the 1826 slides, Hubbard said that "the records of their history are written in indelible characters" (116). The conceit echoed Silliman, who concluded that "centuries may roll by, and the catastrophe of August 1826, will still remain recorded in characters that can neither be effaced, nor misunderstood."[42] And Theron Baldwin, inspecting a similar slide in Vermont, found the sight "convincing." He assented to Silliman's own view of scientific procedure: "And while standing upon that mountain, I realized the force of a remark which you have often made, that we can never be properly prepared to reason upon the phenomena of the deluge, till we have *taken the field*, and witnessed for ourselves, the effects of those convulsions which have devastated the surface of our planet" (232). In other words, scientists learn the most about nature when they sightsee and act like tourists.

Not surprisingly, the boundary between science and tourism was porous. Ordinary tourists geologized and botanized for pleasure. Ethan Crawford guided many botanists over Mount Washington, including William Oakes, a summer regular at the inn who expressed his gratitude by paying for Crawford's tombstone. In fact, Crawford became skilled enough at recognizing plant species that botanists hired him to collect specimens and to pack and ship them to Boston.[43] And scientists themselves promoted tourism. Silliman printed in his *Journal* an article entitled "Popular Notices of Mount Washington and Its Vicinity." It contains little of scientific value even by the standards of the day but, like any guidebook, simply describes the attractions that the tourist would encounter on a loop through Crawford Notch. Scientists also enjoyed Crawford's hospitality, the same as other guests. Silliman remarked in his *Journal* how much he liked hearing Crawford blow the tin horn and shoot off the cannon.[44]

Perhaps the Appalachian Mountain Club (AMC) offers the best example of the convergence of science and tourism. This group was composed mainly of scientists, who founded the organization in 1876 in order to study and promote the White Mountains. The club immediately started a journal, *Appalachia*, which printed articles on White Mountain natural history, lists of the latest books on the region, accounts of hikes in the mountains, and a superb map of the entire area. Another goal was to facilitate travel in the mountains, and hikers still use trails and cabins built by the AMC. One notable event sponsored by the club was a hike to the top of Mount Willey on 28 August 1876 to commemorate the fiftieth anniversary of the disaster. Thus, scientists' enthusiasm for the White Mountains led them to participate in tourism and to contribute a great deal to it. This was a natural outgrowth of science's and tourism's common way of viewing the landscape.

The Pathology of American Land Use

George Perkins Marsh invented one of the most perceptive narratives of American landscape in the nineteenth century. His masterpiece, *Man and Nature; Or, Physical Geography as Modified by Human Action* (1864), still in print today, appeared less than two years after passage of the Homestead Act (1862), which provided for the distribution of free land in an attempt to organize and settle the West and to create Jefferson's nation of small farmers. Marsh wrote at a time when Americans foresaw endless prosperity, secured by a limitless supply of land, but he rejected such notions about nature's abundance. Instead, he pointed out the unintended consequences of ordinary land use: deforestation, erosion, and the depletion of soil nutrients. Far from boosting the earth's productivity, Marsh argued, farmers typically destroy its capacity to support life. However, these symptoms appear only in the aggregate. Agrarians had placed their hopes in the virtue of the individual farmer; Marsh looked at the effects of farmers as a class. With Lyell, he imagined the earth as a self-sustaining environment. For Marsh, humans were a foreign element that disturbed nature's balance by short-sighted exploitation.

In demythologizing Man's relation to Nature, Marsh maintained an anti-individual and antitourist view of the landscape. This attitude stemmed partly from experience, and his life offers interesting contrasts with that of Ethan Crawford. Both were born around 1800 in the newly settled region of Vermont along the Connecticut River. Although Crawford was illiterate, Marsh was a polymath. He knew many languages by the time he graduated from Dartmouth. He published a grammar of Old Icelandic and several books on the English language. He practiced law in Burlington, Vermont, was elected to Congress, and helped found the Smithsonian Institution. Afterward, he became U.S. ambassador to the Ottoman Empire and, for twenty years until his death in 1882, was ambassador to Italy. However, Marsh showed poorer business instincts than Crawford. Having built a carding mill just as Vermont's woolen industry peaked, Marsh, too, went bankrupt in the Panic of 1837. He bankrupted again about 1860, this time in railroads. To recuperate his fortunes both times, he went to Chicago, where a childhood friend set up sweetheart deals for him in real estate, which Marsh rejected, although he would have become rich if he had accepted. Scholarly detachment kept him from fixing himself in one place and exploring its potential, as Ethan Crawford had done, but this very breadth of vision allowed him to see the pathologies of American land use.

Marsh derived his sense of cyclic and self-contained natural processes from Charles Lyell, a longtime correspondent. Marsh owned most of Lyell's books, including two complete editions of the *Principles of Geology*.[45] In *Man and Nature*, Marsh argued that, left to itself, Nature maintains a dynamic equilibrium of forces on the earth's surface but that Man's unwise actions, such as overcutting trees, disturb this balance and destroy the environment's capacity to support life. "Nature, left undisturbed, so fashions her territory as to give it almost unchanging permanence of form, outline, and proportion."[46] Marsh here applies Lyell's doctrine of the uniformity of the geologic past to the ecology of nature as it exists in the present.

This Eden of nearly geometric perfection scarcely resembles that nature in which Wordsworth heard the "still, sad music of humanity." To Marsh, humans are foreign to nature: "But man is everywhere a disturbing agent. Wherever he plants his foot, the harmonies of nature are turned to discords. The proportions and accommodations are overthrown. Indigenous vegetable and animal species are extirpated, and supplanted by others of foreign origin, spontaneous production is forbidden or restricted, and the face of the earth is either laid bare or covered with a new and reluctant growth of vegetable forms, and with alien tribes of animal life."[47] Some of the "disturbances" Marsh described anticipate today's concerns about erosion, desertification, global warming, and species destruction.

But it is certain that man has done much to mould the form of the earth's surface
. . . [so] that the destruction of the forests, the drainage of lakes and marshes, and
the operation of rural husbandry and industrial art have tended to produce great
changes in the hygrometric, thermometric, electric, and chemical condition of
the atmosphere . . . and, finally, that the myriad forms of animal and vegetable
life, which covered the earth when man first entered upon the theater of nature
whose harmonies he was destined to derange, have been, through his action,
greatly changed in numerical proportion, sometimes much modified in form and
product, and sometimes entirely extirpated (18).

Marsh's relationship to late-eighteenth-century aesthetics parallels Cole's.
Both turned the love of natural scenery into a heightened awareness of nature's autonomy. Wordsworth urged people to experience nature to recover
the better part of themselves, but, even more decisively than Cole, Marsh rejected the study of nature for its humane properties. Instead, he observed the
anomalies of landscape with a cold eye. Human society had not only upset the
earth's original balance, but also disrupted the cycles by which the environment restores itself.

But for the intervention of man and domestic animals, the regeneration of deso-
lated landscapes would occur more frequently, proceed more rapidly. The new
scarped mountains, the hillocks of debris, the plains elevated by sand and gravel
spread over them, the shores freshly formed by fluviatile deposits, would clothe
themselves with shrubs and trees, the intensity of the causes of desolation would
be diminished, and nature would thus regain her ancient equilibrium. But these
processes, under ordinary circumstances, demand, not years, generations, but
centuries; and man, who now finds scarce breathing room on this vast globe, cannot retire from the Old World to some yet undiscovered continent, and wait for
the slow action of such causes to replace, by a new creation, the Eden he has
wasted (227–8).

Here is the unacknowledged truth about agrarianism. According to Crevecoeur, the New World was where men such as Andrew the Hebridean could
clear and farm land that would help himself and his community to grow
steadily richer.[48] But Marsh showed that the very methods used by American
farmers rapidly deplete whatever resources nature contains. The way Americans use land, there can be no open-ended "improvement" of the sort the
Physiocrats predicted. By burning off the trees and replacing the great number of indigenous species with a few domesticated animals and plants, the
American farmer damages the environment almost irreversibly. The land's capacity to produce surpluses degenerates rapidly. "But we are, even now,"
Marsh warned, "breaking up the floor and wainscotting and doors and win-
dow frames of our dwelling, for fuel to warm our bodies and seethe our pot-

tage, and the world cannot afford to wait till the slow and sure progress of exact science has taught it a better economy."[49] Perhaps more clearly than anyone else in the nineteenth century, Marsh saw the opportunism concealed behind America's agrarian sentiments.

This is the context in which Marsh discussed the Willey slide, which he thought deforestation most likely caused. As Lyell did in the *Principles of Geology*, Marsh used the Willey slide to illustrate his description of a global geographical process. He embedded his discussion of the disaster in a vigorous analysis of the causes of mountain slides and their influence on the environment: Tree roots hold topsoil firmly in place and help absorb water; trunks and branches block the wind; cutting too many trees on a hillside opens it up to erosion, flash floods, and landslides, all of which leave the land barren. Right after Marsh scolded man for "the Eden he has wasted," he made this conjecture about the Willey disaster:

> I have said that the mountainous regions of the Atlantic States of the American Union are exposed to similar ravages, and I may add that there is, in some cases, reason to apprehend from the same cause even more appalling calamities than those which I have yet described. The slide in the Notch of the White Mountains, by which the Willey family lost their lives, is an instance of the sort I refer to, though I am not able to say that in this particular case, the slip of the earth and rock was produced by the denudation of the surface [vegetation]. It may have been occasioned by this cause, or by the construction of a road through the Notch, the excavations for which, perhaps, cut through the buttresses that supported the sloping strata above.[50]

According to Marsh, the Willey disaster is a warning of what will happen more often if Americans continue to abuse their land. Marsh seemed to think that the Willeys were, like Andrew the Hebridean, interested in clearing land for a farm. Of course, this supposition about the Willeys was mistaken, and the Willey slide did not inaugurate a period of avalanches in New England. Probably neither deforestation nor road building caused the Willey slide. Little wood had been cut from the mountain, and the road cut Marsh referred to was at the Gate of the Notch two miles away. The major cause was probably the excavating action of glaciers, which made the valley sides too steep. It was only a matter of time before a great rainstorm soaked the underlying rock layers until they became slippery enough to give way.[51] Only by chance did it happen on 28 August 1826. The Willeys were victims of circumstances that had been prepared fifteen thousand years before, a span of time unimaginable to most people in the early nineteenth century.

Despite his mistake about the Willeys, Marsh's larger point remains valid. America's demand for progress has dangerous consequences. These appear more clearly when the observer achieves some emotional distance from the figure of the farmer. Marsh considered human acts almost entirely without reference to agency or personality. Humans were defined objectively by their effects rather than subjectively by their desires. Seen in this context, Marsh's account of the Willey slide is incisive. The story's effect is amplified by Marsh's painstaking reconstruction of the geographical context in which the causes and consequences of slides should be understood. The reader has seen how surface vegetation prevents erosion. He has seen analyses of slides from many parts of the world and knows, for instance, that every year since the Roman Empire the Po River has carried "into the Adriatic, the lakes, and the plains, not less than 150,000,000 cubic yards of earth and disintegrated rock" washed down from the northern Apennines.[52] With this background, the lesson Marsh intended the Willeys' story to convey strikes home. The long perspective of geography makes even ordinary, sensible improvements, such as clearing land and building roads, appear short-sighted and opportunistic.

Although he misunderstood the particular enterprise they were engaged in, Marsh was right that the Willeys' view of land was typically American. No doubt, the Willeys had no greater concern for the land's well-being than had those more famous characters in America's frontier history—the miner who works a vein until it runs out and then abandons it, along with slag heaps and open shafts, or the farmer who plants a field with tobacco year after year until he exhausts the soil. Theirs is the mentality of an extraction economy whose object is to siphon off wealth from the land as fast as possible.

Marsh's distance from the behavior he described kept him from recognizing the speculative approach to land taken by Americans such as the Willeys. For one thing, he described humans as agents of geographical change but omitted study of the greed, ambition, and calculation that determine humans' attitude to land. Although these feelings lead to short-sighted land management and eventually to man-made disasters, they do not stop motivating people after the catastrophe has occurred. Indeed, it takes more ingenuity to make money from land after it has become a worthless desert. Marsh understood "desertification" literally, as the result of deforestation and erosion. But the image works just as well to describe other side effects of a modern economy. When Midwestern farms were making those in New England's hill country obsolete, the White Mountain region had become as good as a desert to the people who lived there. The Crawfords and the Willeys knew how to reinvent the land so that it became even more valuable than it had been before. But Marsh was limited by the agrarianism he was critiquing. Like most writers and artists in the nineteenth century, he never thought to ask why the Willeys were in Crawford Notch in the first place.

Epilogue

Six years after Henry James toured the United States, George Santayana went on a farewell trip across the country. Half-European and half-American as was James, Santayana planned to emigrate to Spain, but he was positioned to offer some criticism before leaving. A cross-continent trek had, perhaps, given this Harvard professor of philosophy the distance he needed to speak freely about America's intellectual climate—and especially New England's. And so, on 25 August 1911 at the University of California in Berkeley, Santayana attacked "The Genteel Tradition in American Philosophy."[1] The genteel tradition, he believed, forced intellectuals to view things through the prism of idealism instead of simply studying the world as it is.

Like James, Santayana chose skyscrapers to represent the modern condition, and he summed up his thinking this way: "The American Will inhabits the sky-scraper; the American Intellect inhabits the colonial mansion."[2] This is more than a fancy way to blame colleagues for losing touch with the world of affairs. Rather, Santayana asserted that modern life had far outrun the ability of intellectuals to comprehend it. Moreover, American intellectuals secluded themselves in the mansion of tradition and did not notice the deficit in their understanding. Without the cultural counterweight they should provide, business shaped the landscape at will. Santayana had made an inspired choice to use the skyscraper as a metaphor in his critique of American intellectuals, for perhaps the skyscraper's key feature was its symbolic function. In any case, he came close to naming the hidden relation between business and culture in America: Intellectuals foster images that then become the means by which business gives new value to land. Thus, cultural trappings both promote and camouflage a very sophisticated exploitation of landscape.

However, it would have shocked Santayana and James to learn that this relation had formed well before the age of skyscrapers. Nevertheless, the history of the White Mountains shows that the logic behind skyscrapers originated much closer to the eighteenth century than to the twentieth. Ethan Allen

Crawford and the Willeys understood how America's profound beliefs about nature added pecuniary value to land. These upcountry folk displayed greater mastery of the landscape than the writers, artists, and scientists who went to the White Mountains to explain what the Willey slide meant. Intellectuals saw that the disaster had violated the older, humane view of nature, and they began to formulate more modern ideas about the way nature works. Yet Hawthorne, Cole, Silliman, Marsh, and especially James did not see how speculation had shaped their perceptions of the landscape. The middle-class Willeys and the illiterate Crawford had already discovered how to make money from the changing aesthetic judgments of nature. Literature, art, and science simply helped the enterprise along.

The free appropriation of cultural imagery by business poses a difficult challenge for intellectuals who mainly pay attention to what those images are and where they came from. By contrast, the speculator almost always wins control of the landscape by knowing how to *sell* such images. The way to understand American landscape, therefore, is not through the particular images by which it is imagined, but in how those images are used. The speculator makes money by inventing or promoting a new narrative for a place that had been devalued. He gets to that place before intellectuals become interested and has a freer hand in defining it. Ethan Crawford established his business a decade before the Willey slide drew Cole and Hawthorne to the Notch. More importantly, speculation exercises greater control over the landscape than does high culture because it links culture's prevailing images of landscape to a tangible asset, land. By packaging land in salable units, the speculator offers the means whereby America's profoundest myths can be acted out.

Thus, speculators exercise the most control over landscape because their imagination is the most versatile. Since speculation works by exploiting the *difference* between two images, speculators can operate whatever the terms in which American culture envisions the landscape. They sell their product by changing its image. They can use any image or narrative that comes to hand or invent a new one. They do not believe in the organic theory of the land's value, as Jefferson did, nor are they trapped in the bourgeois fantasy of Nature's purity that Wordsworth described. Thus, a speculator is the kind of businessman Karl Marx never dreamed of. Marx thought that capitalism was simply an ideology that people would see through and reject in due course. But the speculator's speed and versatility provide virtual immunity from questions of ideology and self-interest. Indeed, the speculator succeeds despite a severe public bias against speculation grounded in America's agrarian sentiments. Speculators succeed because they know how to appeal to a deep level of America's collective psychology whose dynamics cannot really be altered by rational analysis.

Just as in Santayana's day, many intellectuals continue to overlook the speculator because they approach American landscape from the perspective of ideology. The routine assumption that cultural productions reflect the economic and social organization from which they come represents today's version of the genteel tradition. In an influential essay on nineteenth-century American painting, Bryan Wolf asserted that "representation refers to a network of social agencies whose work is the manufacture of ways of seeing, the production of perceptual codes."[3] In other words, the social and economic order shapes the way people see landscape. Although this statement is quite true, it explains little, and the critic must find a harder truth to learn how speculation shapes landscape. Discerning the ideology within a myth does not explain the speculator's method. It does not help to declare, "All the World's a Code," as Wolf does in his essay's title. Codes help to explain the consumer's naive acceptance of landscape images; they say nothing about what the speculator does.

The power and value of American landscape rest on the naive enactment of myth that tourism and speculation provide. The myth is simply the hook by which the speculator becomes the unacknowledged controller of American experience. Intellectuals should not underestimate the reach of such myths. After all, the myth of Arcadia beguiled even the keen-witted Henry James on his White Mountain vacation, and scholars such as Leo Marx and Annette Kolodny identify the pastoral as a uniquely American experience. According to Kolodny: "If the American continent was to become the birthplace of a new culture and, with it, new and improved human possibilities, then it was, in fact as well as in metaphor, a womb of generation and a provider of sustenance. Hence, the heart of American pastoral—*the only one in which metaphor and the patterns of daily activity refuse to be separated.*"[4] In America, then, pastoral is not just a cultural artifact, a myth to be decoded: It is a lived experience. And the speculator does not simply manufacture the narratives and images that define the pastoral landscape. He does a more profound service. He turns those images into reality, that is, realty.

NOTES

In the notes, citations are given in shortened form. See the references for complete information.

Chapter One: The Significance of the Willey Disaster

1. Bouton, *Records Relating to New Hampshire*, 7:14.
2. Wood, *Turnpikes of New England*, 225.
3. Crawford, *History of the White Mountains*, 22. This earliest local history of the White Mountains remains the most important source of information on the period before 1850. It is a curious document. Its author is Lucy Howe Crawford, Ethan Allen Crawford's wife. However, she tells the story from his point of view and even writes as if Ethan were the narrator (with some lapses into her own voice). She attributes the creation of their tourist business entirely to Ethan, but she must have played a considerable role herself.

Ethan was illiterate, and Lucy could read and write only passably. Her lack of skill appears in the book's shaky plotting. Though telling the story in rough chronological order, Lucy often gets ahead of herself or leaves out parts of the events she is narrating so that she must return later and sketch them in. In short, the life story of Ethan and Lucy is somewhat fragmented and seems at first "primitive." Bit by bit, however, the reader comes to see the extraordinary cleverness and determination of this couple who, almost by themselves, invented White Mountain tourism.

4. Ibid., 23.
5. Benjamin G. Willey, *Incidents in White Mountain History*, 111.
6. Wood, *Turnpikes of New England*, 225–6.
7. Ibid., 223.
8. Elwell, *Fraternity Papers*, 198.
9. Benjamin G. Willey, *Incidents in White Mountain History*, 111–2.
10. Crawford, *History of the White Mountains*, 177.
11. Ibid., 170, 175.
12. Ibid., 84–6.
13. Benjamin G. Willey, *Incidents in White Mountain History*, 117; Melcher, *Destruction of the Willey Family*, 2.
14. Benjamin Silliman et al., "Miscellaneous Notices of Mountain Scenery," 222.
15. Ramsey, *The Willey Slide*, 8.

16. Benjamin G. Willey, *Incidents in White Mountain History*, 135.
17. Benjamin Silliman et al., "Miscellaneous Notices of Mountain Scenery," 226.
18. Crawford, *History of the White Mountains*, 86, 93.
19. Ibid., 94.
20. Benjamin Silliman et al., "Miscellaneous Notices of Mountain Scenery," 227.
21. Crawford, *History of the White Mountains*, 235.
22. Melcher, *Destruction of the Willey Family*, 3–4, 6.
23. Ibid., 4, 8.
24. Ramsey, *The Willey Slide*, 13.
25. Crawford, *History of the White Mountains*, 93.
26. Benjamin G. Willey, *Incidents in White Mountain History*, 130–1.
27. Ibid., 131–2.
28. For agrarianism and its influence on Jefferson's political philosophy, see Eisinger, "Influence of Natural Rights"; Griswold, "Agrarian Democracy of Thomas Jefferson"; Henry Nash Smith, *Virgin Land*, 128–9; and Appleby, "Commercial Farming." The clearest expression of America's agrarian sentiments appears in Hector St. Jean de Crevecoeur's *Letters from an American Farmer* (1782), esp. in the concluding section of "Letter III," entitled "History of Andrew, the Hebridean." Andrew supposedly arrived from Europe with little money but, through the conditions favorable to farmers in America, soon became a prosperous and respected citizen. Crevecoeur's vision of the sedate course of prosperity corresponds to agrarian landscapes in art, which depicted cultivated valleys with tranquil communities; see Clarke, "Landscape Painting."
29. Of course, nineteenth-century Americans readily accepted the idea of progress as applied to the development of landscape. Scholars now view progress skeptically; nonetheless, they often unwittingly assume that development, or settlement, defines American landscape. They inherit this bias from Frederick Jackson Turner, who had an agrarian bent; see "The Significance of the Frontier in American History," in *Early Writings*. According to Turner, the settlement of a given area proceeds in ascending stages of economic complexity (198). Economic law dictates that land use can move only toward greater intensity (e.g., from pasturing to farming to manufacturing), so development is inevitable. Cf. Cronon, *Nature's Metropolis*, 46–54.

As did Turner, historians still identify *frontier* with the settlement process. In *The American Frontier Revisited*, Margaret Walsh summarized the dominant approaches: "Defining the frontier in three distinct ways, firstly as a *condition* or as unused resources awaiting exploitation, secondly as a *process* of recurring stages of settlement, and finally as a specific *location* or geographic region, then the historian is in effect discussing growth in a newly settled area or the economics of underdevelopment" (15).

However, the example of the White Mountains contradicts such literal conceptions of frontier. The region had few exploitable resources; the most dynamic movements in its economic history occurred after settlement; and tourism, its most lucrative industry, traded on the abandonment and reforestation of upland farms. The term *frontier*, then, should perhaps designate any piece of land—regardless of its state of development—that is undergoing sudden changes in use or perception due to speculation. Land becomes a frontier because a speculator treats it as "free" to receive a new narrative and purpose. Speculation can account for a variety of land-use changes, including both settlement and movements inimical to settlement. Cf. Limerick, *Legacy of Conquest*, esp. "Introduction" and chapter 2, "Property Values," 17–32, 55–77.

30. Cameron, *Hawthorne's "The Ambitious Guest,"* 6.

31. Gidley and Lawson-Peebles, *Views of American Landscapes*, xx.

32. See Harris, *Land Tenure System*. Land tenure in England derives from the manorial system established by William I; according to Harris, "all land was held of the king, and . . . it could be granted successively from one subject to another to be held in turn of the last grantor. The relationship was one of lord and tenant" (3). Holding land "in socage" was the chief form of feudal tenure, and "[t]he most important factor in socage tenure was the rent charge on the land" (29). Because of feudal tenure, most often neither the actual occupant nor the grantor himself had free disposal of the land. (Of course, English tenant farmers enjoyed much more freedom than peasants in France and elsewhere on the continent, at least until the nineteenth century.)

The great exception was in the manor of East Greenwich in Kent, where socage tenure included extra rights, including that of selling land (37–8). The charters of ten of the original thirteen American colonies also granted land tenure on these terms (147). To attract settlers, proprietors had to offer land on the freest terms, and attempts to establish a manorial system, as in England, failed because tenants would simply leave to buy land elsewhere or even to squat. In America, Kentish land tenure evolved into fee simple absolute tenure, which is virtually universal today.

33. For an overview of the availability of and desire for land, see Peter Wolf, *Land in America*. Wolf emphasized two fundamental characteristics of America's land market that are relevant here. First, America has a vast oversupply. Even in 1980, after two hundred years of aggressive settlement and massive government giveaways, only a tiny fraction of the land in the United States was developed (24–5). In practice, this means that the potential supply of land far outstrips the real uses for it. Second, Americans have a deeply ingrained belief in the inherent value of land. "In America, land is magic. And it always has been. Success is owning it with a house. Wealth is owning a lot of it, without a house . . . There is a continuing mystique that land will create wealth. There is a mystique that land, like gold, is a tangible, solid investment that will provide security" (4–5).

34. Crawford, *History of the White Mountains*, 49.

35. Horace Fabyan, who bought Ethan Allen Crawford's inn as well as the Willey House, built the first grand hotel in 1844; see Bulkley, "Horace Fabyan." The quarter century beginning about 1880 is the mature period of grand hotels, when they peaked in size, number, and grandeur (see chap. 3). This period coincides with the first era of skyscraper construction, primarily in Chicago and New York City. The first steel-frame office building was William Le Baron Jenney's Home Insurance Building, begun in Chicago in 1883, although masonry buildings had reached ten or twelve stories in the 1870s; see Fleming et al., *Penguin Dictionary of Architecture*, 181, 299.

36. Rem Koolhaas coined the term *Manhattanism* to describe this phenomenon. Koolhaas stated more explicitly the theory of New York City's growth that James expounded impressionistically. Both treat the city as a problem of narrative. With each new tower, the architect tells a story that reinterprets the city. However, each skyscraper/story is discrete; taken together, they do not form a coherent whole. New York City's high-toned architecture, then, serves two purposes. It makes one building more prominent than its competitors while concealing the fact that the building is merely a business venture.

Thus, Koolhaas explained Manhattanism as "an unformulated theory . . . whose program—to exist in a world totally fabricated by man, i.e., to live *inside* fantasy—was so ambitious that to be realized, it could never be openly stated." Koolhaas's idea describes the White Mountains just as aptly. But, because the fantasies there were not expressed through buildings or development, James did not see the same principle at work. See Koolhaas, *Delirious New York*, 10.

Further discussion of this idea appears in two books on Chicago by Ross Miller. In *American Apocalypse*, Miller described how the trauma of the 1871 fire, which gutted the whole city, became sublimated into Chicago's vigorous optimism. This optimism fueled the rebuilding of downtown, with its stunning collection of skyscrapers, and the White City, the grounds of the World's Columbian Exposition in 1893.

In *Here's the Deal*, Miller showed how real estate speculators helped turn a block at the city's heart into an empty lot. Though full of vibrant small businesses, block 37 was labeled "derelict" by the city and slated for redevelopment. By the time developers acquired the site and razed its buildings, real estate had gone into a deep slump, leaving a hole next to city hall that cost $150 million. Chicago's fantasy of developing land to its "highest and best use," which often contradicts good social and economic sense, simply reverses the fantasy of the White Mountains, where business trades on the supposed *absence* of development and the purity of Nature. The underlying, speculative approach to land is the same.

37. James, *American Scene*, 77.

38. Ibid., 14. James's response differed little from that of many other tourists who took a walk through the woods and found an abandoned farm. These incidents seem to have elicited mainly head shaking, as in Samuel Adams Drake's account: "A brisk pace brought us in a short time to the edge of an ancient clearing, now badly overgrown with bramble and coppice, and showing how easily nature obliterates the mark of civilization when left alone. In this clearing an old cellar told its sad story but too plainly. Those pioneers who first struck the axe into the noble pines here are all gone. They abandoned in consternation the effort to wring a scanty subsistence from this inhospitable and unfruitful region." Drake, "The White Mountains, Part 2," 192.

39. James's criticism of rural New England largely echoed his attack on New York City's landscape, and many of his observations about the White Mountains could have supported the same view. Nonetheless, James exempted the White Mountains from censure.

The whiteness that marks New York City also characterizes the classic New England village, which James described as "exhibiting more fresh white paint than can be found elsewhere in equal areas" (*American Scene*, 38). The white meeting houses, whose simple, tall spires dominate many towns, "blow the ground clear of the seated solidity of religion"; like office towers, they reduce everything to one level and are completely "continuous and congruous, as to type and tone, with the common objects" surrounding them (24). Thus, villages are no easier to tell apart than are skyscrapers. "These communities stray so little from the type, that you often ask yourself by what sign or difference you know one from the other" (39). In English villages, Anglican churches give the landscape a permanent moral significance, whereas New England's Separatist instincts have retarded the establishment of durable values. Likewise, insisted James, the White Mountains are "a room vast and vacant, with a vacancy especially reducible . . . to the fact of that elimination" of permanence (24).

Chapter Two: The Tourism Frontier

1. Winthrop, cited in Kilbourne, *Chronicles of the White Mountains*, 21.

2. Ibid., 22, and see Wilson and Fiske, *Appleton's Cyclopaedia of American Biography*, 2:688.

3. Weeks, *History of Coos County*, 61.

4. Crawford, *History of the White Mountains*, 44, 121.

5. Weeks, *History of Coos County*, 63–71.

6. For early explorations of the White Mountains, see Powers, *Historical Sketches*, and Tuckerman, "Early Visits."

7. Weeks, *History of Coos County*, 57.

8. See Belknap, *History of New Hampshire*, 3:320.

9. Benjamin G. Willey, *Incidents in White Mountain History*, 58–9.

10. Norman Smith, "A Mature Frontier," 4.

11. Hands, "Letter from the Northern States," 122.

12. Wilson, *Hill Country of Northern New England*, 65.

13. Cross, *Dolly Copp*, 6, and F. Allen Burt, *Story of Mount Washington*, 52.

14. Wilson, *Hill Country of Northern New England*, 131.

15. Ibid., 75.

16. Benton and Barry, *Statistical View of Sheep*, 20.

17. See Goetzmann, "Mountain Man as Jacksonian Man." Goetzmann showed that the primary role of the mountain man was not that of a rugged individualist but that of a capitalist.

18. Crawford, *History of the White Mountains*, 28–32.

19. Ibid., 40–1.

20. The efforts of Ethan Allen Crawford typify the birth of tourism throughout the Northeast during the early nineteenth century. The entrepreneurs of tourism had to teach people how to look at natural scenery before the business could take off. Dona Brown described this transformation: "Educated at Niagara Falls and along the Hudson, increasing numbers of American tourists were prepared to approach the mountains of New Hampshire with a new perspective, seeing in them not the rough roads and half-cleared forests of a frontier region but the sublime peaks and picturesque valleys of a romantic landscape. That new perspective was not the result of chance but of hard work." Brown, *Inventing New England*, 43.

21. Crawford, *History of the White Mountains*, 133.

22. Ibid., 69, 142.

23. Ibid., 131–2.

24. Emerson's journal entries on his trip to the White Mountains appear in Emerson, *Journals and Miscellaneous Notebooks*, 4:27–30.

25. Irving described the visit in one or two letters. See Irving, *Life and Letters*, 3:28–9.

26. Cross, *Dolly Copp*, 12.

27. Thomas, "Reminiscences of the White Mountains," 46.

28. Ibid., 48.

29. Ibid., 49.

30. Ibid. The scene was not to everyone's taste, however, as British army officer E. T. Coke discovered when he climbed Mount Washington on what must have been an

overcast day in 1832: "The view from it is most extensive, nearly one hundred mountain tops rising beneath the feet like the billowy swellings of the ocean . . . Here was an unvaried view of mountain and dale alike covered with forest, the small settlements but indistinctly visible from such an altitude, and scarcely relieving so dark a mass." See Coke, *Subaltern's Furlough*, 2:151. Coke preferred the more settled landscape he saw from the top of Mount Holyoke in Massachusetts.

31. Frank H. Burt, "White Mountain Album," 314.

32. Crawford, *History of the White Mountains*, 58, 132–3.

33. Ibid., 102, 106, 112. The carriage road idea was his most far-sighted, however. The Mount Washington Summit Road Company, with assets of $50 thousand, eventually completed the project in 1861 after six years of construction. Its success has continued for more than 130 years; thousands of cars every year still use it to get to the top of Mount Washington; see F. Allen Burt, *Story of Mount Washington*, 73–6.

34. Crawford, *History of the White Mountains*, 111.

35. Ibid., 30, 32.

36. Ibid., 151–2.

37. Ibid., 160. For an account of how speculation causes American real estate markets to follow a boom-and-bust pattern, see Lindeman, "Anatomy of Land Speculation."

38. Kilbourne, *Chronicles of the White Mountains*, 137, 158.

39. Horace Fabyan's career in the White Mountains was almost as important as Ethan Crawford's. For the details of Fabyan's life, see Bulkley, "Horace Fabyan," 52–77.

40. Brown, *Inventing New England*, 25–6.

41. Parkman, *Journals of Francis Parkman*, 1:13–4.

42. Fabyan, *Mount Washington House*, 9.

43. Bulkley, "Horace Fabyan," 61.

44. Ibid., 63.

45. Rogers, *Miscellaneous Writings*, 167.

46. Ibid., 170.

47. Ibid., 184.

48. See Sears, *Sacred Places*, 209–21.

49. Rogers, *Miscellaneous Writings*, 176.

50. In "New City, New Frontier: The Lower East Side as Wild, Wild West," Neil Smith showed how high culture fronted for one recent deal. In the 1980s, the real estate industry used low rents to lure artists into renovated loft space in a once-derelict corner of Manhattan. After the neighborhood had gained a reputation for cultural chic, rents jumped considerably, and wealthier residents supplanted the artists. "However wittingly or otherwise," Smith observed, "the culture and real-estate industries worked together to transform the Lower East Side into a new place—different, unique, a phenomenon, the pinnacle of avant garde fashion. Culture and place became synonymous . . . Good art and good location became fused. And good location means money." As in the White Mountains, art helped speculators make one place seem more desirable than another. See Sorkin, *Variations on a Theme Park*, 78–9.

51. Another important early speculator was Joseph Whipple, who founded the inland town of Jefferson (originally named Dartmouth) in 1772. In several transactions he acquired the town's whole area from its grantees and divided his holdings into one-

hundred-acre lots. To attract settlers, he offered them fifty acres for free, but they could only obtain the other half of their lot for one hundred dollars. This little trick enabled Whipple to obtain the standard price of one dollar per acre for raw land, even though his was located in an isolated area. See Dodge, "Colonel Joseph Whipple," and Weeks, *History of Coos County*, 406.

52. Cameron, *Hawthorne's "The Ambitious Guest,"* 6.

Chapter Three: The Golden Age of Tourism

1. See Wilson, *Hill Country of Northern New England*, 302–20. Logging of original timber stands in nineteenth-century America (unlike western Europe) represented a relatively unintensive use of land. That is, the timber required no cultivation and supported transportation to market over long distances. But dairy farming represents a relatively intensive use of cultivated land and occurs close to urban markets because milk does not last long without refrigeration.

2. Timothy Dwight, *Travels in New England.*

3. Campbell, "Two's Company," 311.

4. Thoreau, *Journal*, 1:89–91.

5. Parkman, *Journals of Francis Parkman*, 7–15.

6. Donald B. Cole, "White Mountains in 1845," 209–13.

7. Ibid., 213.

8. Benjamin G. Willey, *Incidents in White Mountain History*, 309–21.

9. Sweetser, *White Mountains*, 50, 68a.

10. According to Crawford, the first tourist to die was the son of a British M.P., who rashly attempted to climb Mount Washington in the late fall of 1851 and fell to his death. See Crawford, *History of the White Mountains*, 187–8, 240, and Kilbourne, *Chronicles of the White Mountains*, 268.

11. Ball's account appears in Ball, *Three Days*. Ball miraculously suffered only the loss of a toe to frostbite. His ordeal received much public attention.

12. Thoreau, *Journal*, 259–60.

13. Mead, *The Up-country Line*, 49.

14. Weeks, *History of Coos County*, 437.

15. Haskell, *What I Know*, 17–8.

16. Brown, *Inventing New England*, 27.

17. Bulkley, "Horace Fabyan," 63.

18. Ibid., 61; Kilbourne, *Chronicles of the White Mountains*, 220–1.

19. Wallace, "Social History," 28.

20. Ibid., 30.

21. Rideing, "White Mountains," 324.

22. See Bulkley, "Identifying the White Mountain Tourist," 151–4.

23. Quoted in F. Allen Burt, *Story of Mount Washington*, 67.

24. Trollope, *North America*, 43.

25. Murray, *Letters*, 45.

26. Ibid., 50.

27. These are published in Beecher, *Summer Parish*.

28. Derks, *Value of a Dollar*, 11–6, 31.

29. Sweetser, *White Mountains*, 158–61.

30. Rideing, "White Mountains," 323–4.
31. Derks, *Value of a Dollar*, 2.
32. Rideing, "White Mountains," 324.
33. Kilbourne, *Chronicles of the White Mountains*, 163.
34. Peter B. Bulkley's article, "Horace Fabyan, Founder of the White Mountain Grand Hotel," contains valuable information about hotel construction and finances. Bulkley argued that Fabyan's 1848 addition to Ethan Allen Crawford's inn (renamed the Mount Washington House) became the model for later hotels.
35. Bulkley, "Horace Fabyan," 63–4.
36. Kilbourne, *Chronicles of the White Mountains*, 338–41, 344.
37. Wallace, "Social History," 29.
38. Bulkley, "Horace Fabyan," 60.
39. Ibid., 64.
40. Bremer, *Homes of the New World*, 2:586–7.
41. Sears, *Sacred Places*, 10.
42. McGrath, "The Real and the Ideal," 68.
43. Frank H. Burt, "White Mountain Album," 315–6.
44. Theodore Dwight, *Sketches of Scenery and Manners*, 7.
45. King, *White Hills*.
46. George Franklyn Willey, *Soltaire*.
47. Bulkley, "Identifying the White Mountain Tourist," 123.
48. Sweetser, *White Mountains*.
49. See Coffin, "Sylvester Marsh."
50. Wallace, "Social History," 29.
51. F. Allen Burt, *Story of Mount Washington*, 93.
52. Rideing, "White Mountains," 330.
53. Kilbourne, *Chronicles of the White Mountains*, 240–1.
54. Spaulding, *Historical Relics*, 72–4.
55. Benjamin G. Willey, *Incidents in White Mountain History*, 264–5.
56. Unless otherwise noted, facts about land sales come from the Coos County Registry of Deeds in Lancaster, New Hampshire.
57. Weeks, *History of Coos County*, 137.
58. See Crawford, *History of the White Mountains*, 175.
59. Weeks, *History of Coos County*, 406.
60. F. Allen Burt, *Story of Mount Washington*, 174.
61. Ibid.
62. Weeks, *History of Coos County*, 922.
63. Kilbourne, *Chronicles of the White Mountains*, 230.
64. F. Allen Burt, *Story of Mount Washington*, 67.
65. Despite high expenses and high prices, the Summit and Tip-Top Houses were quite popular. "Coal which cost $7 a ton in Portland," remarked Noyes, "cost us $25 when we got it up the mountain" (cited in F. Allen Burt, *Story of Mount Washington*, 66). Dinner cost one dollar, whereas an overnight guest paid $2.50, the highest rates in the area. Nevertheless, Noyes recalled that "we used to average nearly 100 diners a day" (67).
66. Weeks, *History of Coos County*, 921.
67. Kilbourne, *Chronicles of the White Mountains*, 234–6.

68. Ibid., 232.
69. Ibid., 246–7.
70. F. Allen Burt, *Story of Mount Washington*, 175–7.
71. James recognized this most modern aspect of American life because he was also conservative. In some ways, James even seems backward. "Undeniably," wrote Ross Posnock, "*The American Scene* is a peculiar work of social criticism, lacking as it does a theory of capitalism or political economy, of ideology or bureaucracy." See Posnock, "Henry James, Veblen and Adorno," 32. Yet Marxist terminology would not have clarified James's understanding of America's hotel culture because the business practices he described are more simple, subtle, and powerful than is the industrial capitalism that Marx analyzed.
72. James, *American Scene*, 105.
73. Posnock, "Henry James, Veblen and Adorno," 41.
74. James, *American Scene*, 452.
75. Lyons, "In Supreme Command," 533.
76. James, *American Scene*, 438.

Chapter Four: Tourism and Landscape Painting

1. Lyell, *Principles of Geology*, 1:331. The big exception is the eruption of Vesuvius that buried Pompeii and two other towns in A.D. 79, which Pliny the Younger witnessed and described in two letters written at the request of the historian Tacitus (VI.16,20). At the end of the second letter, Pliny apologized for the event's insignificance: "You will read these details but will not write about them since they are by no means worthy of history; you will judge for yourself—you asked for them after all—whether they seem even worth a letter."
2. Dahl, "American School of Catastrophe," 381.
3. Perry Miller, *Nature's Nation*, 129.
4. McGrath, "The Real and the Ideal," 60.
5. Thomas Cole, "Essay on American Scenery," 8.
6. Champney, *Sixty Years' Memories*, 142.
7. Nygren adds: "He is pivotal in the development of American landscape after 1825." See Nygren, "From View to Vision," 63. The best introduction to the Hudson River School as a whole is *American Paradise*.
8. According to C. G. Jung, the term *symbol* "always presupposes that the chosen expression is the best possible description or formulation of a relatively unknown fact, which is none the less known to exist or is postulated as existing." See Jung, *Psychological Types*, 474. In the nineteenth century, most Americans knew of land speculation, but few realized how much speculation shaped American economic life, and fewer still realized that the speculator's attitude pervaded the thinking of ordinary people.
9. Gilpin, "Essay on Picturesque Beauty," 50. The history of the idea of the sublime appears in Monk, *The Sublime*.
10. In Europe, the romantic devotion to nature, which expressed itself through the picturesque, represented a different sublimation; it was an antidote to utilitarian capitalism. By the early nineteenth century, economic thinkers had reduced Nature to the status of "raw materials," which were factored into the economy only in terms of their relative scarcity. Dieter Groh and Rolf-Peter Sieferle pointed out "that, as nature dis-

appeared from economic theory, it was 'discovered' at the same time to be a source of aesthetic experience." See Groh and Sieferle, "Experience of Nature," 573. The picturesque sensibility provided a psychological counterweight to utilitarianism and reinserted moral value into nature.

11. Tuckerman, "Gleanings from the Visitors' Albums," 377. See also Campbell, "Two's Company." According to Campbell, Pratt served as an assistant to Samuel F. B. Morse, who tutored Pratt in painting. Pratt was also the business agent for Morse's most famous painting, *House of Representatives* (309–10).

12. Campbell, "Two's Company," 324.

13. Ibid., 319.

14. Wallach, "Thomas Cole," 65.

15. Elwood C. Parry, *Art of Thomas Cole*, 178.

16. In the 1820s and 1830s, White Mountain tourists had to stay in farmhouses that also served travelers. See chapter 2.

17. Trumbull was the leader of the old guard being challenged by younger artists; his patronage of a great new talent such as Cole helped to bolster his influence.

18. Trumbull is supposed to have said: "This youth has done at once, and without instruction, what I cannot do after 50 years' practice." Cited in Elwood C. Parry, *Art of Thomas Cole*, 26.

19. See Schumpeter, *History of Economic Analysis*, 442. "The oldest and most primitive way" of imagining economic history, according to Schumpeter, "is by constructing typical stages through which an economy must pass." Schumpeter cited the work of Prussian Frederick List as a nineteenth-century example. List's stages were "hunting, agriculture, agriculture plus manufacture, agriculture and manufacture plus commerce." During a visit to the United States, List wrote *The Outlines of American Political Economy* (1827), which expressed a classic agrarian view complementary to his epochal scheme: "The price of land, and the possibility of converting it into money, rises and falls with the price of the produce" (8). He warned that, when loose credit sustains land prices beyond those supported by agricultural produce, a sudden crash will destroy a nation's industry, credit, and morals for fifty years (8). List concluded, therefore, that national prosperity "depends upon the steadiness of the prices of land and property" (9).

20. Quesnay, *Economical Table*, 208–9. For a discussion of Quesnay's ideas within their political and economic context, see Fox-Genovese, *Origins of Physiocracy*.

21. Dahl, "American School of Catastrophe," 384–5.

22. Physical catastrophes still serve to bring to the public's attention the sudden changes in landscape caused by speculation. For example, in 1992 hurricane Andrew shocked the nation with its extensive destruction of south Florida. Its winds ripped roofs off tract houses in whole neighborhoods. The hurricane damage revealed that contractors rushing to build had failed to meet tough construction standards that could have saved most homes. Many called for stricter enforcement of building codes, but in the hurried rebuilding some contractors again cut corners. The public accepts housing "developments" as normal land use and does not fully appreciate the mechanism by which speculators change the landscape. Natural disasters form an objective correlative to this dim awareness of how profits are made from land. For an account of real estate speculation's catastrophic effects on urban and suburban communities, see Ross Miller, *Here's the Deal*, and Downie, *Mortgage on America*.

23. Cole's views on the expanse and importance of nature in America simply varied a common theme about American landscape during the nineteenth century. For example, N. P. Willis wrote: "Certain it is that the rivers, the forests, the unshorn mountainsides and unbridged chasms of that vast country, are of a character peculiar to America alone—a lavish and large-featured sublimity, (if so we may express it,) quite dissimilar to the picturesque of all other countries." See Willis, *American Scenery*, v. The supposedly larger quantity of nature in America portended great things for the nation itself.

24. For the history of panoramas, see Lee Parry, "Landscape Theater in America." Edinburgh artist Robert Barker invented the panorama in 1787 and, in London in 1792, constructed the first theater to display 360-degree, realistic landscape views. After paying admission, a viewer "proceeded along a darkened corridor . . . Then, climbing a flight of stairs, he arrived at a platform that offered an unobstructed view of the entire unframed continuous landscape. By comparison with the entrance passageway, the painted landscape appeared brightly lit (from unseen windows near the outer edge of the conical roof)" (54).

Panoramas came to the United States in 1795 and were popular until about 1850. Serious artists such as Albert Bierstadt and Frederic Church copied not only the panorama's wide viewing angle but also its theatrical presentation. They would commonly send an impressive painting on tour to cities throughout America and would display it for paying customers in large, darkened rooms with just the canvas lit up.

25. The panoramas that Thoreau saw were moving panoramas; viewers sat facing in one direction while they watched the canvas roll in front of them. Thoreau is probably referring to "Benjamin Champney's *Great Original Picture of the River Rhine and Its Banks*, first shown in Boston in the winter of 1848–49" and to "John Banvard's *Panorama of the Mississippi River*," shown in Boston in 1846–47, which used two thousand feet of canvas (ibid., 59). In "Walking," Thoreau reversed the order of viewing them.

26. Thoreau, *Excursions*, 274.

27. See Alan Taylor, "Creation of Cooper's Town," 4–14.

28. Weeks, *History of Coos County*, 72.

29. Environmentalism in the strict sense did not appear in the White Mountains until much later. In 1876, a group of White Mountain enthusiasts founded the Appalachian Mountain Club (AMC) to promote research and recreation. The AMC's journal *Appalachia* published much scientific work on the region, while the club itself helped build trails and huts to make the mountains more accessible for hikers (see Kilbourne, *Chronicles of the White Mountains*, 348–57).

Later still, environmentalists defended the White Mountains against the timber industry: "Thousands of tons of saw-mill refuse, and of earth from sloping land denuded of forest growth, are being deposited in the reservoirs and the slack-water portions of the rivers." J. B. Harrison, "Our Forest Interests," 423. Harrison called for "honest and thorough reporting and description of what is done each year by the men who are despoiling and destroying the mountain forests, water sources, and scenery" (420). As with Cole, catastrophic exploitation required a more detailed awareness of landscape.

30. Hubbard, "Observations, 1837," 116.

31. Marx, *Machine in the Garden*, 89.

32. Novak, *Nature and Culture*, 234.

33. Shepard, "New England Landscape," 38.

34. Durand best articulated the philosophy of the Hudson River School: Art has "no other purpose surely than to aid, perchance, the growth of our perceptions." See Durand, *Letters on Landscape Painting*, 1:275. Not surprisingly, Durand started the trend among nineteenth-century American artists of painting *en plein air.*

35. Again, Durand said it best: "Although painting is an imitative Art, its highest attainment is representative, that is, by the production of such resemblance as shall satisfy the mind that the entire meaning of the scene represented is given." For a painting's trees, e.g., to show bark lines distinctive of species will more clearly represent the landscape's meaning. See *Letters on Landscape Painting*, 1:146.

36. After Cole, many American landscape painters followed Durand in transforming Cole's emphasis on detail into a gentler naturalism, which conceals a surprisingly modern attitude toward form. Barbara Novak linked the "naive" vision of Durand's art to the self-conscious primitivism of early modernism: "This is doubtless due not to Durand's avant-gardism, of which he was totally unconscious, but to his empiricism, which responded, like Cezanne's, to the weight of objects in reality . . . Courbet's rocks are weighty largely because of the heavy paint that depicts them. Durand's have weight because he takes care to cut the volume of the rocks themselves into the pictorial space in which they are set. In this spontaneous American proto-impressionism, which appears not only with Durand, but at the same time in Kensett's studies of rocks and waterfalls, paint surface is never allowed to dominate the depicted scene." Novak, *Nature and Culture*, 239.

37. Whittredge, "Autobiography, 1820–1910," 56.

38. European landscape painting apparently arose from Renaissance Italy's demand for soothing images of the countryside; see Gombrich, *Norm and Form*, 111–2. For the sixteenth- and seventeenth-century Dutch and Flemish painters who established the genre, *landscape* meant the activities of farming and pasturing found at the edge of cultivation. Landscape was "[t]he antithesis of wilderness," according to John Stilgoe. "Originally the word was German—*landschaft* . . . A landschaft was not a town exactly, or a manor or a village, but a collection of dwellings and other structures crowded together within a circle of pasture, meadow, and planting fields and surrounded by unimproved forest or marsh." See Stilgoe, *Common Landscape of America*, 12.

39. Of early nineteenth-century landscape painting in Europe, Martin Rudwick wrote that "the 'romantic' movement encouraged attempts to depict the wild mountain landscapes that had previously been considered unfit for serious artistic expression; but at the same time the artists generally exaggerated the vertical scale with scant regard for 'realism' in order to heighten the romantic impact of the scene, and often obscured the topography by his interest in swirling clouds and other atmospheric effects." See Rudwick, "Emergence of a Visual Language," 173–4.

40. Elwood C. Parry III, "Acts of God, Acts of Man," 55–6.

41. Ibid., 57–8.

42. Bedell, "Anatomy of Nature," 1:55–6.

43. Ibid., 61–2. See also N.P.C., "Geology and Landscape Painting," 6:255–6.

44. Durand, *Letters on Landscape Painting*, 1:354.

45. Perhaps the best examples are such works as *Heart of the Andes* and *Cotopaxi*, painted by Thomas Cole's only pupil, Frederic E. Church. "Church was identified and respected as the most scientific of painters," according to Stephen Jay Gould. "His

penchant for accuracy in observation and rendering, both for intricate botanical details in his foregrounds and geological forms in his backgrounds, was admired as a primary source of quality in his art and as a key to success in awakening feelings of awe and sublimity in his viewers." See Gould, "Church, Humboldt, and Darwin," 99.

46. Shepard, "New England Landscape," 41.
47. Bedell, "Anatomy of Nature," 13n.
48. Shepard, "New England Landscape," 33.
49. Agassiz, *Geological Sketches*, 1–28.
50. Shepard, "New England Landscape," 33.
51. See Mitchell, "Caspar David Friedrich's *Der Watzmann*."
52. Shepard, "New England Landscape," 37.
53. Kilbourne, "White Mountain Artist," 451.
54. MacAdam, "Proper Distance from the Hills," 22.
55. Ibid.
56. Keyes, "Perceptions of the White Mountains," 44.
57. McGrath, "High and Holy Meaning," 14.
58. MacAdam, "Proper Distance from the Hills," 34.
59. Ibid., 27.
60. McGrath, "High and Holy Meaning," 15–6.

Chapter Five: The Literature of the White Mountains

1. Tatham, "Franklin Leavitt's White Mountain Verse," 222.
2. Hale, *Excursion to the Highlands*.
3. For more on the relationship between early nineteenth-century painting and literature, see Callow, *Kindred Spirits*.
4. Book 4, stanza 108. See also Wallach, "*Course of Empire*," 378.
5. Benjamin G. Willey, *Incidents in White Mountain History*, 140.
6. "Late Storm," 626.
7. Bohls, "Disinterestedness and Denial," 17.
8. Perry Miller, *Nature's Nation*, 199.
9. Frank H. Burt, "White Mountain Album," 312.
10. Theodore Dwight, *Sketches of Scenery and Manners*, 4.
11. Ibid., 62–3.
12. Cited in Sears, *Sacred Places*, 78.
13. Theodore Dwight, *Sketches of Scenery and Manners*, 6.
14. Mellen, *Martyr's Triumph*, 267–300.
15. See Sigourney, "The White Mountains," 340–2.
16. Kilbourne, *Chronicles of the White Mountains*, 84.
17. Mellen, *Martyr's Triumph*, 276–7.
18. Sigourney, "The White Mountains," 341.
19. Mellen, *Martyr's Triumph*, 282.
20. Dickinson, no. 1624, in *Complete Poems*, 667–8.
21. Warner, *Their Pilgrimage*.
22. Scribner, *Laconia*.
23. Parkman, "Scalp-Hunter."

24. There were at least a couple of similar adventure stories set in the White Mountains. See Larcom, *Leila among the Hills*, and Moore, *Wild Nell*.

25. Mellen, *Martyr's Triumph*, 281.

26. Oakes, *Scenery of the White Mountains*.

27. Campbell, "Two's Company," 327.

28. Drake, "White Mountains, Part 1," 10.

29. Mellen, *Martyr's Triumph*, 281–2.

30. Joseph W. Turner, *Orange Blossoms*, n.p.

31. Cited in King, *White Hills*, 198–9.

32. Mellen, *Martyr's Triumph*, 282.

33. *Avalanche of the White Hills*, 5. The work is attributed to McLellan.

34. Cited in King, *White Hills*, 200.

35. For a discussion of George F. Willey's *Soltaire*, see chapter 3.

36. Mellen, *Martyr's Triumph*, 288.

37. "The Ambitious Guest" appeared first in 1835 in the *New England Magazine;* Hawthorne revised it slightly in 1842 for the second volume of *Twice-Told Tales*. See Hawthorne, *Twice-Told Tales*, 324–33.

38. See Cameron, *Hawthorne's "The Ambitious Guest,"* 17–22.

39. Ibid., 17.

40. Hawthorne, *Letters, 1813–1843*, 226.

41. For an account of the Thomases' trip, see chapter 2.

42. Hawthorne, *American Travel Sketches*, 226.

43. Ibid., 29.

44. The first American translation is *Henry of Ofterdingen: A Romance* (Cambridge: John Owen, 1842). However, Thomas Carlyle wrote his "Novalis" in 1829, which Emerson included in an American edition of Carlyle's essays in 1838. *Heinrich von Ofterdingen* contains both geologic myth and science, which Novalis learned while studying with Abraham Gottlob Werner, the most influential geologist before Charles Lyell; see Laudan, *From Mineralogy to Geology*. Both Werner and Novalis influenced the painting of Caspar David Friedrich (see chap. 4). These romantics believed in "the interplay of natural forces that unified everything from the crystalization of granite to the strivings of the human intellect" (Laudan, 111). In short, the transcendental coincides with the empirical. During the nineteenth century, American intellectuals and tourists, whom German romantic ideas influenced heavily, approached landscapes such as the White Mountains with the same sensibility.

45. In *History of the White Mountains*, Ethan Crawford explained:

> I recollect a number of years ago, when quite a boy, some persons had been up on the hills and said they had found a golden treasure, or carbuncle, which they said was under a large shelving rock and would be difficult to obtain for they might fall and be dashed to pieces. Moreover, they thought it was guarded by an evil spirit, supposing it had been placed there by the Indians, and that they had killed one of their number and left him to guard the treasure, which some credulous, superstitious persons believed, and they got my father to engage to go and search for it . . . They set out and went up Dry river, and had hard work to find their way through the thickets and over the hills, where they made diligent search for a number of days, with some of the former men spoken of for guides, but they could not find the

place again, or anything that seemed to be like it, and worn out with fatigue and disappointment, they returned (97–8).

This account also probably owes something to the story of Field's 1642 trip to the White Mountains found in Winthrop's *Journal* (see chap. 2).

46. Hawthorne, "Sketches from Memory," in *Tales and Sketches*, 338–51, quotation on 343.

47. Cohen, "Sources of 'The Ambitious Guest,'" 223.

48. Sears, "Hawthorne's 'The Ambitious Guest,'" 363.

Chapter Six: Science and Sightseeing

1. "It is rather curious," wrote local historian Frederick Kilbourne, "that the great wonder of the New Hampshire highlands seems not to have impressed him sufficiently to call forth any recorded description of it or comments upon its aspects." Kilbourne, "Thoreau and the White Mountains," 366, 359.

2. Cited in Kilbourne, "Thoreau and the White Mountains," 366.

3. Thoreau, *Journal*, 11:57.

4. See Gray, "Obituary," 139–40.

5. Thoreau, *Excursions*, 161–2.

6. The title of Burnet's work, *Telluris Theoria Sacra*, or *Sacred Theory of the Earth*, suggests the mixture of Biblical and mechanical ideas. Both led Burnet to adopt a view of the geologic past which proved too clean and regular.

7. Daniels, *American Science*, 65.

8. Ibid., 96–7.

9. Gray, "Obituary," 139–40.

10. See chapter 5, note 34.

11. Samuel Tyler, cited in Daniels, *American Science*, 200.

12. Kant, *Kant*, 471.

13. See, e.g., the thoughts of Augustus Silliman, Benjamin Silliman's brother, on what one ought to feel atop Mount Washington:

> Oh! my brother-man—thou that dost toil, and groan, and labour, in continual conflict with what appears to thee unrelenting fate—thou to whom the brow-sweat appears to bring nought but the bitter bread, and contumely, and shame;—thou on whom the Sysiphean rock of misfortune seems remorselessly to recoil—ascend thou hither. Here, on this mountain-peak, nor King, nor Emperor are thy superior. Here, thou *art* a man. Stand thou here; and while with thy faculties thou canst command, in instant comprehension, the scene sublime before thee, elevate thee in thy self-respect, and calmly, bravely throw thyself into the all-sheltering arms of Him, who watches with like benevolence and protection, the young bird in its grassy nest, and the majestic spheres, chiming eternal music in their circling courses!

See Augustus E. Silliman, *Gallop among American Scenery*, 168.

14. In the early nineteenth century, geologic events such as mountain formation were understood as having been sudden and cataclysmic. Perhaps they appeared thus because scientists were used to thinking about the past as a relatively short span. Lyell was the first to think out fully what the geologic scale of time meant to the interpreta-

tion of such events. As Martin Rudwick explained, "there was perhaps a gap between the rational acceptance of a vast time-scale and the imaginative appreciation of what such a time-scale might imply." See Rudwick, *Meaning of Fossils*, 171.

15. Nicolson, *Mountain Gloom and Mountain Glory*, 252–3.
16. Gould, *Time's Arrow*, 5–6.
17. Hutton, *System of the Earth*, 128.
18. Lyell, *Principles of Geology*, 192.
19. Lyell, *Second Visit*, 1:62.
20. Kant, *Kant*, 498.
21. The major contemporary critic of Lyell's theory of uniformity (with its cyclic view of the geologic past) was William Whewell, an early philosopher of science. In challenging Lyell, Whewell argued that whether events happen "uniformly" or "catastrophically" is a question of the viewer's relative position. "The course of things is *uniform*," he wrote, "to an Intelligence which can embrace the succession of several cycles, but it is *catastrophic* to the contemplation of man, whose survey can grasp a part only of one cycle." See Whewell, *Philosophy of the Inductive Sciences*, 671.
22. Hooykaas, *Natural Law and Divine Miracle*, 131.
23. Lowenthal, *George Perkins Marsh*, 275.
24. Marsh cited in ibid., 377 n. 50.
25. Lyell, *Second Visit*, 97.
26. English women played a key role in the development of botany. See Rudwick, *Great Devonian Controversy*, and Shteir, *Cultivating Women, Cultivating Science*.
27. Rudwick, "Emergence of a Visual Language," 153.
28. "Description of the White Mountains," 139.
29. Cutler, *Life*, 2:220–1. Mercury barometers were awkward to carry and use and gave unreliable results. The primitive instruments in use around 1800, combined with the difficulty of climbing mountains, left scientists almost entirely ignorant of mountain elevations. Early in the nineteenth century, Alexander von Humboldt called for a concerted effort to measure the world's mountains; see Laudan, *From Mineralogy to Geology*, 163.
30. Cutler, *Life*, 1:104.
31. Thoreau, *Journal*, 11:52.
32. Cutler, *Life*, 2:224.
33. Belknap, *History of New Hampshire*, 3:51.
34. Bigelow, "White Mountains."
35. Shattuk, "Excursion to the White-Hills," 29.
36. Goodrich, *Wonders of Geology*, 35.
37. Jackson, *Geology and Mineralogy*, 1.
38. Ibid., 78.
39. Benjamin Silliman et al., "Miscellaneous Notices of Mountain Scenery," 220.
40. Daniels, *American Science*, 18.
41. Hubbard, "Observations, 1837," 105.
42. Benjamin Silliman et al., "Miscellaneous Notices of Mountain Scenery," 222.
43. Crawford, *History of the White Mountains*, 126–7.
44. See Nichols, "Popular Notices of Mount Washington," 80.
45. *Catalogue of the Library*, 423.
46. Marsh, *Man and Nature*, 29.

47. Ibid., 36.
48. See chapter 1, note 28.
49. Marsh, *Man and Nature*, 52.
50. Ibid., 228.
51. Lobeck, *Geomorphology*, 89. Lobeck illustrated the role of glaciers in scooping out valleys and making them susceptible to landslides with a sketch of Tuckerman's Ravine on Mount Washington's eastern slope. The bowl-like cross-section shown in this sketch closely resembles paintings of Crawford Notch looking down the valley, such as *The Willey Slide*, attributed to Charles Codman (1800–1842), which hangs in the Conway Library.
52. Marsh, *Man and Nature*, 223–4.

Epilogue

1. Santayana, *Genteel Tradition*, 36.
2. Ibid., 40.
3. Bryan Wolf, "All the World's a Code," 334.
4. Kolodny, *Lay of the Land*, 9 (italics added). See also Marx, *Machine in the Garden*.

References

In addition to the works listed below, which are referenced in the notes to this book, readers interested in researching the history and culture of the White Mountains prior to the twentieth century should consult the two following works: Allen H. Bent, *A Bibliography of the White Mountains*. Boston: Houghton, Mifflin, 1911 (very thorough; its entries are arranged by type of publication, and it also has a good index). Catherine H. Campbell and Marcia Schmidt Blaine, eds. *New Hampshire Scenery: A Dictionary of Nineteenth-Century Artists of New Hampshire Mountain Landscapes*. Canaan, N.H.: Phoenix Publishing, 1985 (exhaustively lists paintings, sketches, drawings, engravings, maps, and other images and arranges them according to artist).

Agassiz, Louis. *Geological Sketches*. Boston: Fields, Osgood, & Co., 1862.

American Paradise: The World of the Hudson River School. New York: Metropolitan Museum of Art, 1987.

Appleby, Joyce. "Commercial Farming and the 'Agrarian Myth' in the Early Republic." *Journal of American History* 68, no. 4 (1982): 833–49.

Ball, Benjamin Lincoln. *Three Days on the White Mountains: being the perilous adventure of Dr. B. L. Ball on Mount Washington during October 25, 26, and 27, 1855*. Boston: Nathaniel Noyes, 1856.

Bedell, Rebecca Bailey. "The Anatomy of Nature: Geology and American Landscape Painting, 1825–1875," vol. 1. Ph.D. diss., Yale University, 1989.

Beecher, Henry Ward. *A Summer Parish: Sabbath Discourses and Morning Service of Prayer*. New York: J. B. Ford & Co., 1875.

Belknap, Jeremy. *The History of New Hampshire*. Vol. 2. Boston: Thomas & Andrews, 1791. Vol. 3. Boston: Belknap & Young, 1792.

Benton, C., and S. F. Barry. *A Statistical View of the Number of Sheep in the Several Towns and Counties in Maine, New Hampshire, ...* Cambridge, Mass.: Folsom, Wells, & Thurston, 1837.

Bigelow, Jacob. "Some Account of the White Mountains of New Hampshire." *New England Journal of Medicine and Surgery* 5, no. 4 (1816): 321–38.

Bohls, Elizabeth A. "Disinterestedness and Denial of the Particular: Locke, Adam Smith, and the Subject of Aesthetics." In *Eighteenth-Century Aesthetics and the Reconstruction of Art*, edited by Paul Mattick Jr., 16–51. Cambridge: Cambridge University Press, 1993.

Bouton, Nathaniel, ed. *Documents and Records Relating to the Province of New Hampshire, from 1764–1776*. Vol. 7. New York: AMS Press, 1973.

Bremer, Fredrika. *The Homes of the New World: Impressions of America*, 2 vols. Translated by Mary Howitt. New York: Harper & Brothers, Publishers, 1854.

Brown, Dona. *Inventing New England: Regional Tourism in the Nineteenth Century.* Washington, D.C.: Smithsonian Institution Press, 1995.

Bulkley, Peter B. "Horace Fabyan, Founder of the White Mountain Grand Hotel." *Historical New Hampshire* 30, no. 2 (1975): 52–77.

———. "Identifying the White Mountain Tourist, 1853–1854: Origin, Occupation, and Wealth as a Definition of the Early Hotel Trade." *Historical New Hampshire* 35, no. 2 (1980): 106–62.

Burt, F. Allen. *The Story of Mount Washington.* Hanover, N.H.: Dartmouth Publications, 1960.

Burt, Frank H., ed. "White Mountain Album: Excerpts from the Registers of Ethan Allen Crawford." *Appalachia*, n.s., 7, no. 7 (1941): 302–19.

N.P.C. "Relation Between Geology and Landscape Painting." *Crayon* 6, no. 8 (1859): 255–6.

Callow, James T. *Kindred Spirits: Knickerbocker Writers and American Artists, 1807–1855.* Chapel Hill: University of North Carolina Press, 1967.

Cameron, Kenneth Walter. *Genesis of Hawthorne's "The Ambitious Guest."* Hartford, Conn.: Transcendental Books, 1955.

Campbell, Catherine Crawford. "Two's Company: The Diaries of Thomas Cole and Henry Cheever Pratt on Their Walk through Crawford Notch, 1828." *Historical New Hampshire* 33, no. 4 (1978): 308–33.

Catalogue of the Library of George Perkins Marsh. Burlington: University of Vermont, 1892.

Champney, Benjamin. *Sixty Years' Memories of Art and Artists.* 1900. Reprint, New York: Garland Publishing, 1977.

Clarke, Graham. "Landscape Painting and the Domestic Typology of Post-revolutionary America." In *Views of American Landscapes*, edited by Mick Gidley and Gilbert Lawson-Peebles, 146–66. Cambridge: Cambridge University Press, 1989.

Coffin, Charles Carleton. "Sylvester Marsh: The Projector of the Mount Washington Railroad." *Bay State Monthly* 3, no. 2 (1885): 65–8.

Cohen, B. Bernard. "The Sources of Hawthorne's 'The Ambitious Guest.'" *Boston Public Library Quarterly* 4, no. 4 (1952): 221–4.

Coke, E. T. *A Subaltern's Furlough*, 2 vols. New York: J. & J. Harper, 1833.

Cole, Donald B. "The White Mountains in 1845: From the Journal of Benjamin Brown French." *Historical New Hampshire* 44, no. 4 (1989): 202–25.

Cole, Thomas. "Essay on American Scenery." In *The Collected Essays and Prose Sketches*, edited by Marshall Tymn, 1–17. St. Paul, Minn.: John Colet Press, 1980.

Crawford, Lucy. *Lucy Crawford's History of the White Mountains*, edited by Stearns Morse. 1846. Reprint, Boston: Appalachian Mountain Club, 1978.

Crevecoeur, Hector St. Jean de. "Letter III: History of Andrew, the Hebridean." In *Letters from an American Farmer.* 1782.

Cronon, William. *Nature's Metropolis: Chicago and the Great West.* New York: W. W. Norton & Co., 1991.

Cross, George N. *Dolly Copp and the Pioneers of the Glen.* Baltimore: Press of Day Printing Co., 1927.

Cutler, Manasseh. *Life, Journals, and Correspondence of Rev. Manasseh Cutler, LL.D.*, edited by William Parker Cutler and Julia Perkins Cutler, 2 vols. Cincinnati: Robert Clarke & Co., 1888.

Dahl, Curtis. "The American School of Catastrophe." *American Quarterly* 11, no. 3 (1959): 380–90.

Daniels, George H. *American Science in the Age of Jackson.* New York: Columbia University Press, 1968.

Derks, Scott, ed. *The Value of a Dollar: Prices and Incomes in the United States, 1860–1989.* Detroit: Gale Research, 1994.

"Description of the White Mountains in New Hampshire." *Monthly Review* 76 (February 1787): 138–9.

Dickinson, Emily. *The Complete Poems of Emily Dickinson*, edited by Thomas H. Johnson. Boston: Little, Brown & Co., 1960.

Dodge, Levi W. "Colonel Joseph Whipple and His Dartmouth Plantation." *Granite Monthly* 15 (January 1893): 20–31.

Downie, Leonard, Jr. *Mortgage on America: The Real Cost of Real Estate Speculation.* New York: Praeger Publishers, 1974.

Drake, Samuel Adams. "The White Mountains, Part 1." *Harper's New Monthly Magazine* 63, no. 373 (1881): 1–23.

———. "The White Mountains, Part 2." *Harper's New Monthly Magazine* 63, no. 374 (1881): 190–213.

———. "The White Mountains, Part 3." *Harper's New Monthly Magazine* 63, no. 375 (1881): 355–76.

Durand, Asher B. *Letters on Landscape Painting*, ser. Crayon 1–2 (1855).

Dwight, Theodore, Jr. *Sketches of Scenery and Manners in the United States*, edited by John F. Sears. Delmar, N.Y.: Scholars' Facsimiles & Reprints, 1983.

Dwight, Timothy. *Travels in New England and New York.* Vol. 2. London: William Baynes & Son, 1823.

Eisinger, Chester E. "The Influence of Natural Rights and Physiocratic Doctrines on American Agrarian Thought during the Revolutionary Period." *Agricultural History* 21, no. 1 (1947): 13–23.

Elwell, Edward Henry. *Fraternity Papers.* Portland, Maine: Elwell, Pickard & Co., 1886.

Emerson, Ralph Waldo. *The Journals and Miscellaneous Notebooks of Ralph Waldo Emerson.* Vol. 4, edited by Alfred R. Ferguson. Cambridge: Harvard University Press, 1964.

Fabyan, Horace. *Mount Washington House, White Mountains, N.H.* New York: Baker, Goodwin & Co., Printers, 1852.

Fleming, John, et al., eds. *The Penguin Dictionary of Architecture.* 3d ed. London: Penguin Books, 1980.

Fox-Genovese, Elizabeth. *The Origins of Physiocracy: Economic Revolution and Social Order in Eighteenth-Century France.* Ithaca: Cornell University Press, 1976.

Gidley, Mick, and Gilbert Lawson-Peebles, eds. *Views of American Landscapes.* Cambridge: Cambridge University Press, 1989.

Gilpin, William. "Essay on Picturesque Beauty." 1792. In *Nineteenth-Century Theories of Art*, edited by Joshua C. Taylor, 47–61. Berkeley and Los Angeles: University of California Press, 1987.

Goetzmann, William H. "The Mountain Man as Jacksonian Man." *American Quarterly* 15, no. 3 (1963): 402–15.

Gombrich, E. H. *Norm and Form: Studies in the Art of the Renaissance*. London: Phaidon, 1971.

Goodrich, Samuel. *The Wonders of Geology*. Boston: Bradbury, Soden & Co., 1845.

Gould, Stephen Jay. "Church, Humboldt, and Darwin: The Tension and Harmony of Art and Science." In *Frederic Edwin Church*, edited by Franklin Kelly, 94–107. Washington, D.C.: National Gallery of Art, 1989.

———. *Time's Arrow, Time's Cycle: Myth and Metaphor in the Discovery of Geologic Time*. Cambridge: Harvard University Press, 1987.

Gray, Asa. "Obituary." *American Journal of Science and Arts* 37, no. 19 (1849): 139–42.

Griswold, A. Whitney. "The Agrarian Democracy of Thomas Jefferson." *American Political Science Review* 40, no. 4 (1946): 657–81.

Groh, Dieter, and Rolf-Peter Sieferle. "Experience of Nature in Bourgeois Society and Economic Theory: Outlines of an Interdisciplinary Research Project," translated by Peter Vintilla. *Social Research* 47, no. 3 (1980): 557–81.

Hale, Nathan. *Notes Made During an Excursion to the Highlands of New Hampshire and Lake Winnipiseogee*. Andover, Mass.: Flagg, Gould, & Newman, 1833.

Hands, T. "Letter from the Northern States of America." *Monthly Magazine* 52, no. 358 (1821): 121–2.

Harris, Marshall. *Origin of the Land Tenure System in the United States*. Ames: Iowa State College Press, 1953.

Harrison, J. B. "Our Forest Interests in Relation to the American Mind." *New England Magazine* 9, no. 4 (1893): 417–24.

Haskell, Ray I. *What I Know About Mount Agassiz, Bethlehem and the White Mountains*. Lancaster, N.H.: Journal Printshop, 1914.

Hawthorne, Nathaniel. *Hawthorne's American Travel Sketches*, edited by Alfred Weber et al. Hanover, N.H.: University Press of New England, 1989.

———. *The Letters, 1813–1843*, edited by Thomas Woodson et al. Columbus: Ohio State University Press, 1984.

———. *Tales and Sketches*. New York: Library of America, 1996.

———. *Twice-Told Tales*. Columbus: Ohio State University Press, 1974.

Hooykaas, R. *Natural Law and Divine Miracle: The Principle of Uniformity in Geology, Biology and Theology*. Leiden: E. J. Brill, 1963.

Hubbard, Oliver P. "Observations Made During an Excursion to the White Mountains, in July, 1837." *American Journal of Science and Arts* 34, no. 1 (1838): 105–24.

Hutton, James. *James Hutton's System of the Earth, 1785, ...* Reprint, Darien, Conn.: Hafner Publishing Co., 1970.

Irving, Pierre. *The Life and Letters of Washington Irving*. Vol. 3. New York: G. P. Putnam, 1864. Reprint, 1967.

Jackson, Charles T. *Final Report on the Geology and Mineralogy of the State of New Hampshire with Contributions Towards the Improvement of Agriculture and Metallurgy*. Concord, N.H.: Carroll & Baker, State Printers, 1844.

James, Henry. *The American Scene*. Bloomington: Indiana University Press, 1968.

Jung, C. G. *Psychological Types*, translated by H. G. Baynes and R. F. C. Hull. Princeton: Princeton University Press, 1971.

Kant, Immanuel. *Kant,* edited by Robert Maynard Hutchins. Chicago: Encyclopaedia Britannica, 1955.

Kelly, Franklin, ed. *Frederic Edwin Church.* Washington, D.C.: National Gallery of Art, 1989.

Keyes, Donald D. "Perceptions of the White Mountains: A General Survey." In *The White Mountains: Place and Perceptions,* 41–58. Hanover, N.H.: University Press of New England, 1980.

Kilbourne, Frederick W. *Chronicles of the White Mountains.* 1916. Bowie, Md.: Heritage Books, 1978.

———. "Thoreau and the White Mountains." *Appalachia* 14, no. 4 (1919): 356–67.

———. "A White Mountain Artist of Long Ago: John Frederick Kensett, 1816–1872." *Appalachia* 26, no. 4 (1947): 447–55.

King, Thomas Starr. *The White Hills: Their Legends, Landscape, and Poetry.* 2d ed. New York: Hurd & Houghton, 1870.

Kolodny, Annette. *The Lay of the Land.* Chapel Hill: University of North Carolina, 1975.

Koolhaas, Rem. *Delirious New York: A Retroactive Manifesto for Manhattan.* New York: Monacelli Press, 1994.

Larcom, Lucy. *Leila among the Hills.* Boston: Bradley & Woodruff, 1861.

"The Late Storm at the White Mountains." *Christian Spectator* 12 (1826): 625–33.

Laudan, Rachel. *From Mineralogy to Geology: The Foundations of a Science, 1650–1830.* Chicago: University of Chicago Press, 1987.

Limerick, Patricia Nelson. *The Legacy of Conquest: The Unbroken Past of the American West.* New York: W. W. Norton & Co., 1987.

Lindeman, Bruce. "Anatomy of Land Speculation." *Journal of the American Institute of Planners* 42, no. 2 (1976): 142–52.

List, Frederick. *The Outlines of American Political Economy.* Philadelphia: Samuel Parker, 1827.

Lobeck, A. K. *Geomorphology: An Introduction to the Study of Landscapes.* New York: McGraw-Hill Book Co., 1939.

Lowenthal, David. *George Perkins Marsh: Versatile Vermonter.* New York: Columbia University Press, 1958.

Lyell, Charles. *Principles of Geology.* Vol. 1, edited by Martin J. S. Rudwick. 1830. Reprint, Chicago: University of Chicago Press, 1990.

———. *A Second Visit to the United States of North America,* 2 vols. New York: Harper & Brothers, Publishers, 1850.

Lyons, Richard S. "'In Supreme Command': The Crisis of the Imagination in James's *The American Scene.*" *New England Quarterly* 55, no. 4 (1982): 517–39.

MacAdam, Barbara J. "'A Proper Distance from the Hills': Nineteenth-Century Landscape Painting in North Conway." In *"A Sweet Foretaste of Heaven": Artists in the White Mountains, 1830–1930,* 21–38. Hanover, N.H.: University Press of New England, 1988.

Marsh, George Perkins. *Man and Nature,* edited by David Lowenthal. Cambridge: Harvard University Press, 1965.

Marx, Leo. *The Machine in the Garden: Technology and the Pastoral Ideal in America.* New York: Oxford University Press, 1964.

Mattick, Paul, Jr., ed. *Eighteenth-Century Aesthetics and the Reconstruction of Art.* Cambridge: Cambridge University Press, 1993.

McGrath, Robert L. "'Lessons of High and Holy Meaning': Artists and the White Mountains." In *"A Sweet Foretaste of Heaven": Artists in the White Mountains, 1830–1930,* 10–20. Hanover, N.H.: University Press of New England, 1988.

———. "The Real and the Ideal: Popular Images of the White Mountains." In *The White Mountains: Place and Perceptions,* 59–70. Hanover, N.H.: University Press of New England, 1980.

[McLellan, Isaac]. *The Avalanche of the White Hills, August 28, 1826.* Boston: Jones Power Press Office, 1846.

Mead, Edgar T. *The Up-country Line: Boston, Concord & Montreal RR to the New Hampshire Lakes and White Mountains.* Brattleboro, Vt.: Stephen Greene Press, 1975.

Melcher, Edward. *A Sketch of the Destruction of the Willey Family by the Mountain Slide, On the Night of August 28, 1826, ...* Lancaster, N.H.: J. S. Peavey, Book & Job Printer, 1880.

Mellen, Grenville. *The Martyr's Triumph; Buried Valley; and Other Poems.* Boston: Lilly, Wait, Colman, & Holden, 1833.

Miller, Perry. *Nature's Nation.* Cambridge: Harvard University Press, 1967.

Miller, Ross. *American Apocalypse: The Great Fire and the Myth of Chicago.* Chicago: University of Chicago Press, 1990.

———. *Here's the Deal: The Buying and Selling of a Great American City.* New York: Alfred A. Knopf, 1996.

Mitchell, Timothy. "Caspar David Friedrich's *Der Watzmann:* German Romantic Landscape Painting and Historical Geology." *Art Bulletin* 66, no. 3 (1984): 452–64.

Monk, Samuel H. *The Sublime: A Study of Critical Theories in Eighteenth-Century England.* New York: Modern Language Association of America, 1935.

Moore, Mrs. H. J. *Wild Nell, the White Mountain Girl,* ser. *Household Monthly* (1858–59).

Murray, Amelia Matilda. *Letters from the United States, Cuba, and Canada.* 1856. Reprint, New York: Negro Universities Press, 1969.

Nichols, G. W. "Popular Notices of Mount Washington and the Vicinity." *American Journal of Science and Arts* 34, no. 1 (1838): 73–80.

Nicolson, Marjorie Hope. *Mountain Gloom and Mountain Glory: The Development of the Aesthetics of the Infinite.* Ithaca: Cornell University Press, 1959.

Novak, Barbara. *Nature and Culture: American Landscape and Painting, 1825–1875.* New York: Oxford University Press, 1980.

Nygren, Edward J. "From View to Vision." In *Views and Visions: American Landscape before 1830,* edited by Edward J. Nygren et al., 3–81. Washington, D.C.: Corcoran Gallery of Art, 1986.

Oakes, William. *Scenery of the White Mountains: with Sixteen Plates from the Drawings of Isaac Sprague.* Boston: Wm. Crosby & H. P. Nichols, 1848.

Parkman, Francis. *The Journals of Francis Parkman.* Vol. 1, edited by Mason Wade. New York: Harper & Brothers Publishers, 1947.

[———]. "The Scalp-Hunter." *Knickerbocker* 25, no. 4 (1845): 297–303.

Parry, Elwood C. *The Art of Thomas Cole: Ambition and Imagination.* Newark: University of Delaware Press, 1988.

Parry, Elwood C., III. "Acts of God, Acts of Man: Geological Ideas and the Imaginary

Landscapes of Thomas Cole." In *Two Hundred Years of Geology in America: Proceedings of the New Hampshire Bicentennial Conference on the History of Geology*, edited by Cecil J. Schneer, 53–71. Hanover, N.H.: University Press of New England, 1979.

Parry, Lee. "Landscape Theater in America." *Art in America* 59, no. 6 (1971): 52–61.

Posnock, Ross. "Henry James, Veblen and Adorno: The Crisis of the Modern Self." *Journal of American Studies* 21, no. 1 (1987): 31–54.

Powers, Grant. *Historical Sketches of the Discovery, Settlement, and Progress of Events in the Coos Country and Vicinity, Principally Included Between the Years 1754 and 1785*. 1840. Reprint, Haverhill, N.H.: Henry Merrill, 1880.

Quesnay, Francois. *The Economical Table* (Tableau economique). 1766. Reprint, New York: Bergman Publishers, 1968.

Ramsey, Floyd W. *The Willey Slide: A New Chronicle of the Famous Tragedy in Ample Detail and Soberly Recounted*. Franconia, N.H.: Thorn Books, 1990.

Rideing, William H. "The White Mountains." *Harper's New Monthly Magazine* 55 (August 1877): 321–32.

Rogers, Nathaniel Peabody. *A Collection from the Miscellaneous Writings of Nathaniel Peabody Rogers*. 2d ed. Manchester, N.H.: William H. Fisk, 1849.

Rudwick, Martin J. S. "The Emergence of a Visual Language for Geological Science, 1760–1840." *History of Science* 14 (1976): 149–95.

———. *The Great Devonian Controversy: The Shaping of Scientific Knowledge among Gentlemanly Specialists*. Chicago: University of Chicago Press, 1985.

———. *The Meaning of Fossils: Episodes in the History of Palaeontology*. 2d ed. New York: Science History Publications, 1976.

Santayana, George. *The Genteel Tradition*, edited by Douglas L. Wilson. Cambridge: Harvard University Press, 1967.

Schneer, Cecil J., ed. *Two Hundred Years of Geology in America: Proceedings of the New Hampshire Bicentennial Conference on the History of Geology*. Hanover, N.H.: University Press of New England, 1979.

Schumpeter, Joseph A. *History of Economic Analysis*, edited by Elizabeth Boody Schumpeter. New York: Oxford University Press, 1955.

[Scribner, I. W.]. *Laconia; or, Legends of the White Mountains and Merry Meeting Bay*. Boston: B. B. Mussey & Co., 1854.

Sears, John F. "Hawthorne's 'The Ambitious Guest' and the Significance of the Willey Disaster." *American Literature* 54, no. 3 (1982): 354–67.

———. *Sacred Places: American Tourist Attractions in the Nineteenth Century*. New York: Oxford University Press, 1989.

Shattuk, George. "Some Account of an Excursion to the White-Hills of New Hampshire, in the Year 1807." *Philadelphia Medical and Physical Journal* 3, pt. 1 (1808): 26–35.

Shepard, Paul, Jr. "Paintings of the New England Landscape: A Scientist Looks at Their Geomorphology." *College Art Journal* 17, no. 1 (1957): 30–47.

Shteir, Ann B. *Cultivating Women, Cultivating Science: Flora's Daughters and Botany in England, 1760 to 1860*. Baltimore: Johns Hopkins University Press, 1996.

S[igourney], L[ydia] H. "The White Mountains." *Ladies Magazine* 1 (August 1828): 340–2.

Silliman, Augustus E. *A Gallop among American Scenery: or, Sketches of American Scenes and Military Adventure*. New York: D. Appleton & Co., 1843.

Silliman, Benjamin, et al. "Miscellaneous Notices of Mountain Scenery, and of Slides and Avalanches in the White and Green Mountains." *American Journal of Science and Arts* 15, no. 2 (1829): 217–32.

Smith, Henry Nash. *Virgin Land: The American West as Symbol and Myth*. Cambridge: Harvard University Press, 1950.

Smith, Neil. "New City, New Frontier: The Lower East Side as Wild, Wild West." In *Variations on a Theme Park: The New American City and the End of Public Space*, edited by Michael Sorkin, 61–93. New York: Noonday Press, 1992.

Smith, Norman. "A Mature Frontier: The New Hampshire Economy, 1790–1850." *Historical New Hampshire* 24, no. 3 (1969): 3–19.

Sorkin, Michael, ed. *Variations on a Theme Park: The New American City and the End of Public Space*. New York: Noonday Press, 1992.

Spaulding, John H. *Historical Relics of the White Mountains. Also a Concise White Mountain Guide*. n.p.: J. R. Hitchcock, 1862.

Stilgoe, John R. *Common Landscape of America, 1580–1845*. New Haven: Yale University Press, 1982.

"A Sweet Foretaste of Heaven": Artists in the White Mountains, 1830–1930. Hanover, N.H.: University Press of New England, 1988.

[Sweetser, Moses F.]. *Views in the White Mountains*. Portland, Maine: C. R. Chisholm & Brothers, 1878.

Sweetser, Moses F. *The White Mountains: A Handbook for Travellers*. 8th ed. Boston: Ticknor & Co., 1887.

Tatham, David. "Franklin Leavitt's White Mountain Verse." *Historical New Hampshire* 33, no. 3 (1978).

Taylor, Alan "The Creation of Cooper's Town in Fact and Fiction." *Ideas* 2, no. 2 (1994): 4–14.

Taylor, Joshua C., ed. *Nineteenth-Century Theories of Art*. Berkeley and Los Angeles: University of California Press, 1987.

Thomas, Mary Jane. "Reminiscences of the White Mountains," edited by Harriet S. Lacy. *Historical New Hampshire* 28, no. 1 (1973): 37–52.

Thoreau, Henry David. *Excursions*. Boston: Houghton Mifflin Co., 1893.

———. *The Journal of Henry David Thoreau*. Vol. 1, edited by Bradford Torrey and Francis H. Allen. Salt Lake City: Gibbs M. Smith, 1984.

Trollope, Anthony. *North America*. Philadelphia: J. B. Lippincott & Co., 1862.

Truettner, William H., and Alan Wallach, eds. *Thomas Cole: Landscape into History*. New Haven: Yale University Press, 1994.

Tuckerman, Frederick. "Early Visits to the White Mountains and Ascents of the Great Range." *Appalachia* 15, no. 2 (1921): 111–27.

———. "Gleanings from the Visitors' Albums of Ethan Allen Crawford." *Appalachia* 14, no. 4 (1919): 367–83.

Turner, Frederick Jackson. *The Early Writings of Frederick Jackson Turner*. Madison: University of Wisconsin Press, 1938.

Turner, Joseph W. *Orange Blossoms: Poems*. East Boston: Published by the author, 1877.

Wallace, R. Stuart. "A Social History of the White Mountains." In *The White Mountains: Place and Perceptions*, 17–40. Hanover, N.H.: University Press of New England, 1980.

Wallach, Alan. "Thomas Cole: Landscape and the Course of American Empire." In

Thomas Cole: Landscape into History, edited by William H. Truettner and Alan Wallach, 23–111. New Haven: Yale University Press, 1994.

Wallach, Alan P. "Cole, Byron, and *The Course of Empire*." *Art Bulletin* 50, no. 4 (1968): 375–9.

Walsh, Margaret. *The American Frontier Revisited*. Atlantic Highlands, N.J.: Humanities Press, 1981.

Warner, Charles Dudley. *Their Pilgrimage*. Hartford, Conn.: American Publishing Co., 1904.

[Weeks, James W.] *History of Coos County, New Hampshire*. Syracuse, N.Y.: W. A. Ferguson & Co., 1888.

Whewell, William. *The Philosophy of the Inductive Sciences Founded upon Their History*. 2d ed. 1847. Reprint, New York: Johnson Reprint Corporation, 1967.

The White Mountains: Place and Perceptions. Hanover, N.H.: University Press of New England, 1980.

Whittredge, Worthington. "The Autobiography of Worthington Whittredge, 1820–1910," edited by John I. H. Baur. *Brooklyn Museum Journal* 1942: 7–68.

Willey, Benjamin G. *Incidents in White Mountain History*. Boston: Nathaniel Noyes, 1856.

Willey, George Franklyn. *Soltaire: A Romance of the Willey Slide and the White Mountains*. Manchester: New Hampshire Publishing Corp., 1902.

Willis, Nathaniel P. *American Scenery; or, Land, Lake, and River: Illustrations of Transatlantic Nature*. 1840. Reprint, Barre, Mass.: Imprint Society, 1971.

Wilson, Harold Fisher. *The Hill Country of Northern New England: Its Social and Economic History, 1790–1930*. New York: Columbia University Press, 1936.

Wilson, James Grant, and John Fiske, eds. *Appleton's Cyclopaedia of American Biography*. Vol. 2. New York: D. Appleton & Co., 1888.

Wolf, Bryan. "All the World's a Code: Art and Ideology in Nineteenth-Century American Painting." *Art Journal* 44, no. 4 (1984): 328–37.

Wolf, Peter. *Land in America: Its Value, Use, and Control*. New York: Pantheon Books, 1981.

Wood, Frederic J. *The Turnpikes of New England and Evolution of the Same through England, Virginia, and Maryland*. Boston: Marshall Jones Co., 1919.

INDEX